Sami Zubaida is Emeritus Professor of Politics and Sociology at Birkbeck, University of London and a specialist in the religion, culture and politics of the Middle East. He is author of *Law and Power in the Islamic World*, *Islam, the People and the State* and co-editor of *A Taste of Thyme: the Culinary Cultures of the Middle East*.

BEYOND ISLAM

A New Understanding
of the Middle East

Sami Zubaida

I.B. TAURIS

LONDON · NEW YORK

Published in 2011 by I.B.Tauris & Co Ltd
6 Salem Road, London W2 4BU
175 Fifth Avenue, New York NY 10010
www.ibtauris.com

Distributed in the United States and Canada Exclusively by
Palgrave Macmillan
175 Fifth Avenue, New York NY 10010

Library of Modern Middle East Studies, Vol 84

ISBN: 978 1 84885 069 9 (HB)
       978 1 84885 070 5 (PB)

A full CIP record for this book is available from the British Library
A full CIP record is available from the Library of Congress

Library of Congress Catalog Card Number: available

Typeset in Clifford by Pindar NZ, Auckland, New Zealand
Printed and bound in Great Britain by TJ International Ltd, Padstow,
Cornwall

Contents

Acknowledgements

Chapters in this book other than the Introduction, are based on previously published material. Chapter 1, Is There a Muslim Society? Ernest Gellner's Sociology of Islam, was first published in *Economy and Society*, 24:2, 1995. Chapter 2, Political Modernity in the Middle East, appeared in Khalid Masud, Armando Salvatore and Martin van Bruinessen, eds., *Islam and Modernity*, Edinburgh University Press 2009. Chapter 3, Shifting Social Boundaries and Identities in the Modern Middle East, is developed from an earlier paper presented at a conference in Aix-en-Provence, France in 2005 and published in the Proceedings, G. D. Khoury and N. Meouchy, eds., *Etat et Societie de l'orient arabe en quete d'avenir, 1945–2005*, Volume 2, Paris: Guenther 2007. Chapter 4, Cosmopolitans, Nationalists and Fundamentalists in the Modern Middle East, draws on various of my writings on the topic, and my Inaugural Lecture at Birkbeck College in 2004, with that title. Chapter 5, The Public and the Private in Middle East History and Society, was published in an earlier version in A Filali-Ansari and S. K. Ahmed, eds., *The Challenge of Pluralism: Paradigms from Muslim Contexts*, London: the Agha Khan University and Edinburgh University Press 2009. Chapter 6, Islam and Nationalism, draws, in part, on my article by that title in *Nations and Nationalism*, 10:4, 2004.

I have too many intellectual debts to list fully. The Middle East Study Group has been a constant stimulus over many years. Fred

Halliday, who sadly died just before the time of writing these lines, was a giant presence in my intellectual and political universes, as he was for many others. Many long and challenging discussions with Mohammad Nafissi have had their influence on much of what is written, and I thank him for a critical reading of the Introduction. Nelida Fuccaro also read the Introduction and provided thoughtful comments.

The Department of Politics and Sociology at Birkbeck College was my institutional home for most of my working life. Colleagues and friends there have provided intellectual nourishment over the years, and in particular my late friend Paul Hirst. SOAS, and in particular its London Middle East Institute, has been my second home, and its Library is my regular resource.

I thank Iradj Bagherzade and Abigail Fielding-Smith at I.B.Tauris for their idea for this book, and their patience and encouragement in the process of putting it together.

I thank Charles Peyton for his meticulous editing of the text.

Introduction

Beyond Islam

These are essays about aspects of culture, religion and politics in Middle Eastern histories and societies. A common thread in the essays is to 'de-sacralize' the region, questioning the predominant role attributed to religion in so much of the writing on these histories and societies, where the adjective 'Islamic' is applied to every aspect of culture and society. We may question what can be 'Islamic' about art, science, music and politics, which are often so attributed. Religion is an important element in Middle Eastern societies, as indeed it is, or was, in Europe and elsewhere. But it is one among many factors, and one with varying inputs into social forms. Those social forms, however, are only explicable in terms of politics, sociology and economic and cultural processes, just like any other social formation. Within these configurations religion is 'materialized' or 'embedded' in social institutions and practices that are open to determination by economic and political factors. That is not to deny the independent role of religious inputs, only to say that these have to be viewed in relation to the other social relations. In the history of Europe, Christianity was materialized in the churches and monasteries as well as the courts, their economic and legal functions, the ebbs and flows of their political and institutional powers and their relations to monarchies and markets. This was also the case with Islam (and Christianity) in the Middle East, perhaps with less crystallized church-like institutions, but in the case of the Ottomans, for instance, with extensive hierarchical bureaucracies in legal and educational systems and numerous interfaces with government and the military. *Awqaf* (endowments) – systems of property with religious sanction – dominated the landscape and the politics of the cities of the region for much of their history, and represented a crucial intersection between economic and political institutions and powers. These are among the many aspects of the 'materialization' of religion.

At the time of writing, themes and issues of 'Islam' are prominent in public discourses of politics, ideology and policy. Religion, therefore, has become essential in conceiving and explaining the diverse societies, cultures and histories that are dubbed 'Islamic'. The intention of this book is to go 'beyond Islam', to advance concepts and analyses of Middle Eastern societies, histories and cultures in their diverse mutations.

Religion and modernity

One theme in the chapters that follow is the transition to modernity in various spheres of culture, politics and religion. 'Modernity' is not a precise concept. It refers to a whole range of phenomena that accompany the spread of capitalism and the inclusion of ever-more regions of the world in its revolutionary processes. Outside its native Western Europe, capitalism was spread by colonial expansion and the dominance of European power. These processes affect different regions unevenly and at different periods. For most of the Middle East it occurred from the late eighteenth century, gathering momentum at exponential speed in the nineteenth and twentieth centuries. These processes include a 'dis-embedding' of religion from social institutions and practices. In both Europe and the Middle East, at different periods of time, law, education, productive property and institutions (church and monastic lands in Europe, *awqaf* in the Middle East) were disengaged from religious control. New institutions and practices, products of modern economic and technical developments, of transport and communication, media, sports, arts and entertainment, all arose without reference to religion or its institutions. This is a process that many historians and sociologists have called 'secularization'. It does not refer to the intensity or weakness of belief and observance, but precisely to the structural and institutional separation of social spheres from religion and its authorities. Yet, this concept of 'secularization', which seems so obvious, has been controversial, challenged by many (often with ideological motives) as to what counts as 'secular'. Perhaps all can agree if the process is instead described as the 'dis-embedding' of religion. This is accompanied by an increasingly exclusive focus on faith and observance in more narrowly defined spheres of religion and morality. Religious authorities and their flocks in many regions, and certainly in much of Western Europe, have been largely reconciled to this specialization, but retain their claims to authority over morality, especially on sexual and family matters. These are the spheres of religious contention in much of the world – over issues such as contraception, abortion, homosexuality and extramarital sexuality.

This dis-embeddedness of religion from social materiality brings to the fore in many modern societies another aspect of religion, which is that of identity and difference. Religion has always acted as a communal and political marker, drawing boundaries around faith groups and their institutions, and crystallizing as frontiers of conflict and violence under particular circumstances. Wars of religion, inter-communal strife, pogroms and, latterly, genocides are common in the histories of many societies. In modern societies, while religion has been stripped of many of its social functions and authority, its communal-identity aspect has come centrestage nowhere more dramatically than in the case of Islam. Capitalism, modernity and secularization had all come to the Middle East as aspects of European/Western domination, and were conceived by many as 'Christian'. Religious definitions and boundaries have always played an important part in the ideologies of resistance, as has opposition to Western dominance, and have fed, to a greater or lesser extent, into nationalist ideologies and movements (see Chapters 2 and 5). For much of the twentieth century, however, nationalist and anti-colonial ideologies and movements had affiliations with secular ideologies: liberal constitutionalism; fascism; and, in the later decades of the twentieth century, mostly with the political left, aided by Soviet patronage towards Third World liberation struggles. Marxist and liberationist motifs and concepts played an important part in these movements until the 1970s, and even into the 1980s. 'Socialism' and leftist rhetoric were integral to Nasirism, Ba'thism and the Palestinian Liberation Organisation. While religious nationalisms, such as that of the Muslim Brotherhood in Egypt, constituted important elements, they were by no means dominant. The combination of the Iranian Revolution (dubbed 'Islamic') in 1979, then the collapse of communism in the following decade, blunted the force and appeal of leftist and secularist elements in nationalism, and brought to the fore identity elements of ethnic and religious contestation. We see this clearly in the Balkans, especially with the break-up of Yugoslavia. Islamic advocacy in much of the Middle East shares in this trend.

In the Middle East, and in so much of the 'Muslim world', we have the paradox of largely secularized societies and polities combined with the espousal of sacralized ideologies by regimes and oppositions. The societies are secularized in that many of their institutions and practices have no relation to religion, not even in 'Islamic' Iran.[1] But the more secular the societies, the keener religious authorities and oppositional movements are to paint them as Islamic, giving rise to what I call 'spray-on Islam'. We shall later consider a prominent example of this in the section entitled 'Islamic finance'.

Alternative or multiple modernities?

The concept of 'alternative' or 'multiple' modernities has come to prominence in academic literature.[2] It describes and implicitly justifies the ideological projects of identity politics – defined as 'alternative', presumably, to Western modernity, which is assumed to have some uniformity deriving from a Western essence. This essentialism is explicitly articulated in the notion of 'axial civilizations' emerging in remote histories and continuing to animate civilizational traditions in their particular regions, culminating in modern renaissances renewing those traditions in modernity. Shmuel N. Eisenstadt, in a critique of what he terms 'Orientalist' approaches, argues that they 'barely touch on a problem central to Weber's analysis. The problem relates to the various broad symbolic and institutional frameworks of these [Oriental] civilizations – whether Brahmanic or Sanskrit or Confucian cosmopolis, or of the Islamic Umma and its dynamic'[3] (there is more on Hoexter et al. (2002) below and in Chapter 6). It seems odd that this should be presented as a critique of 'Orientalism' when this Weberian approach can be seen as a form of 'Orientalism', namely, the presentation of Oriental societies and cultures as totally other to an equally essentialized 'West', and claiming to identify an essence whose dynamics have persisted through the ages and into the present, expressed respectively in their unique modernities. Armando Salvatore, an advocate of this approach, writes of 'religious traditions that ingrained into the history and societies of the Muslim world'.[4] The 'alternatives' are routes to modernity emanating from those specific cultures, histories and religions. It is supposed, for instance, that there is a specifically Islamic modernity, not following the Western pattern, but somehow 'modern' *and* authentically Islamic. Ernest Gellner's sociology of Islam, considered in Chapter 1, argues one interesting version of this notion.

To clarify and elucidate these issues, we must first identify the primary motor of modernity. It is capitalism that ushers in diverse processes of social transformation, which are not merely cultural imitation, but solvents of old social and cultural patterns. From this perspective, modernity in diverse parts of the world is not the product of cultural influences, imitations and 'invasions' from the West (though these do occur in varying forms), but the consequence of transformations of social relations, powers and authorities brought about by sweeping socio-economic forces. These forces, while sharing common elements (to be discussed presently) produce different patterns of cultural and political transformations, depending on local historical and cultural conjunctures. It is crucial to understand, however, that these differences are not of the West versus the Rest, but include both the West and the Rest. Modern capitalism may have originated in England, but it has had distinct effects in France, Germany and Italy, not relating specifically to different 'cultures', but to historical totalities of economy, class structure, government and patterns of power, as well as to cultural processes. And it is important to keep in mind that 'culture' is a process intertwined with the dynamics of economy and power, and not a fixed essence working itself out through history. I should add that Islam as culture is itself shaped by widely divergent histories and cultural traditions. Clifford Geertz's classic *Islam Observed* presents vivid pictures of total contrast between Indonesian and Moroccan Islam as forms of religious expression, shaped by the different cultural universes of the two countries.[5]

The common processes and effects of capitalism that shape modernity include the break-up of primary communities of production and exchange dependent on kinship, governed by patriarchal authority, reinforced by religion and custom, and buttressed by religio-political institutions and powers. Commodity production, monetized exchange, individualization of labour, the development of 'the economy' as an autonomous sphere regulated by state and international authorities[6] – all lead to profound social transformations, which are by now familiar in most parts of the world. These processes provide conditions that favour the liberation of individuals, including women, from the patriarchal authorities of household and community, who lose some, maybe most, of their control over their life chances, which increasingly come to be determined by educational and economic fields outside communal control (though in many cases they retain the influences of family and patronage as gatekeepers of opportunity). Crucially, these processes affect 'the economy of desire': capitalism creates avenues, means and commodities of gratification, material and symbolic, often related in one way or another to sexuality. These are the processes which theorists like Theodore Adorno, Max Horkheimer and Herbert Marcuse considered to be part of the insidious repressions of capitalism and of its 'instrumental reason', and which are celebrated by more recent theorists like Jean Baudrillard as part of the postmodern condition. However we evaluate these effects, the fact remains that capitalism enters into the formation of the modern psyche and the pattern of its desires, and this is always a component of modernity. Patriarchal and religious authorities, while participating in these economies of desire, are at the same time fearful at their loss of control over social spheres and spaces, and over women and the young.[7] They respond with moralistic campaigns aimed at re-establishing control, sometimes supported by the 'ressentiment' of sectors of society who feel deprived and excluded by social transformations. But they are fighting a losing battle, as we can see, for example, in the case of the youth of Iran rebelling against the moralistic authoritarianism of the clerics.

Since the nineteenth century these processes of modernity/capitalism have transformed the individual and society in most parts of the world, including the diverse Muslim world, but they were accelerated and enhanced in the second half of the twentieth. There are always winners and losers in these processes. The losers were mainly the poor, many of whom were deprived of their land, which became a commodity, and of their livelihood – their crafts and guilds hit by cheap imports; many were forced to migrate, ending up in urban slums and shanties. These developments favoured the emergence of new elites and the decline of the old. Many of the old and new elites who benefited from these transformations nevertheless disliked their social and cultural effects, and the challenge they presented to patriarchal and religious controls and authorities. Among the losers in many places were the religious classes, who, from the nineteenth century, incited the losers among the poor in Ottoman lands and elsewhere against the reforms and transformations. They fought losing battles, but much of their ideological ground was taken over by new elites and authorities, who, like the Ottoman Sultan Abdul-Hamid II (r. 1876–1909), while continuing the processes of reform and capitalism, adopted Islamic rhetoric against democrats and constitutionalists, identifying them with hostile foreign powers.[8] This resort to religious ideology in defence of reactionary power has been a regular strategy of despots until the present. It also generated its opposite: the radical religious claims of oppositional forces, as we see in Saudi Arabia and elsewhere now. This ideological instrumentalization of religion and tradition has a common target: the liberated individual of modernity, struggling to escape the re-imposition of patriarchal and political authority.

The question of modernity, then, is not one of cultural essences leading to 'alternative modernity', but of basic conflicts and contests between different social forces and desires. We see this clearly in present-day Iran. A religious clique dominated a popular revolution to impose its arbitrary and corrupt rule (at the time of writing, it is being transformed into a clerical–military despotism). The children of the revolution, those born on its terrain, are struggling against this enforced morality not by seeking an 'alternative' modernity, but by pursing modernity tout court, identified in their minds with the USA and its cultural products. In Egypt a different pattern prevails: religious rhetoric and identification have emerged as Egyptian nationalism, if not chauvinism, nourished by a paranoid view of the world as one of clashes of hostile religions. Within this framework, however, the capitalist economy of desire asserts itself: in patterns of consumption; in the media; in modern fashions (even behind female veils); in imported TV soap operas; in expressions of sexuality outside patriarchal bonds – as in the simmering sexuality, including *'urfi* (informal) marriages, among students and other young people; in the culture of shopping malls and of mixing of the sexes in their halls; and in the brands of cigarettes and soft drinks.[9] The fact that popular preachers and religious zealots continue to fulminate against deviance, looseness and immorality, to demand the stern legal enforcement of morality in this world and to threaten hellfire in the hereafter, is testimony to the continued popularity of sin.[10] Modernities are not alternative: they are ideologically contested. The notion of 'alternative modernities' takes sides in these contests, by legitimizing the 'cultural' standpoint of patriarchal and traditional advocates as somehow more 'authentic' than that of the advocates of liberation and diversity.

Is Islam a distinct culture and civilization that must be 'understood' by the West?

This question is acutely raised in relation to the increasingly prominent presence of Islam in Europe. It is raised in the related context
of 'multiculturalism'. This term seems at first to refer to a clearly dis-
cernible fact: so many aspects of modern urban societies in the West
manifest multiple cultural traits and origins. Witness 'world music'
as a prominent genre, or the great variety of culinary delights: from
pizza to curry, sushi and Thai delicacies, in addition to the pasta and
pesto from nearer home. Traits originate from different cultures and
are mixed into various hybrid forms and 'fusions' – from *rai* (North
African rock) to Indian jazz, to Hispano-Moroccan flamenco. Yet the
term 'multicultural' is taken to imply a multiplicity of *unit* cultures:
how are these units to be labelled and distinguished? By nationality,
religion or ethnicity? As Indian, Muslim or Kurdish? Do these really
form distinct units? I am reminded of the well-intentioned efforts of
London education authorities in the 1970s to instil multiculturalism in schools by teaching Bengali in East London schools with a
preponderance of Bangladeshi pupils, only to discover that London
Bangladeshis don't know Bengali, but speak its remote relative
Sylheti! The Indian subcontinent is itself multicultural, but with
illusive units, hard to categorize as distinct entities. When it comes
to 'Muslim culture' the unit becomes even more indeterminate, not
only because of the multiplicity of nationalities and ethnicities, but
also the varieties of identification of the religion itself, and its adap-
tations to ideologies, generations and styles of life. In fact, modern
forms of Islam, whether reformist or radical, tend to reject ethnic culture and its colouring of religion in favour of a 'pure' Islam derived
from scriptures and Prophetic sources. Islam as a distinct culture,
then, is illusory. As a religion it has certain constants, such as the
holy book and the belief in the unity of God and the prophethood
of Muhammad. But even these constants are constructed through
a variety of discourses and practices enshrined in differing institutions. 'Culture' is best viewed as a *process*, in flux in relation to other
socio-economic and political processes and situations, rather than

a distinct unit with an essential identity. I am here reminded of the classic advocacy of the politics of recognition by Charles Taylor and colleagues. Taylor et al. argued for a liberalism that recognized collective goals of cultural groups (for example, in Quebec), with the object being the defence of 'cultural integrity'. The demands made on liberal polities is to 'let cultures defend themselves, within reasonable bounds', and, further, to recognize the equal worth of different cultures.[11] The clear assumption here is that there are recognizable, well-bound and integral cultural units, which act as collective subjects. This view does not see culture as a process, and one that involves ideological contests as to its boundaries and contents. It is precisely propositions of multiculturalism such as Taylor et al.'s that inspire diverse parties to make ideological and political claims, speaking for an assumed cultural group, whose presumed members in fact often question the credentials of self-appointed spokespersons.

Are these Muslim 'cultures', beliefs and institutions alien to Westerners, requiring special study and understanding? I would argue not. Islam shares with Christianity and Judaism a wide range of doctrines, practices and moral precepts. The issues of sexual morality and its codification in state law, for instance – so prominent in Islamic distinctiveness today – were until recently also part of Christian advocacy in Europe and North America, and remain so in the latter. Homosexuality was a criminal offence in Britain until the legal reforms of the 1950s and 1960s, and so was abortion. Religious authority, while separated from most social and cultural spheres in the process of modernity, continued to claim dominion over matters of family and sexuality. In Britain, the liberties of belief and expression remain limited by laws of blasphemy, though they are largely in disuse. The assertion of the precedence of religious truths over scientific is a feature of Christianity and Judaism as much as it is of Islam, and the Muslim denunciation of Darwinian evolutionism has well-known precedents and parallels in the USA (and earlier in Europe). Enforced religious worship and observance – a feature of some Muslim polities and communities today – were also present in many European societies in the past.

In the liberal societies of Western Europe, modernity has led to the decline of religious authority (which is not necessarily to say of faith, though that is also the case for the most part). The mainstream churches have largely adapted to this loss of authority, and have directed their appeal in terms of spirituality and the 'good life'. That is to say, the authorities of the main churches have accepted the secularization of life, the evolution of sexuality, the equality of women and the supremacy of science as a form of knowledge. The papacy continues to fight a rearguard action on some of these issues, but in the process is losing support and authority among the faithful. The fringe elements who refused to accept these reforms have become anomalous in Europe (though not in the USA). These elements are the first referents of the term 'fundamentalist': those who insist that the scriptures mean what they say. 'Fundamentalism', whether Christian or Muslim, is essentially a phenomenon of secularization.

In relation to this history, the manifestations of militant Islam are not alien, but echo many of the features and episodes of assertions of religious authority in the history of the West. What worried liberal Westerners at the 1989 scenes of the burning of Salman Rushdie's *Satanic Verses* in public demonstrations in British cities and elsewhere is precisely that it was reminiscent of similar events in their own histories. The so-called fatwa against Salman Rushdie cannot be considered strange in countries that until recently had persecuted heresy, and slightly earlier burned heretics. After all, Martin Luther was himself the object of a papal fatwa, which he escaped, and then himself proceeded to burn heretics and dissenters. So, what is mysterious or alien about these particular Islamic manifestations? The fact is that many European citizens are worried about Islam in their midst precisely because it parallels elements in their past that they thought had been combated and overcome. On some of these issues of religious and moral enforcement there are tactical alliances between Muslim clerics, conservative Christians and Orthodox Jews.

This is not to imply that Muslims in Europe are uniform in their moral conservatism and assertive authoritarianism. Most surveys carried out in Europe (especially before September 2001 – after that there is a tendency towards retrenchment around the umma) found that a majority of nominal Muslims (between 60 and 70 per cent) are non-observant, and that, of those who are, many are 'private' believers, not involved in political or cultural advocacy. Of those who are active, many are reformists and modernists – like many active Muslim feminists, as well as advocates of Euro-Islam. Some are Salafists[12] and jihadists. Do any of these groups represent distinct 'cultures'?

Second- and third-generation members of Muslim groups in Europe are largely acculturated to the host societies.[13] Many have grown away from the cultural milieux, motifs and social controls of their parents, but in different directions. Some, probably a majority, have adopted the ways of the host society. Others have developed various religious ideas and affiliations, but often not those of their parents. If we divide religious orientations (crudely) into reformist and Salafist, we find that both have rejected the religion of their parents as 'ethnic' religion that departs from correct Islam in pursuit of saint worship and superstition. The parents also (mistakenly) cast their ethnic ways as religious Islam. Thus, horrific practices such as 'honour killing' and female circumcision are seen by their practitioners as religious duty, and are denounced by reformists as folk practices, alien to the true Islam. In a sense, then, both modernists and Salafists have embraced a culture-free 'pure' Islam. Their advocacy is not one of cultural difference, but of ideological and social objectives. They pursue these objectives, however, on the convenient pretext of the multiculturalism so prominent in the public discourse of the host societies. In fairness, some reformist advocates of 'Euro-Islam', notably Tariq Ramadan, reject the rubric of multiculturalism in favour of a common European outlook, in which Islam takes its place alongside other religions embraced by European citizens.[14]

Historical constructions of identity

'Identity politics' requires an emphasis on difference, which goes hand in hand with the essentialization of what is 'Islamic' as opposed to what is 'Western'. Thus, a whole range of what are considered vices – alcohol, sexual looseness and homosexuality, dealing in loans on interest – are defined as Western intrusions into Islamic culture, part of the Western cultural invasion, and to be resisted by asserting historically given

Islamic values. I shall deal with these histories in what follows. Let me start with the question of Shari'a as law and the call for its application. The Shari'a is key to the ideological profile of Islamic advocacy and the assertion of its values. It is a major demand of almost all Islamist movements, and even features in the demands of some elements speaking for 'Muslim communities' in Western countries. It is assumed by many that the Shari'a is a determinate body of law based on canonical sources, embodying Islamic virtues. It is also assumed that this form of 'law' prevailed in historical Muslim societies, and was disrupted by colonial or other dominant Western intrusions imposing alien legal systems on Muslims, and that Westernized elites and corrupt rulers acquiesced in this cultural domination. But, of course, there is little agreement on what constitutes this Shari'a, and in what legal institutions it should be embedded.[15] Reformist advocates, fearing outright secular advocacy, have resorted to historicizing the Shari'a, asserting that each generation of Muslims had to follow variable understandings of the divine and prophetic message, in accordance with time and place. 'Fundamentalists' have rejected such historicization, seeing it, quite rightly, as creeping secularization, and insisted on the literal import of the message (which is what we mean by 'fundamentalist'). Of course, the contests between Muslims are their own affair, and it is not for the historian or sociologist to arbitrate. What concerns us as students, however, are the assertions or implications regarding the history of law and religion in the Middle East and the nature of those historical polities. Chapter 2 deals with those polities and the nature of politics, including law and its institutions. One of the contentions of the advocates of the Shari'a is that its rule consisted of a kind of constitution binding on the rulers, corresponding to the modern notion of 'the rule of law'. This idea has been put forward forcibly by an influential American legal scholar, Noah Feldman, in recent articles and a book.[16] Feldman's was an effort at sympathetic understanding of modern Islamist demands for the Shari'a: it indicates a desire to restore the rule of law, now disrupted under the arbitrary repressive regimes prevailing in much of the Muslim world. Feldman (echoing many other, mostly Muslim, commentators) supposed that this rule of law was upheld by the ulama as guardians of the Shari'a, independent from the ruler though often appointed by him, and holding him to account while dispensing justice to the subjects in accordance with its dictates. As many have pointed out, notably Said Amir Arjomand (see note 15), this is a highly idealized view of the scholars and their law, conforming to the image that Islamic apologists have sought to project. It is not clear through which institutions, procedures and powers this guardianship is supposed to be effected. This kind of sympathetic presentation of an essentialized Muslim history and civilization, while insisting on its total alterity to the West, is common among many historians and social scientists. It is well exemplified in the collection of essays edited by Miriam Hoexter, Shmuel N. Eisenstadt and Nehemia Lavtzion on *The Public Sphere in Muslim Societies*.[17] This is an interesting collection of essays on aspects of Muslim history featuring Shari'a courts, *awqaf* and Sufi orders, all examples of the 'public sphere' (the public sphere will be discussed in Chapter 6). In historical temporality, the examples range from the *mihna* (inquisition) of Ibn Hanbal in the ninth century to late Ottoman times in the early twentieth century. Somehow, these remain in essence 'Muslim societies' with a continuity of the constituents of a common public sphere throughout these centuries. In the introduction we read:

> The picture that emerges from the contributions to this volume is that of a vibrant public sphere, accommodating a large variety of autonomous groups and characterized by a relatively stable yet very dynamic nature. The community of believers was the center of gravity around which activity in the public sphere revolved. Its participation in the formation of the public sphere was a matter of course; its well-being, customs, and consensus were both the motives and the main justifications for the introduction of changes in social and religious practices and in the law and policies governing the public sphere. The independence of the Shari'a and the distribution of duties toward the community between the ruler and the ulama, established very early in Islamic history, were crucial factors in securing the autonomy of the public sphere and putting limits on the absolute power of the ruler.[18]

What a remarkable picture of a utopian society, of harmony, consensus and balance, of social autonomies and checks of absolute power! And it continued from 'very early in Islamic history' into late Ottoman times, encompassed a vast geographical area, all as a continuing manifestation of an essential Islamic civilization. This is the picture that modern Islamic apologists would like to project of Islam as religion and civilization. We shall see in Chapters 1 and 2 that the ulama were a diverse body, and occupied shifting positions at different historical points. Senior members held positions of power by virtue of the patronage of rulers, bureaucratic rank (especially under the Ottomans) or social connections, such as association with powerful tribes or factions. Some were also doyens of rich and influential Sufi orders with powerful royal patronage (which does not conform to the 'orthodox' image desired by modern apologists). As figures of power and influence, they acted like other politicians, participating in patronage, control of resources and factional struggles, but with the advantage of being able to invoke religious sanction. In the various rebellions that unseated Ottoman sultans, for instance, the rebels (mostly military garrisons) would seek legal and religious sanction for their action from the senior clerics, usually Shaykhulislam (head of the religious hierarchy), which was forthcoming once it was clear that the sultan had been defeated. Otherwise, the senior scholars, as muftis, were quite inventive in formulating legal justifications for whatever their patron rulers wished to institute. Abussu'ud Efendi, chief mufti to Suleiman the Magnificent, was famous for legalizing forms of land rent as well as cash *waqf* (religious endowments in the form of cash that can only generate income through lending on interest), which were considered illegal in the traditions of the Hanafi school that he followed.[19]

The contention that the Shari'a constituted 'rule of law' also ignores the essential institutional underpinning of this notion in the modern context: evolved institutions, codes and procedures of legal enactments with checks and balances, fallible and imperfect as they might be. The legal, administrative and fiscal reforms of the nineteenth and twentieth centuries in Ottoman lands, and later in Iran, were steps in the direction of such institutionalization: they are the reforms decried by the historical mythologizers as colonial and alien incursions. It is precisely the weakening and near collapse of these institutions and procedures at the hands of nationalist and Islamic 'revolutionaries' since the 1950s that have characterized these arbitrary and repressive regimes. These are symbiotic with the Islamist moralizing and repressive drives that appear to oppose them.

Islamic finance

Islamic finance is another sphere of identity claims that involve historical mythologies, as well as providing lucrative avenues for many entrepreneurs, Muslims and others. It rests on the claim that dealing in loans on interest is prohibited in Islam. Alternative forms of investment, mostly supposed partnerships and profit-sharing, are instituted in Islamic banking. *Riba* (which may be translated as usury) is explicitly decried in the Quran, and is equally decried in all ethical systems. But is all interest usury? Or does the term denote only exorbitant and exploitative rates and arrangements? These are questions that have featured in Islamic as well as other religious thought, historically and in modern reforms. Usury is also banned in Christianity and Judaism. The Catholic church instituted the ban in the European societies of the Middle Ages and the Renaissance, but, of course, the ban was evaded. The formulae and devices for the evasion were called by an Arabic name – *hiyal*, meaning subterfuges – because the Catholics learned it from the Muslims.[20] In any case, in many Muslim contexts, dealing in interest was taken for granted, and *riba* was confined to classifying excessive interest above some notional rate. Interest contracts could be enforced in Ottoman Shari'a courts in the eighteenth century.[21] As we saw, in the sixteenth century even religious endowments in the form of interest-bearing cash were justified by an Ottoman chief mufti. Modern Islamic reformers from the nineteenth century were inclined to legalize interest dealing as part of normal economic activity if it conformed to the normal capitalist calculation as a percentage of profit, but not if it was oppressive, as in the case of much rural peasant debt.[22] Rural debt, however, was used by many landlords, including rich clerics, with no religious sanction.

The countries of the Middle East and the Muslim world featured modern financial practices throughout the nineteenth and twentieth centuries, with normal banking and finance, including loans and investments accruing interest. It was only from the 1970s that the idea of Islamic banking developed and grew as a highly profitable niche, which also gave rise to fraudulent 'Ponzi' schemes in Egypt and the Gulf.[23] Again, the assumption behind it was that Muslims had, historically, avoided the sin of *riba* and were corrupted only by the impact of colonialism and Western dominance. In fact 'Islamic banking' is wholly an innovation, having no historical roots or parallels. It differs from 'normal' banking only in its conceptualization of returns on loans and investments as shares of profit and loss, the rates of return being remarkably close to prevalent interest rates. Clients would be unlikely to continue dealing with a bank that posted losses to be shared. Yet again, we have Islam superimposed on normal modern activity, with pretence of an historically and religiously based difference of identity. Still, the bulk of banking transactions in most of the Islamic world, including the ultra-Islamic Saudi Arabia, continue to be those of conventional banking.

Sexuality and gender

Questions of sexuality and gender feature prominently in the current discourses on difference and identity. A dominant stereotype is that Islam oppresses women: veiling, Shari'a rules on family, marriage (including plural marriage) and divorce are seen as aspects of this oppression. Muslim reactions have varied. Conservatives have insisted that these are divinely decreed rules that are in conformity with human nature and the natural differences between men and women, elaborating on the idea of the complementariness of the sexes determining different rights. For reformists these have been central issues of reform; they have argued that these provisions are historically relative and not a necessary feature of the religion, and they are thereby subject to revisions and modifications, which are sanctioned by a correct reading of the Quran and the canonical sources. Women's liberation, then, is consistent with the spirit of the religion and departs from the historical *fiqh*, whose prescriptions were more in line with traditional patriarchal ideologies than with that spirit.[24] Various elements of the reformist agenda have, over the course of the twentieth century, entered into the personal-status legislation of the main Middle Eastern states. Apart from the Turkish Republic, which banished the Shari'a from its legislation, the main Arab states (though not Saudi Arabia and the Gulf, which retained traditional Shari'a forms) drew on the Shari'a for their personal-status legislation, but always selectively – placing limits on polygamy or limiting divorce prerogatives for the husband, among various other liberalizations. Those reformist legislative concessions have, with the Islamic currents of the later decades of the century, been the object of Islamic campaigns, conservative and radical, seeking the restoration of the full provisions of the historical Shari'a. Such contestations have been particularly prominent in Egypt.[25] The family law reforms in Iran under the Shah were reversed by the Islamic Republic, but subsequently modified in reformist directions under pressure from influential women's campaigns and the contingencies of an economy that needed women's employment outside the home.

Conservatives, radicals and reformists all agree, however, that Islamic norms contain superior moral prescriptions to those of the permissive West, ensuring virtue and the dignity of women, who are protected from exploitation. An added dimension among modernists – especially those who sprang from the political left, like the Iranian Ali Shari'ati (d. 1977) – is that of the critique of capitalism and consumer culture. This culture is said to exploit women, both financially and sexually, pursuing fashions and ornament, encouraging the wearing of revealing garments and make-up and thereby sexual exploitation through the pressures and the models of loose living. These were powerful motifs in the ideological ferment leading up to the Iranian Revolution of 1979[26] – a site of convergence between the anti-capitalist, anti-Western political left and the Islamic radicals.

Gender and sexuality do constitute grounds of marked differences between the West and the Middle East – mostly the Muslim Middle East, though Middle Eastern Christianity and Judaism contain related attitudes. What Europe and the Middle East had in common is the strict regulation of sexuality by religious and legal sanction, confining it to the sanctified marriage bond and punishing extramarital sex. They also shared a general oppression of women in social and familial status and relations, with more or less severe restrictions on roles and statuses of women outside the domestic setting. 'Women's liberation' is a recent development in Western societies – the result of successive campaigns for legal and social rights that gained momentum in the course of the twentieth century, and are still ongoing. Campaigns for women's liberation have also occurred in the various countries of the Middle East in the course of the last century, but in most countries have had limited results and continuous religious and patriarchal challenges. Alongside these parallels, there are considerable and well-known differences. The West has maintained strict monogamy in contrast to the Muslim man's entitlement to four wives and unlimited concubines, as well as temporary marriages for the Shiʻa. Western Christianity had forbidden divorce, while Muslim law allows the husband to divorce at will, though severely restricting that privilege for the wife. The veiling and even confinement of women have also been common features of Muslim communities, often enforced by law and custom, with the corollary of the segregation of the sexes in public spaces and in worship. All these are features not generally shared in Western societies. Indeed, a common theme of surprise, censure and ridicule prevalent in Muslim comments on Western styles since the encounters of the Crusades, is the parading of uncovered women in public and their free association with unrelated men.

How does the Islamic discourse of difference deal with these real differences in framing the virtue of Islamic practice as against Western decadence? Many conservatives and fundamentalists would defend the features of Islamic practice in historical and some contemporary societies in relation to the confinement and oppression of women and the licensing of men to a wide range of licit sexuality, as well as the freedom to divorce at will. Most of the discourse of difference, however, is reformist and apologetic: all these oppressive features, they argue, are distortions of the 'true' Islam, which grants equality of rights while recognizing 'natural' differences between the sexes. Quranic texts, it is argued, have been misconstrued in historical *fiqh* (and in contemporary Islamic states such as Saudi Arabia, Sudan, Iran and elsewhere): allowing four wives was really meant for special circumstances, to take care of orphan girls and war widows, and other such formulations. The Prophet took multiple wives, it is argued, because of the special privileges and circumstances of his prophethood: the multiple marriages and concubinage of his kin and companions are overlooked in these apologetics. In the face of this massive historical record and prevalent current practice, it is argued by many public voices, including 'Muslim feminists', that Islam contains the only true key to the liberation and dignity of women. Western permissiveness, it is argued, combined with consumerist pressures, exploits women, renders them frivolous playthings and diminishes their dignity, in contrast to the protection and respect they are accorded in Muslim practice, in its idealized version advanced by modern apologists. Thus, an alleged Muslim ideal, largely unrealized, is favourably contrasted with a caricature of the West to seal the discourse of difference.

Homosexuality

The discourse of difference is particularly insistent on the issue of homosexuality. This 'deviance' is proclaimed to be the product of Western permissiveness and decadence, alien to Islam, which condemns and punishes such conduct. Homosexuality thus becomes a central plank in the discourse of difference and identity. We shall see presently that this proclaimed difference has a complicated history. Homoerotism was and is prevalent in Middle Eastern societies and elsewhere in recent history – but is 'homoerotism' the same as 'homosexuality'?

A number of recent books have dealt with the question of homoerotism in Middle Eastern societies. A common theme is, perhaps, summed up in the title of one such book, Khaled El-Rouayheb's *Before Homosexuality in the Arab-Islamic World*.[27] They distinguish between 'homoerotism', prevalent in many societies including the Middle East, and 'homosexuality', a more recent concept. Homosexuality designates a sexual orientation as a personality trait, a condition and an identity pertaining to particular individuals. Homo- and heterosexuality are more or less fixed sexual orientations. Prevalent homoerotism in the Middle East, as well as the European past, related to desires and acts rather than to enduring orientations. In many Middle Eastern communities, 'normal' men were likely to fancy boys and (beardless) youths, and in some contexts such attachments were instituted in bonds of concubinage and slavery. Boy servants and craft apprentices could also serve as sexual objects. These relations between a socially superior man and an inferior boy were typically unequal.[28] Neither the man nor the boy was expected to be fixed in his sexual preferences: the man would also be married to one or more women, and might have female concubines; the boy would 'grow out of it'. If an adult man, however, continued to act as a passive, penetrated partner, then this might be considered a shameful effeminacy, stigmatized and punished. The modern concept of 'homosexuality', by contrast, assumes love and sex between homosexual men and women as equal partners. The designation 'homosexual', a more or less definitive distinction from 'heterosexual', has also given rise in more recent times to the cultural identification of a 'gay' community, often incorporating a pressure group for gay rights, as well as fostering styles of life and venues of entertainment and sociability specific to its members. It is this proclaimed presence, confidence and advocacy that have been the object of denunciation, censure and persecution by Islamic, as well as nationalist and conservative, sources and authorities. It should be recalled, however, that such prohibition of homosexuality was shared by most Western societies and their laws until recent times. Homosexual acts constituted criminal offences in British law until the 1960s. Such acts are denounced just as vociferously in Christianity and Judaism as grave sins eliciting severe punishment, and continue to be an issue of contention between conservatives and liberals in many churches. The inscription of such prohibitions into the discourse of difference does not, therefore, designate some essential difference between Islam and the West, but an ideological contest of forms of sexuality and culture shared between dominant Islamism and conservative religious factions in the West.

Afsaneh Najmabadi (2005) and Janet Afary (2009) show how modern thinkers and publicists in Iran, from the start of the twentieth century, have denounced homoerotism, so prevalent and institutionalized in their society, as a perversion and a sickness – a product of the 'backward' society that segregated the sexes and oppressed women, making homoerotism an outlet for the frustrations of its members. Love of boys, then, becomes an aspect of the problematic of 'backwardness', the condition of a traditional society to be reformed in line with the norms of modernity and civilization. Secular intellectuals and religious reformers shared these attitudes, having internalized the European gaze on Islam, which included characterizations of libidinous excess and the 'unnatural' practice of sodomy. In the context of the nineteenth-century Ottoman reforms, Sukru Hanioglu wrote:

> Another important factor [in regard to changing sexual norms] ... was the intrusion of European sexual mores into Ottoman society, and the consequent stigmatisation of homosexuality. The same [contemporary] historian recounts: 'Renowned upper-class boy lovers, such as Kamil and Ali Pashas, vanished along with their entourage. In fact, Ali Pasha tried to conceal his interest in boys out of fear of the criticism of foreigners.'[29]

Progress, rationality and civilization thus required the suppression and punishment of those desires and acts. Women's liberation and the healthy social mixing of the sexes (while preserving chastity) were supposed to liberate individuals from the exclusively male society that gave rise to those desires. Such stigmatization of homosexuality continues into the present day and, in Middle Eastern attitudes, is shared between the religious and the secular, and between Muslims and Christians.

The rise of a public and vociferous gay culture in the West has constituted a challenge to those attitudes to homosexuality, and put down a potent marker for the discourse of difference. Open displays of gay culture and its prominent milieux have been seen by Muslim commentators as a confirmation of the decadence and corruption of the West. This has also led to a forgetting or denial of homoerotic proclivities in many Muslim communities, historically and in the present, and of the general tolerance of these relations and acts in religious circles and discourses. Indeed, the campaigns of persecution of homosexuals in Egypt and elsewhere are directed against 'gays': usually educated middle-class men attracted to the modes of expression and display of their Western counterparts. They represent the provocation of an ideologically driven self-assertion, seen by their detractors as carriers of Western cultural invasion and degeneracy. Invisible in this context are the village men – including religious functionaries – who sodomize boys. In the discourse of difference between essential Islamic virtue and Western vice, homosexuality is a potent element, representing a further denial of history and culture, as well as a blurring of the communalities of conservative thought between Muslim, Christian and Jewish advocacies.

Alcohol

Alcohol consumption is another symbolic marker in the discourse of difference. In the current context of widespread assertions of Islamic identity, many individuals and groups have marked their difference from the decadent other by insisting on abstention as an Islamic virtue. The long history, symbolism and poetry of wine and of drinking cultures in the past and present of Muslim societies are overlooked or derided as deviant. Chapters 4 and 5 will elaborate on these histories and cultures of drinking in Muslim societies.

The adjective 'Islamic'

The discourse of difference is reinforced by the practice of attaching the adjective 'Islamic' to a wide range of aspects of the histories and cultures of the Middle East, North Africa, Central Asia and India, each encompassing a wide diversity, as well as differing from the others. We have 'Islamic history', 'Islamic art', 'Islamic science', 'Muslim society' (the subject of Chapter 1), and many other such usages. The term implies that those regions have Islam as their essence, and confirms their otherness from the 'Christian' West. Yet this 'West' is hardly ever given the adjective 'Christian' with regard to its history, art, science and so on. So, the history of Europe and its offshoots is not 'Christian history', even though Christianity and its churches play prominent parts in it. The monarchs and princes always emphasized their Christian credentials as defenders of the faith and prosecutors of heresy. The church and the papacy are prominent actors in this history, and faith is a central plank in their discourses of legitimacy. So many wars are wars of religion, between the pope and kings, between Catholic and Protestant. The Crusades were wars against another religion. In all these respects, Christianity is at least as prominent a factor in European history as Islam is in diverse regions – yet it is not 'Christian' history, but European, or English, or French, while the history of the church is a specific branch thereof. European art was imbued with religious imagery and symbolism until the nineteenth century and after: the crucifixion, the Madonna and child, the resurrection, the lives of Christ and the saints – all are central themes to centuries of European art. Yet it is not 'Christian' art, but Italian or Flemish; Renaissance, Baroque or Gothic. 'Islamic' art, on the other hand, has almost always avoided religious themes, the portrayal of sacred figures being taboo (exceptions occur in Shi'ite popular iconography, seldom considered 'art'). Mosaics and calligraphy decorate mosques. But despite the supposed ban on portraiture there are vibrant traditions of pictorial art in particular regions and periods. Persian and Indian miniatures, proceeding partly from Chinese influences, are well known, and are the main example of 'Islamic' art. But what is 'Islamic' about them? They portray kings and heroes, battles and hunts, beauties and gardens, legends and myths, but hardly ever religious themes. So, we have European art, which is heavily imbued with religious themes and images but not called 'Christian', and so-called 'Islamic' art which avoids religious themes.

Similar points can be made about 'Islamic' architecture. There are the iconic themes of domes and arches, mostly developments from Byzantine architecture, the Byzantine Aya Sophia in Istanbul being the inspiration for so much that followed. Beyond that, however, there is a great array of styles, specific to particular regions and historical periods. The Abbasid *malwiya* of Samurra in Iraq, following the Mesopotamian ziggurat, replicated in early examples in Egypt (the Ibn Tulun mosque in Cairo); the unique high-rises and decorative architecture of Yemen; the desert mud and stone constructions of Timbuktu, and other African styles. All these become 'Islamic', but there is no unity in their diversity, and no obvious connection to 'Islam' as such. By contrast, European architecture is Renaissance, Gothic, Bauhaus, modernist, postmodern, and so on – but never 'Christian'.

Part of the reason for this terminological oddity is the difficulty of finding alternative attributions. National attributions of 'Arab' or 'Persian' are never entirely accurate, given the multinational and cosmopolitan milieux of politics, urban society, art, science and philosophy; so 'Islamic' is judged to be general and inclusive. But this attribution then feeds into the discourse of difference and the religious essentialism on which it is based. This is particularly pertinent to the concept of 'Islamic' science.

'Islamic' science?

Islamic reformists, modernists and apologists have all insisted on the compatibility of modern science with Islam – insisted, indeed, that Islam actively encourages the seeking of knowledge. A supposed tradition of the Prophet (*hadith*) urges believers to seek knowledge even as far as China! This is regularly quoted to confirm Islam's friendliness to science. The term used in the *hadith* is *'ilm* (knowledge), which is also the modern term for science. Historically, however, science as such was not identified as a distinct branch of knowledge: indeed, in both Europe and the Middle East it was philosophy that subsumed what we now call science – which, in any case, was not separate from philosophical speculation, mysticism and magic. Above all, *'ilm* was religious knowledge, of the canonical sources and of *fiqh* (jurisprudence), and its most common derivative is *'alim* (pl. ulama), which designates clerics and religious scholars. So, *'ilm* in the Prophet's injunction could mean any of these forms of knowledge – most commonly religious knowledge – rather than science in our sense. Through the ages, Islamic academies, *madrasas*, taught a curriculum devoted almost exclusively to the religious sciences.

How do these modern Muslims react to instances where science contradicts revelation – most commonly at present in relation to creation versus evolution? The reformers and modernists of earlier times, such as Muhammad Abduh (d. 1905), favoured science and found formulae to deal with the scriptural stories, much in the manner of Christian liberals. This positivism has not been in favour in more recent utterances, and most Islamic commentators and apologists would assert the priority of revelation over any other form of knowledge, thus they deny and attack evolutionism. Like their fundamentalist Christian counterparts, they present their sacred myths as alternative scientific theory. The discourse of difference (and superiority), however, requires that 'science' is appropriated for religion, and this takes the form of the assertion of the historical priority of Muslims in the field of science.

The immense contribution made by Middle Eastern savants to the development of mathematics and science is not in doubt. Over the period roughly between the ninth and fourteenth centuries, they combined the Greek heritages of mathematics and philosophy (in turn from the earlier civilizations of Egypt and Mesopotamia) with Indian mathematics, especially the crucial decimal number system and the concept of 'zero', to arrive at many creative and advanced syntheses, which contributed to the formation of the science of the modern world. Mathematics aided sophisticated developments in astronomy, anticipating the later Copernican Revolution of the sixteenth century.[30] What relation did these advances have to Islam as a religion, and to its institutions and personnel? In terms of content and intellectual ancestry, such developments had nothing to do with any religion. They may have, however, in terms of education and personnel – similar to the case of Medieval Europe, in which a lot of education, and literate and scholarly activity, was carried out by church institutions and personnel, as these had a near-monopoly of literacy and book culture. Greek philosophy, especially that of Aristotle, was hugely important for the intellectual endeavours of both Christian and Muslim philosophers and theologians, and the translations and commentaries on Aristotle of the Andalusian Ibn

Rushd (1126–98) were to be highly influential in Europe through their adoption by Thomas Aquinas. But, whereas Aristotelianism became part of orthodox doctrine in the medieval church, and went on to feed into the Renaissance, in the Muslim context it came to be seen as suspect in relation to religious orthodoxy. Philosophy continued to develop in Muslim contexts, but separately from the religious sciences, in which the religious disciplines of the Quran, *hadith*, and above all *fiqh* were dominant.[31] Ibn Rushd got into trouble because he brought Aristotelian reason to bear on his religious pursuits. Science, or more correctly proto-science, was part of philosophy. It was carried out by individuals who may have been part of religious institutions (teachers in *madrasas*) – given the close affinity between mosques and literacy – but their philosophical, scientific and medical pursuits were separate from any religious functions they may have had.

As I have said, the *madrasas* were primarily seminaries of religious learning, to which their curricula were devoted; any philosophical or mathematical subjects were at best marginal. Training in astronomy/astrology, alchemy/chemistry and medicine was carried out in a sort of apprenticeship, making use of personal networks, and often under princely patronage. Toby Huff has contrasted this arrangement with the European university institutions that were legally incorporated and autonomous.[32] The latter maintained a locus for the continuity and accumulation of the sciences, as well as relative protection from interference by religious and secular authorities (it did not always work, as in the case of Galileo). Huff explains the decline or arrest of scientific advance in the Muslim world in terms of the absence of such corporate continuities. This thesis may be, and has been, criticized on many levels (see note 31), but its central argument of institutionalization and continuity is important – though it has to be put in the wider social context of the socio-economic development of Europe through the Renaissance, the discovery of the New World and the development of capitalism. Islam as such, then, had no intrinsic connection to science, but its orthodox forms and institutions of learning were always suspicious of philosophical speculation and assertions of the claims of reason against revelation.

The fact is that religious authority and institutions, whether

Christian or Muslim, typically laid claim to guardianship of knowledge, and asserted the supreme priority of revelation over all other sources. They therefore always tried to censor and punish rivals as heretics and rebels, including those making scientific claims that fell foul of religious truths. The ability of alternative and opposing forms of knowledge and discourse to prevail depended on the balance of power in the societies in question. For whatever reason, and some of the above explanations are pertinent, science lost out and religious authority triumphed in much of the 'Muslim world'. The Renaissance Revolution in the West, followed by capitalist expansion, aided the development and institutionalization of science and technology. Religion continued to fight a rearguard action, which it largely lost. Islam, as religion, at best bypassed philosophy and science when these did not pose direct challenges. Modern reformist Islam, beginning in the nineteenth century, adopted a positivist outlook and favoured science as a path of enlightenment and progress. More recent Islamist advocacies have largely accepted scientific and technical progress, but continue to refuse any scientific conclusions that contradict religious verities – most notably in the case of evolutionary science in biology.

Ultimately, bodies of knowledge and theory that have culminated in 'science' have been universal, and have done so through a series of syntheses occurring in a number of civilizational locations at different points in time. The Greek synthesis was developed further by the Middle Eastern savants, also drawing on Indian mathematics. China innovated many of the ideas and techniques that fed into the Renaissance Revolution in Europe. Events then moved to Europe, which later, with the help of capitalism and industry, became the dominant centre for the development of 'science' in its modern sense. Science cannot be claimed as the property of any national or religious group. The enormous resources of wealth, education and organization that are required to advance modern science have favoured advances in the rich economic centres and stable political entities of the world, from where it is then diffused.

* * *

This introductory chapter has advanced a number of themes and debates on the history, culture and society of the 'Muslim world' – more specifically its Middle East region. It has tried to demonstrate, in these various contexts, that religion is only an effective factor in those histories as part of configurations of social relations and ideologies – of economy, power and institutions. Modernity in these societies cannot be explained as a writing-out of some historical or cultural essence of Islam as religion or 'civilization'. The appeal to such an essence, however, has proved a powerful ideological motif both for ethno-religious nationalism in the region and for certain approaches in Western writing that present Islam and the region as totally other. These themes will be explored in relation to various aspects of those histories and societies in the chapters that follow.

1

Is There a Muslim Society?

Ernest Gellner's Sociology of Islam

Ernest Gellner, renowned philosopher, social theorist and anthropologist with fieldwork studies in Morocco to his credit, wrote on
Muslim societies against a wide canvas of philosophical, theoretical
and cross-historical references, making the subject more familiar and
absorbing to the Western reader. Above all, he advanced a coherent
model of 'Muslim society' that allows the reader to gain a clear conceptual hold on the subject. The historical components of this model
are given an impeccable Muslim ancestry in Gellner's extensive
drawing upon the fourteenth-century Arab historian Ibn Khaldun.
This ancestry of his ideas would appear to dispel any suggestion of
ethnocentrism or Western arrogance. Gellner's analysis of Muslim
history has the further virtue of being sociological: it advances a
sociology of Muslim society based on the dialectic between the city
and the tribe, as well as on the provisions of the Islamic religion and
the components of its historical and ideational formation.

This model of Muslim society is not only historical. The modern
developments in politics and society in the region can be analysed
within its terms: the demise of the tribe entails the ascendancy of
the city, with its peculiarly urban socio-religious ethos: rational,

scriptural, puritanical (the Weberian cluster), and is, as such, conducive to modernity and economic development. This aspect of the theory has the liberal virtue of combating ethnocentric and hostile perceptions of Islam as medieval obscurantism. While Gellner's formulations insist on the separateness and alterity of Islam as a coherent and unitary entity distinct from the West, it nevertheless assigns it the virtue of being an alternative route to modernity.

Like all general models of complex historical phenomena, Gellner's may be said to suffer from over-generalization and from the neglect of awkward elements that do not fit in. This line of critique is the familiar historian's resort against theorists. Antiquarian nit-picking, however, does little to diminish the cognitive hold of a good model. Specialists on the region may be critical of many elements of the model, and may cite facts and examples to support their objections, but the generalist reader is much more impressed by the integral picture presented, especially when it seems to offer equally coherent deductions to illuminate pressing political issues of the day. The following critical review, then, confronts a difficult task. It will examine and analyse historical and contemporary episodes and examples, with the intention not just of throwing doubt on the model in terms of 'facts', but of challenging the very idea of a homogeneous 'Muslim society'. It is argued that there are many Muslim societies, and that the range of their variation is comprehensible in terms of the normal practice of social and political analysis, like any other range of societies. Of course, there are certain cultural themes common to the Muslim lands and epochs, arising from religion and common historical reference, much like the common culture arising from Christian religion and history. It would be a mistake, however, to think that these cultural items and the entities they specify are sociological or political constants: they are assigned different meanings and roles by different socio-political contexts. The discussions and examples of the category of 'ulama' in what follows will illustrate this point.

Gellner does not stand alone in this theoretical position. His work is supported and enhanced by modern contributions in history and historical sociology. The work of Patricia Crone on early Islamic history lends Gellner's model a historical foundation: the formative period of the Islamic polity cast it in a mould from which it cannot escape. Important works in historical sociology or comparative history, including Gellner's own as well as those of John Hall and Michael Mann, elaborate similar types of analyses of the West and the rest, including 'Islam'.[1] In the contrast drawn between the totalized entities of Islam and the West, these writers pursue a common tradition in Western writing, dubbed 'Orientalist'. However, as Yahya Sadowski has pointed out,[2] this group differs from its predecessors in crucial respects. While previous writers have emphasized aspects of the Islamic polity conforming to Oriental despotism, with an all-powerful state and a helpless, unorganized society, Gellner, Crone and others present the opposite picture of a weak state, short on legitimacy and vulnerable to both internal threats from a solidary community under ulama leadership and external threats from the tribes. In the modern context, this Muslim-led solidary community – the descendant of the unvarying historical form – is now the adversary of the modern state, still challenging its legitimacy in terms of what Gellner calls the 'Islamic Norm'. Modern Islamism is illuminated in this model in terms that are coherent within a general and historical view of Islam as a unitary entity. The cogent statement of this analysis in terms of social theory is appealing to the generalist reader seeking illumination on the 'Islamic phenomenon'.

This framework of analysis constitutes the familiar philosophy of history asserting the 'uniqueness of the West', deriving from Max Weber among others, in which the West's historical achievements of capitalism, industrialism, modernity, democracy and so on, together constitute a reference point for an analysis of world history. This history is divided into civilizational areas (typically India, China and Islam) whose respective histories are searched for configurations that might be responsible for their failure to measure up to the achievements of the West (the history and sociology of an absence). A more recent, and much debated, variation on this theme is Samuel Huntington's thesis of the 'clash of civilizations', presenting world history and present patterns in terms of distinct unitary 'civilizations' standing apart and in potential conflict with one another – certainly in the case of Islam versus the West. It is not my aim here to address this philosophy of history; much has been written on it already, especially with regard to the much debated Weber thesis. The main concern of this chapter is 'Islam' as a category in this analysis.[3] My intention is not so much to show that they are wrong about Islam, but to challenge 'Islam' as a coherent sociological or political entity.

In what follows I shall concentrate on reviewing the elements of Gellner's model of 'Muslim society' contained in his book of that title,[4] and schematically repeated in his later *Postmodernism, Reason and Religion*.[5]

Gellner's model of Muslim society

Gellner starts from Ibn Khaldun's characterization of the cycles of rule. The theory, however, is not confined to Ibn Khaldun's historical examples, but aspires to a general interpretation of all Muslim societies, past and present. As we shall see, Gellner is obliged at one point to concede exceptions, notably the Ottoman Empire, but these exceptions are soon forgotten and the general sweep restored in further elaborations. Let us examine the elements of this theory.

First, the Khaldunian model. It rests on the distinction and contrast drawn between tribe and city. The ruling dynasty in the city is of tribal origin, but urbanized and civilized. Tribal forces outside the city are armed and militant. They are subordinate to the power of the ruling dynasty only insofar as the latter is sufficiently powerful to subdue the tribes, or sufficiently wealthy to buy them off. For much of the time, the power of the ruler over the tribes is nominal; they enjoy virtual autonomy and pose a potential threat. This threat becomes operative if and when the rulers are weakened and their forces in decline and decadence. Decadence of power is a necessary phase in the cycle supposed in this model. Dynasties that have conquered the city and its wealth do so with the militant vigour of their nomadic stock, and the solidarity (*asabiyya*) of their kinship bonds. In time, the rulers become settled and accustomed to the comforts and luxuries of the city, the branches of their kin develop factional interests and competition over wealth and power, which saps their solidarity. The cost of their expanding retinue and luxury spending leads to an intensification of the taxation burden on the urban population and their growing discontent. The growing weakness of the rulers encourages aspiring tribal dynasties, lusting for the city, to organize military campaigns, which ultimately topple the rulers and replace them, only for the cycle to be repeated.

Gellner expressed no doubts regarding the validity or accuracy of Ibn Khaldun's representation of the political dynamics of history. Can we accept without question the testimony of past historians regarding their own time and society, let alone their generalization from that to the whole of human history? Do we accept Herodotus, Xenophon or Tacitus in this manner? Surely, we must at least consider the historicity of Ibn Khaldun's utterances?[6] In fact, Ibn Khaldun was writing at a time of exceptional political turmoil in the Maghreb, with almost constant wars between dynasties and tribes. He himself was deeply involved in the politics and intrigues of dynastic rivalries as a servant of one ruler or another, deftly switching loyalties, sometimes getting caught and imprisoned.[7] Should we not at least consider this context in our evaluation of the author and his model?

For Gellner, if not quite for Ibn Khaldun, religion plays an important part in the cycle of rulers, which makes it peculiarly Islamic. Islam, for Gellner, is distinguished by a holy law, Shari'a, of divine inspiration and is, therefore, eternal and unchangeable by human volition. This law is based on the Quran and prophetic utterances and examples. It is elaborated, upheld and applied by a class of ulama. These, while lacking in institutional organization (and are, therefore, unlike a church) are nevertheless distinguished by their common attachment to the law. Their training and practice are concerned with the reading, ordering and interpretation of the holy text. Their orientations are scriptural and legal. These traits clearly distinguish them and their religious style from popular and tribal styles of religiosity.

Tribal religiosity, for Gellner, is orientated to personality and charisma, not text and learning – to cults, rituals and ceremonies, not to law.[8] For Gellner, urban religion is Weberian (textual and puritanical), while tribal religion is Durkheimian (his characterization). For the tribes, religion and religious leaders are to do with solidarities and boundaries, with war, alliance and mediation, whereas for the townsfolk they are to do with the sober regulation of peaceful communities of pious merchants and artisans.

The city and its ulama represent the 'High Culture' of Islam – literate, legalistic, unitarian, sober and puritanical – as against the 'Low' or 'Little Cultures' of the nomads – centred around the saint, the saintly lineage, magic and ceremony.[9] The nomads, however, recognize the superiority of the High Culture of the city and the sanctity of the law by which it lives, but cannot themselves aspire to its style, unless and until they are themselves urbanized.

Religion plays a crucial part in Gellner's version of the Khaldunian cycle and the dialectic between tribe and city. Urban religion constitutes a 'nomocracy' headed by the ulama as the guardians of the divine law. This norm demands an ideal government ruling in accordance with divine revelation on the model set up by the Prophet and the early caliphs. This ideal is unattainable in practice, and rulers are always found wanting by these standards. While the ulama and their bourgeois followers acquiesced in the rule of the powers that be, especially because this power protected the city from the threat of the barbarian tribes, they did not fully accept their legitimacy. The ulama controlled the symbols of legitimacy. However, the ulama and their pious followers held themselves separate from the powers and institutions of the rulers, not wishing to be contaminated by their illegality.

Gellner characterizes Muslim society as '[a] weak state and a strong culture'.[10] The state has a double weakness: vis-à-vis the tribes that it cannot control and which pose a constant threat, and the urban nomocracy that holds and can withhold the symbols of legitimacy. Culture is strong because it is entrenched in this nomocracy, which forges the bonds of community based on the law and on the authority and leadership of the ulama.

The precariousness of political power is demonstrated periodically when the two threats it confronts are combined. A disaffected urban preacher addresses himself to the militant tribes, denouncing the impious rulers in the name of the sacred law. While the tribesmen are not known for their legal observances, they are nevertheless impressed by the superior religion of the city and its representatives.

When this combination of urban preacher and militant tribe coincides with the right moment in the cycle, the moment of enfeeblement of rule through decadence and fragmentation, then it can make the push against the rulers and establish a new vigorous dynasty. The most important recent example of this process for Gellner was that of the Wahhabis of Arabia. We shall return to this example.

Before we proceed to examine the different components of this model, we should note that it is posed in contrast to the historical development of Europe and Christianity. Gellner has often drawn attention to the differences between, on the one hand, a European Christianity in which the established church fosters ritual, ceremony and the mediation of a priesthood, while the non-conformist fringes are puritanical and scriptural, rejecting mediation in favour of a direct relation between the believers and their God; and, on the other, an Islam, on the opposite shores of the Mediterranean, which is the mirror-image of this: in Islam it is the established urban religion that is scriptural and puritanical, rejecting magic, ceremony and personal saintly mediation, and the tribal fringes that uphold these latter elements. The European pattern also fosters eventual secularization, accompanying the processes of industrialization and modernity, while the Muslim case is just the opposite: not only resistant to secularization, but pursuing its modernity through religion – a perfect case of what later theorists, discussed in the Introduction, have advanced as 'alternative' or 'multiple' modernities.

In response to critiques of earlier formulations of his model, Gellner recognized that the Ottoman Empire posed problems for the Khaldunian cyclical model. In a section of his essay entitled 'The Terrible Turk',[11] Gellner acknowledged that the longevity of a centralized and bureaucratized Ottoman state, including Egypt, was clearly at variance with the Khaldunian model, in that it did not succumb to its cycles. We should remark in passing that, if the model is supposed to cover the generality of Islamic society, then this is a pretty large exception, considering that it covered much of the greater part of the central Islamic lands from the fifteenth to the twentieth century. How is this exception to be explained? The *devshirme* system of military and bureaucratic recruitment (enslaved children levied from the Christian population of the Balkans, then trained as servants of the sultan), Gellner argued, insulated the Ottoman state from both tribes and ulama by providing loyal servants, divorced from kinship bonds and loyalties, who bypassed both these dangerous sources. In addition, the central parts of the Empire – Anatolia, the Balkans and Egypt – were inhabited by quiescent, tax-paying peasants and not militant tribesmen. Gellner noted, however, that other Muslim rulers had attempted a solution to the dilemma of political organization through recruitment of 'non-tribal mercenary or slave armies',[12] but, as Ibn Khaldun noted, that 'only aggravates the disease of a declining state'. This anomaly made Gellner give up on sociology and merely add another essentialist model:

> It is probably best not to make any attempt to explain away the phenomenon [of the successful Ottoman state] at all, but simply accept it as an alternative model: within the general conditions imposed both by nature and the technical and cultural equipment of Muslim civilisation, there exist at least two possible solutions to the problem of political organisation.[13]

We are back to the essence of 'Muslim civilization' and away from sociology/politics/economics. In fact, as we shall see, the *devshirme* system degenerated and came to an end by the seventeenth century; the janissaries who had initially been the product of this system were then recruited from the native Muslim population, which had very close links with kin, craft guilds and urban quarters. This did not lead to the collapse of the Empire under the pressures of tribal dissidence or ulama intransigence.

The elements of the model

The ulama
Following his statement that Muslim society consists of a weak state and a strong culture, Gellner proceeded to describe the guardians of this culture as follows:

The culture was in the keeping of a relatively open, non-hereditary and thus non-exclusive class, but without a central secretariat, general organisation, formal hierarchy or any machinery for convening periodic councils. Its authority, though in part explicable by the need in such a society for urban services, the capacity of clerkly faith to express the urban ethos, and by the ever-present threat of a reforming-preacher/tribal-fronde alliance, nevertheless remains a sociological mystery ... Perhaps we cannot go beyond describing this self-perpetuating circle.[14]

If this were so, it would indeed be a sociological mystery. We should note, however, that Muslim society, as it emerges from Gellner's work, does not seem to have much of a sociology or a politics or an economics, beyond constantly re-enacting its basic essence. Hall, following Gellner's characterization to its logical conclusion, makes the following remarkable statement:

And what *was* [Muslim] society? It was a large cultural area within which polities of various sizes came and went, or more theoretically, it was an area held together by an ideology. Islam, in other words, had considerable extensive powers. Ideology did not 'reflect' more basic social processes, as Durkheim and Marx believed: it was society.[15]

The source of ulama power, then, insofar as it can be identified, is the urban ethos and its hold over the means of legality and the symbols of legitimacy, upheld by a scholarly/commercial bourgeoisie, remarkable for 'its homogeneity within Islam over many countries and continents, and [for] the source of its astonishing authority'.[16] The Ottoman world did not constitute an exception in the character of this class, its homogeneity and its organization, or lack of it. It is just that the Ottomans had cleverly neutralized this class, at least in part, through their *devshirme* administrators and systematic bureaucratization. Hall, following Gellner's characterization of the ulama in Muslim society, attributes the success of the Ottomans in subduing their ulama to the fact that they paid them well![17] It is strange that all other Muslim dynasties had not resorted to this simple expedient.

The Ottomans, however, progressively from the sixteenth century, had also bureaucratized the ulama (as Hall does recognize); established the religious institution as a department of state; and taken charge of the training, recruitment, remuneration and control of the ulama qua jurists and legal functionaries and qua teachers and preachers.[18] The sixteenth-century sultan known in English as 'Suleiman the Magnificent' is known in Arabic as 'Suleiman al-Kanuni' – the lawgiver. It was under him that the *kanun-name*, an early attempt at codifying the Shari'a and mixing it with sultanic edicts, was introduced. The Ottoman state declared its own competence in matters of law and legally based legitimacy, and the ulama were its functionaries and servants. Like other functionaries, they were differentiated by function, such as law and education, and by rank, ranging from Shaykhulislam (highest religious office, head of religious institutions) and *kadiaskar* (two deputies), to ordinary *madrasa* teachers and mosque preachers. In these capacities, each rank had its own sphere of power and support, which varied from time to time, and which brought the various ranks of the ulama into the political struggles and intrigues both of the *askari* (military/bureaucratic) class and of popular agitation. At the heart of the Ottoman state, then, the ulama were organized: not as a church, but as a department of state and, as such, as full participants in the bureaucratic politics of the state. This form of organization of the ulama, as we shall see, was particular to Istanbul and the heart of the Empire. Elsewhere, the ulama did not lack organization or politics, they just had different modes of organization.

Gellner's characterization of the power of the ulama and their control of symbols of legitimacy must be viewed, then, in the contexts of: (1) institutional locations (not unorganized free-floating figures of authority); (2) differentiated powers and interests following from these locations, which include conflicts and struggles between different sections of the ulama; and (3) involvement in political struggles and intrigues of both the elites and the populace.

Gellner's assertion that the ulama were 'without a central secretariat, general organisation, formal hierarchy, or any machinery for convening periodic councils' implicitly highlights contrasts to the

Christian churches. It is true that they were not organized like a church, but, in the Ottoman case, they had a clear form of organization and a formal hierarchy. As we shall see, however, these are not the only forms of organization of the ulama. In Ottoman lands and elsewhere we also find the *awqaf* administrations (based on religious endowments; see Chapter 2); the Sufi orders (antithetical to the ulama's ethos in Gellner's characterization); political interest groups and councils of notables, guilds and military factions; and informal family and social networks.

The effect of Gellner's picture of the ulama in Muslim society is to assign them a fixed and unvarying political role, part of the essential and repetitive cycles of the society's politics. They are the guardians of the sacred law and the controllers of the symbols of legitimacy. In that capacity they are the natural leaders of the urban community, enjoying unquestioned authority: all this without institutional locations or formal organization. In this way, they are excluded from the exigencies and rhythms of the processes of social affiliation and political struggles that we would expect to affect any social group. We should evaluate this picture through examples. A particularly pertinent example is that of the involvement of the Istanbul ulama in the politics of reform initiated and carried out by successive sultans from the closing decades of the eighteenth century.

From the sixteenth century, and possibly earlier,[19] an aristocracy of ulama was forming around the high offices of state in the learned hierarchy. Families and clans of ulama increasingly monopolized and competed for these offices. Young men with little learning assumed high offices through nepotism and bribery. This process divided the ulama, producing a stratum of rank and privilege set against the common run of teachers, preachers, functionaries, students and the unemployed. By the eighteenth century this process was far advanced, with keen competition for the high posts between members of the ulama aristocracy, and seething resentment from the lower ranks at their exclusion.[20] The formation of political alliances and conflicts followed this split. The aristocratic clans of the ulama became integrated into the ruling classes, and into the life of the court and high office. Anxious for position and privilege in a situation of intense competition, this sector of the ulama displayed loyalty and support for the sultan, including his projects of military and administrative reform. The first obstacle to these reforms was the resistance of the janissary corps. In the struggle between Selim III and the janissaries in 1807[21] many of the high-ranking ulama were firmly behind the sultan; others, like the Shaykhulislam, vacillated opportunistically; while the lower ranks, especially the students (known as *softas*) participated in the janissary-led riots and preached religious righteousness on their side, denouncing the reforms as the works of foreign infidels. A brief look at the janissaries is necessary at this point.

From the seventeenth to the nineteenth centuries the janissary corps played a central part in the politics of the Empire, and especially of Istanbul. This corps, which had emerged earlier as part of the *devshirme* system, had, by the seventeenth century, become deeply entrenched in the social and economic life of the main cities, including the capital.[22] The recruits were native Muslims (as against the former *devshirme*), who also became attached to particular trades and crafts, soldiering only part-time if at all, but drawing military stipends – an important factor in the military enfeeblement of the Empire. Successive sultans tried to ameliorate or alter this situation, but were confronted by the power of the armed janissaries leading the urban classes to which they were affiliated in riots and disturbances defending their position and privileges. This defence of the status quo was often supported by sectors of the ulama afraid for their own privileges. Here we have an inversion of Gellner's disgruntled *'alim* (singular of ulama) leading dissident armed tribesmen against the city. We have instead militant urban soldiers leading the urban classes against feared assaults by the government, and the ulama riding on the bandwagon. A further twist is added to this configuration if we consider the religious affiliation of the janissaries, which was firmly to the Bektashi order, considered by the orthodox to be heretical, and tainted by heterodox Shi'i doctrines and rituals. These struggles were intensified towards the end of the eighteenth century, when military reforms became an urgent necessity if the Empire was to survive against the European powers. Sultan Selim instituted a new European-style military corps known as *nizam-i-jedid* ('new order'). The janissaries saw this development as a threat and rioted, initiating disturbances in the capital that were to end in the dethronement of the Sultan. His later successor, Mahmud II, renewed the reform plans and, with greater subtlety and cunning, succeeded in ridding himself of the janissaries once and for all in 1825. Let us consider the role of the ulama in these struggles.

Mahmud's strategy was to isolate the janissaries from their erstwhile religious allies.[23] He set out to appease the lower orders of the ulama and the students by providing avenues of employment and gain. In 1824, for instance, he issued a decree forbidding parents to withdraw their sons from *mektebs* (religious schools) before they had attained adequate religious knowledge.[24] This measure pleased the neighbourhood imams greatly, assuring as it did more secure income and higher standing. The plan for the new military order included an imam for each of the 51 proposed companies, thus offering possibilities of state employment for the lower ranks of ulama and the students. The period of service of the military imam was to be five years, thus providing opportunities for larger numbers. At the same time, retired military imams could enter the ranks of the judiciary.[25] Mahmud also involved the higher ulama in the councils that made the decisions on military reforms, giving them shared responsibility for those decisions. This strategy was to be crowned with success. When the crunch came and the janissaries made their expected move in June 1825, they were weakened and isolated. The ulama of all ranks stood against them and preached obedience to the sultan, especially in his efforts to strengthen the armies of Islam.[26]

The following century of reforms divided the ulama. Many of the high-ranking ulama continued their support for successive sultans and vezirs, even when their reforms threatened the long-term continuation of their authority and position. Some of them participated in the drafting of the *tanzimat* (reform) decrees and in the projects of legal reform. Others resisted on some occasions and acquiesced in others.[27] The lower-ranking ulama and the students returned to their opposition and discontent; Mahmud's measures of appeasement soon dissipated after their objective had been achieved.

These episodes illustrate the divisions within the ulama of Istanbul and the shifting political affiliations of the different sectors in line with political developments and strategies. The Ottoman Empire, however, was not just Istanbul and the Terrible Turk. The various provinces offered a wide range of diversity. The ulama (or sectors thereof) occupied different positions and were involved in different political games in the various provincial centres. This variety is systematically analysed and compared in the now classic essay by Albert Hourani, 'Ottoman Reform and the Politics of Notables'.[28] In Hourani's analysis, 'notables' are the patrician class of the major cities who have access to the rulers or governors and may sit in their councils. At the same time, they have bases of social and economic power, such as networks of clients and followers, as well as control of the provisions of the city from a rural hinterland that they control. They are thus important intermediaries between the governors and the governed. The ulama, or at least the higher ulama, formed an important part of this class. They were part of the old, established families of the Middle Eastern and North African cities whose members alternated in religious office. Hourani presented a typology of the different cities in terms of their natures, their sources and instruments of power, and the forms of political association and manoeuvring they consequently engaged in (see Chapter 2 for further elaboration).

In this picture, Istanbul was unique in not featuring politics of notables. It lacked the ancient families of other cities because it had not been a Muslim city before the conquest, and its trading bourgeoisie remained predominantly non-Muslim. The politics of Istanbul, right up to the late nineteenth century, were the politics of court and bureaucracy. As we have seen, the ulama were largely bureaucratized, and participated in the politics of court, bureaucracy and military formations – especially of the janissaries, until their destruction.

The cities of Egypt and the Fertile Crescent present a number of different pictures. What they have in common is that the presence of the central Ottoman bureaucracy and the military units within them was partial and sometimes precarious. The governors could rule only through the medium of the local power elites: the notables, including the ulama, and localized military formations, notably janissary regiments that established local connections with guilds and urban quarters and thereby became part of the politics of the notables.

Here is how Hourani characterized the sources of the power held by the ulama component of the notables:

> [The ulama] were necessary to the Ottoman government because they alone could confer legitimacy on its acts. But while in Istanbul they were an official group, in the provinces they were local groups: apart from the *qadi*, the others – *mufiis, naqib, na'ibs* – were drawn from local families. Their positions alone would have given them influence, but they derived it also from other sources: from the inherited reputation of certain religious families, going back many centuries perhaps to some saint whose tomb lay at the heart of the city; from the fact that, in spite of this, the corps of ulama lay open to all Muslims; from the connection of the local ulama with the whole religious order and thus with the palace and the imperial *divan*; and from their wealth, built up through the custody of *waqfs* or the traditional connection with the commercial bourgeoisie, and relatively safe from the danger of confiscation because of their religious position.[29]

Hourani, then, attributes the power of the ulama partly to their religious position and partly to material considerations of connections and wealth – and the relative safety of this wealth. Note that religious standing is understood in large part to be derived from the inherited charisma of family and sacred ancestry (many of the religious families claimed descent from the Prophet, and the *naqib* is precisely the doyen of these *ashraf*, the holy lineages).

But this is only a very general picture, and Hourani went on to outline much more specific configurations for particular cities. In eighteenth-century Cairo, for instance, the main source of power was the control of the land tax:

> [The local leadership] did not come either from the religious class or from the leaders of the military corps. It is true, the religious leaders (not so much the teachers of the Azhar as the heads of families which possessed a hereditary leadership of important *turuq*) had certain weapons in their hands: a connection with the Muslim merchants

who engaged in the Nile and Red Sea trade, control of *waqfs*, a close link with the population of the small towns and countryside, and of course the prestige of religious ancestry and learning. But the long experience of military rule, and the whole tradition of the Sunni ulama, had taught them to play a discreet and secondary role, and taught the people to look elsewhere for political leadership.[30]

Hourani goes on to show that the main loci of power were the rival mamluke (military slave dynasties) households, 'elites created by men possessing political or military power and inheriting their prestige, composed of freedmen trained in the service of the current heads of the household, and held together by solidarity which would last a lifetime'.[31] The leaders and politicians of each household knew how to make of it a core around which clustered religious leaders, commanders of regiments, popular guilds and urban quarters. These households competed for offices and titles offered by the Ottoman governor, and the rich tax farms that went with them, which were the ultimate source of their wealth and influence. Within this configuration, then, the ulama entered political struggles as followers of one or other faction, and not altogether as a corps of ulama. Hourani, in the passage quoted, is careful to distinguish the more powerful ulama from the teachers of al-Azhar (typical of Gellner's 'guardians of the Norm'), and to indicate that the sources of power of the religious leaders consisted of inherited charisma, *awqaf* associated with Sufi *turuq*, and lucrative commercial connections. Hourani then went on to delineate yet other patterns for Syrian, Iraqi and Arabian cities. In each case the ulama's forms of power and influence were related to the sources and instruments of the power of the local elites and the place of the ulama within them.

Hourani's analysis relates to relatively modern times – the eighteenth and nineteenth centuries. Are these, then, exceptional? And do they differ from the formations of earlier centuries? Well, of course they do, but only in the patterns of politics and the nature of factions and their sources of power. That is to say, we are looking at variant patterns of politics, not at some eternal Muslim society. We shall see in Chapter 2 how political modernity affected those patterns from the nineteenth century. Let us now consider an example from much earlier mamluke Egypt and Syria – that of the turbulent times of the famous jurist Ibn Taymiyya.

In many respects, Ibn Taymiyya (1263–1328) is a Gellnerian ideal-type *'alim*. A Hanbali,[32] he was a textual literalist and strict legalist, militantly intolerant of what he considered heterodoxy or heresy, a scourge of the Sufis and bitter enemy of the Shi'a. He issued a famous fatwa against Islamized Mongols who were at the time the rulers of Mardin. He declared that they were not Muslims because they ruled in accordance with the *yasa* of Mongols alongside the Shari'a. That fatwa is now widely quoted by modern Islamists denouncing their governments as non-Muslim for not ruling by the Shari'a alone. Ibn Taymiyya is also venerated by the Wahhabis and Salafis for his strict literalism and fight against Sufis and the Shi'a.

Ibn Taymiyya, though conforming to Gellner's image of an *'alim*, lived through events and struggles that illustrate the diversity and conflicts of religious life at his time. He lived in a non-Gellnerian world of differentiated society and religious schism involved in political struggle, in alliance or opposition to one mamluke amir or another.

As a Hanbali teacher and judge, Ibn Taymiyya entered into polemics against the *qadis* and scholars of other schools – the Ash'aris in theology and the Shafi'is in law. He also polemicized against the Sufis, especially against the followers of the mystical ideas of Ibn 'Arabi. One of his prominent antagonists was 'Ala' al-Din al-Qunawi – Shafi'i Qadi-ul-Qudat (chief judge) of Damascus, and at the same time a Sufi follower of Ibn 'Arabi (a coincidence of legalism and mysticism that, though anomalous for Gellner, is common, as we shall see). They replied in kind and criticized him for anthropomorphism (*tajseem*, attributing human character to God). These disputes often ended up in councils of inquisition presided over by mamluke amirs. On several occasions Ibn Taymiyya ended up in jail and in disgrace. On others he had the better of his opponents. The relative ascendancy of different mamlukes seems to have determined his fortunes. Muhammad bin Qalawun favoured Ibn Taymiyya, while Baybars al-Jashinkir favoured his opponents.

We catch a glimpse of a situation in which ulama, doctrine, law and rule were involved in a complex, differentiated society and polity, and can be understood only in terms of their dynamic and conjunctures. It is a far cry from the unitary class of non-organized ulama enjoying undisputed authority guaranteed by the divine law. The example of Ibn Taymiyya, his adversaries and patrons does not seem to fit in easily with Gellner's formulae: 'The social norms and ideals ... are available, in final and definitive form, to anyone who can read. The Norm is extra-ethnic and extra-social, and not too easily susceptible to political manipulation. This is of very great importance'.[33]

We have also noted, in passing, that the ulama were closely involved in urban Sufism – another interesting anomaly in Gellner's model. We should consider this aspect further.

The ulama and Sufism

Gellner recognizes urban Sufism,[34] its pervasiveness and its diversity. There are many different kinds of Sufi orders, some more ecstatic than others. These cater for the religious needs of various urban strata, especially the illiterate lower orders, who, like their tribal brethren, are not satisfied with a diet of scripture and law, but need audio-visual excitement. In the urban setting, however, Sufism, according to Gellner, does not play the vital (Durkheimian) social role it does in the tribes. It does, nevertheless, provide forms of organization, charisma, leadership and following, which satisfy needs and are not to be found elsewhere in this supposedly egalitarian and unorganized religion. Gellner's characterization of urban Sufism is perhaps best summed up in a passage from another of his essays:

> Roughly speaking: urban Sufi mysticism is an alternative to the legalistic, restrained, arid (as it seems to its critics) Islam of the ulama. Rural and tribal 'Sufism' is a substitute for it. In the one case, an alternative is sought for the Islam of the ulama because it does not fully satisfy. In the other case, a substitute for it is required because, though its endorsement is desired, it is, in its proper and urban form, locally unavailable, or is unusable in the tribal context.[35]

In either case, Sufism, for Gellner, is distinct from the Islam of the ulama. The fact of the matter is that the ulama themselves, for much of Muslim history, were involved as members and leaders of Sufism. As we saw in the case of Ibn Taymiyya's antagonist, the Shafi'i *qadi* of Damascus, he was also a Sufi follower of the doctrines of Ibn al'Arabi. This is not the exception, but almost the norm. It was Ibn Taymiyya's uncompromising hostility to Sufism that was the exception.

Sufism, as Gellner appreciated, was a primary form of organization and association. Craft guilds and urban quarters were organized as Sufi orders. The factions of urban popular as well as princely and notable politics were, consequently, tied up with Sufi organization. The ulama, being closely involved in these forms of organization and politics, were inevitably included in these orders. In the Ottoman context, the janissaries and their associates in the urban classes were predominantly Bektashi – an order distrusted by the establishment for its Alawi and Shi'i sympathies and its heterodox practices, including ritual consumption of *rakı* (a Turkish alcoholic drink). On the other hand, the Mevlevi order attracted for the most part members of the court circles and the ruling elites, including ulama. Other *turuq*, branches of the Qadiriyya, and later the Nakshibandi, also became important in urban affiliations and politics, and most had their complement of ulama. Here is another form of social organization in which the ulama were involved, often as ulama. How does this square with sober scripturalism?

'Within the enormous mass of these movements,' wrote Gellner, 'some are much nearer the ecstatic, non-scripturalist end of the spectrum than others. Some, on the other hand, are close to the sober-urban-unitarian-puritan scripturalist end.'[36] The latter end of the spectrum was for those who sought a compromise between legalism and a minimum of social organization. This is true of the Nakshibandi orders, and the Khalwatiyya in Egypt, which are scriptural and legalistic. While these have many ulama members, they are by no means the only resort of Sufi ulama. As we saw, the Mevlevi order included many ulama. This order is best known for its dance (inspiring the name 'whirling dervishes'), known as the *sema* ceremony, by any standards ecstatic and ceremonial. What Gellner does not seem to realize is that you can engage in ecstatic, mystical and ceremonial activity, including music and dancing, and still be 'dignified'. The high and the low in the social order engaged in different ceremonies and musical styles. This difference can be readily observed at the present time if you contrast, say, the popular celebrations on the night of the *mawlid* (Prophet's birthday) in the popular religious quarters of Cairo (Al-Husain or Al-Sayida Zeynab) with the Mevlevi *sema* ceremony in their Istanbul *tekke* (lodge). The first comprise raucous music and chanting, open to all comers – men in peasant dress, jeans or soldiers' uniforms, and women with sundry covers, some high on hashish, rolling their heads and occasionally going into a trance. The second features classical music with religious chants accompanying a highly disciplined and well-rehearsed whirling dance, the dancers dressed in uniform robes and headgear, the whole designed to produce an aesthetic experience, musical and visual. In fact, there is ample evidence that, at different points in Muslim history, the ulama fully participated in the mysticism, ceremonies, rituals and heterodox beliefs that went with them. It is worth quoting at length from John Kingsley Birge's *The Bektashi Order of Dervishes*:

> When the writer first visited Turkey in 1913 he went about under the impression that Turkey was a Sunni ... country. He quickly found to his surprise that an enormous proportion of the people not only were affiliated with dervish brotherhoods, but even the leaders who appeared on Friday as Imams in the formal worship (*namaz*) in the mosque, were on other days to be found acting as *Seyhs* in dervish tekkes. During Muharrem, the month when Shi'ites especially remember the death of *Huseyin* ... the writer visited tekke after tekke, and found in them dervishes passionately mourning the death of *Hasan* and *Huseyin*.

The writer questions 'one of Turkey's greatest scholars' about this phenomenon:

> The scholar replied that there in Constantinople where the proportion was presumably less than in the rest of the country, probably

sixty per cent of the people belonged directly or indirectly to dervish fraternities . . . In Muslim lands, he continued, the practice of *takiye*, dissimulation, has grown up to make possible a man continuing his standing as an orthodox member of the religious body while at the same time being a member of a mystic fraternity which emphasised an experiential rather than a traditional and formal approach to reality.[37]

The significance of this testimony is clear enough for our argument. There remains the question of 'dissimulation'. For the most part, an *'alim*'s membership or leadership of dervish brotherhoods was no secret. Birge's informant, however, may have been referring to Shi'i sympathies as an aspect that was hidden: for most of Ottoman history, such sympathies were not only religiously heterodox, but politically subversive, implying association with Iranian religion. It may be more accurate to say that some ulama kept their official legal and scholarly role separate from their participation in mystic orders. Others, as we have seen, were leaders, officers and spokesmen of these orders.

The urban ethos

Gellner invokes Weber's concept of 'elective affinity' to explain the special link of the urban bourgeoisie to puritan, ethical, scriptural religiosity.[38] He does cite contrary examples, notably the entrepreneurial but non-puritanical Chinese; but the concept does apply in the Muslim case with 'remarkable homogeneity' across all Islamic lands throughout their history. This homogeneity is due not only to the said elective affinity, but to the special position of 'astonishing authority' of the ulama as the upholders of the Norm, and as possible allies of the militant tribesmen in displacing the ruler.

We have seen in the previous section that scriptural orthodoxy and the Shari'a were upheld by the ulama in their official capacity as scholars and jurists, but that many of the same ulama also participated in Sufi brotherhoods, some of whose beliefs and practices bordered on the heterodox and the subversive, and openly included music and dancing. Does this suggest that many of the ulama and the urban bourgeoisie to which they belonged were scriptural only in certain situations but not in others (which would make a nonsense of the elective affinity thesis, dependent as it is on the notion of a deep psychological commitment)?

Sufism apart, we may ask: do scripturalism and orthodoxy in Islam necessarily entail 'puritanism' and a distaste for ceremony? The religious calendar of orthodox Islam is dotted with ceremonial occasions. Just consider the fasting month of Ramadan throughout the Islamic lands: festivities interlaced with prayer and worship (for the especially religious and the old), overeating, conviviality both at home and in the streets and cafés, including musical recitals and storytelling, and many games. This can be aptly described as a 'mixture of the sacred, the profane and the commercial', as Gellner described the *counter*-example of the pagan Chinese.[39] We also note the ceremonies of Muharram and Ashura – occasions of mourning for some (and as we have seen, not just Shi'a), but joyful celebration for others (for example, in North Africa); or the routine ceremonies of marriage and circumcision. All these are elaborate ceremonies with considerable input of ritual, much of it 'superstition', against the evil eye (which, as I shall show, is recognized in the Quran), in seeking the blessing of saints and the propitiation of evil spirits. All these regular and frequent ceremonial indulgences, in terms of pleasures as well as 'superstition', constitute an essential part of the lifestyle of the urban bourgeoisie throughout the Muslim world, with the exception of the Wahhabis and modern reformists. With few departures, the ulama fully condone and participate in these activities. The Wahhabis, as represented by the Saudi regime, are considered by most Muslims to be harsh and un-Islamic killjoys for prohibiting ceremony and music – especially during such honoured occasions as the celebration of the *mawlid*. Indeed, this prohibition is commonly broken in the Hijaz and its sacred capital Mecca, which has remained resolutely Shafi'i. This Wahhabi puritan zeal, however, is characteristic of many of the modern Salafis and radical Islamists, and it is perhaps this uniquely modern phenomenon that misled Gellner into interpreting puritanism as a universal trait of orthodoxy.

Does puritanism follow from scripturalism? An obvious point that is often overlooked in discussions of the Weber thesis is that there is nothing 'puritanical' about the Bible as such, which includes passionate love poems and accounts of lascivious sexuality as well as magic and occult forces – the very stuff of 'superstition' (which, as we know, is other people's religion). It is the puritans who rendered a puritanical reading of the Bible. Similarly, there is nothing puritanical about the Quran. After all, it allows a man four wives and as many slave girls as he can afford! Nor is the Quran antithetical to the props of magic and the rituals against evil spirits.

Every recitation of the Quran starts with a banishment of the Devil. Al-Shaytan (Satan) is a prominent character in many Quranic verses, and believers are constantly enjoined to beware his traps.[40] It follows, therefore, that the Devil and his servants are potent forces to be banished by rituals and incantations, and to be harnessed by those intent on evil. This recognition of evil forces is explicit in Surat al-Falaq (Chapter of the Daybreak), which, being short, can be quoted in full:

> Say: 'I take refuge with the Lord of the Daybreak
> from the evil of what He has created,
> from the evil of darkness when it gathers,
> from the evil of women who blow on knots,
> from the evil of an envier when he envies.'[41]

The evil eye of the envier (a deeply entrenched belief among members of all religions in the Middle East and elsewhere), the magic of 'blowing on knots', the mysterious forces of darkness – are the common ingredients of magic and ritual: these lines are widely recited as an invocation against magic and spells, but also as a commencement of spells. It is believed by some that repetition of this chapter (7, 15 or 40 times), combined with other procedures, can summon up powers for magical spells or for undoing them. Marcel Mauss, in his *A General Theory of Magic*, defines magic as the appropriation of the collective symbols of religion for instrumental individual ends.[42] The procedure described here conforms to this definition and may be argued to be alien to orthodox scriptural observance. It should be noted, however, that these procedures are not alien to ulama, and that many of them, especially from the lower orders of teachers and preachers, also offer their magical services to the populace. The urban bourgeoisie, especially their women, are among their regular clients. Above all, the entities and powers in question are not the product of the imagination of superstitious folk – rather, their existence and danger are actually specified in the scriptures.

Scriptural recognition of folk beliefs is not confined to this chapter, but crops up in many others, most specifically in the chapter on the jinn.[43] It reveals that some of the jinn have heard the Quran and have accepted Islam. At the same time, there are 'certain men of mankind who would take refuge with certain men of the jinn, and they increased them in vileness'. Jinn are repeatedly mentioned in other parts of the holy book as an order of creation parallel to mankind, with good and bad individuals, some Muslim and some pagan, and they have connections and intercourse with humans. The concepts of the jinn and of their character are the pillars of magical and ritual beliefs and practice in the Near East (for Jews and Christians as much as for Muslims). Their existence and character are firmly attested in the Quran, and over the centuries entered the beliefs and services of many of the ulama as well as the common people.

Gellner is, of course, correct to distinguish between the Great Tradition of urban and scholarly literacy and the Little Traditions of folk belief and practice, but he is wrong to draw the boundaries between the two in terms of ceremonies, ritual and magic – these elements are common to both, as we have seen; it is the style of performing them that differs. Gellner is surprised to note: 'It is not only the urban and literate Great Tradition which is significantly similar in Islam ... the rural and folk tradition also displays astonishing similarities'.[44] He goes on to say that these Little Traditions cannot be based on pre-Islamic local paganism – otherwise they would not display such similarities across geographical barriers. This mystery is partly solved, however, once we realize that many of these 'traditions' have a basis in the Quran, which, in turn, shares these concepts with ancient Middle Eastern ideas and practices. These similarities, therefore, are not confined to Islam, but are to be found among Christianity, Judaism and other religions.[45]

The pleasures of the flesh

Weber's puritans were 'this-worldly' ascetics, who, supposedly, exercised methodical restraint in matters of bodily pleasures: indulgences in sex, food, drink and other intoxicants; entertainments; and even love of close kin, spouses and children. Gellner explicitly transfers this Weberian characterization to the Muslim urban bourgeoisie and their ulama members. The 'Muslim bourgeoisie' is a broad category; there have been many such bourgeoisies, and each one no doubt included a wide range of personal dispositions. However, if we are to look at the main historical examples in the central Islamic lands, then the picture we get is very far from the puritan characterization. We have already mentioned their fondness for ceremony, often including music and dancing. Let us look at the pleasures of the flesh.

Sexuality

Original sin and man's fallen nature are the essential doctrinal props of Christian puritanism, and these are absent in Islam. For a Muslim man many forms of sexuality are allowed, providing they are enacted within a legitimate relationship of marriage or slavery.[46] The Quran is very positive about sexual activity; its injunctions, mostly addressed to men, are clear: 'Your women are a tillage for you; so come unto your tillage as you wish, and forward for your souls.'[47] A man is allowed up to four wives at any one time, with the right of instant divorce and re-marriage, and an unlimited number of slave concubines. The *sunna*, the example and traditions of the Prophet and his Companions, offer further encouragement in this direction. In the literature of *fiqh* (jurisprudence), man's sexual desire is considered powerful and dangerous if not controlled and regulated.[48] But the mode of control prescribed, unlike Christian puritanism, is legal access, through marriage or concubinage, to one or more women from an early age. Celibacy, abstinence, even restraint, are not in the spirit of Orthodox Islam, and are confined mostly to the ascetic practices of some Sufis and sectarians.

The picture of Paradise drawn in many places in the Quran, and elaborated on in the literature of commentary and interpretation,[49] is one of the sensual delights of food, drink (pure waters, milk and honey, wine) and sex:

> In the Gardens of Delight ... upon close-wrought couches reclining upon them, set face to face, immortal youths going round about them with goblets, and ewers, and a cup from a spring (no brows throbbing, no intoxication) and such fruits as they shall choose, and such flesh of fowl as they desire, and wide-eyed houris as the likeness of hidden pearls.[50]

It is made clear in other chapters that those *houris* are virgins, untouched by men or jinn. Note also the mention of 'immortal youths' serving heavenly drinks, their presence and service being one of the pleasures.[51] While sodomy is strictly forbidden in Islam, the love of boys is a constant theme in the culture of the Middle East – and not just for Muslims – over the centuries. It is celebrated in poetry and song, and considered by the pious to be a regular temptation. Ibn Hanbal is reported to have allowed the believer one look at a comely boy, but insisted that a second would incriminate his soul. This model of heavenly pleasure contrasts starkly with the Jewish and Christian versions, with sombre worship and sacred music, the greatest pleasure being the presence of the Lord.

It is not surprising, therefore, to find in the large corpus of Arabic erotic literature many notable contributions by distinguished jurists, exploring through explicit tales and reflections what is proper and licit in sexual conduct, the nature and (physical) types of women and how to treat them (the discourse being addressed to the male Muslim) and the techniques of pleasure.[52] The list of such works includes those of the Hanbali *'alim* and student of the stern Ibn Taymiyya Ibn Qayyim al-Jawzia, entitled *The Lovers' Garden* and *Tales about Women*. Another distinguished jurist, Jalaluldin al-Suyuti (1445–1505), whose prolific oeuvre included compilations and verifications of *hadith* and commentaries on the Quran, also wrote erotic *belles lettres*, one of which was a description of the wedding nights of members of twenty different crafts and professions in the respective idioms of their vocations.[53] The two most renowned and widely diffused pornographic works in Arabic literature, *The Perfumed Garden* and *How an Old Man Can Regain His Youth through Sexual Potency* were both written, in the twelfth and fifteenth centuries respectively, by men with religious titles – the first by Shaykh Sidi Muhammad Nefzawi, the second by Mawla Ahmad Ibn Sulayman.[54]

For these pious men, writing erotic literature was nothing to be ashamed of, for the sexual conduct described is legitimate, being within the frame of a legal relationship of marriage or slavery. And if it is not illegal, then it is not immoral: what is halal is not shameful. This is not to say, of course, that there are no examples of prudery among ulama or others. After all, the whole thrust of the argument here is to highlight the diversity of Muslim societies. There are no grounds, however, for attributing puritanism (in Weber's sense) to urban religious cultures in the Muslim world.

Alcohol and other intoxicants

The interdiction of alcohol made the pleasure of its consumption ever more piquant. No one familiar with the social history of urban Muslim society – its literature and poetry, its philosophy and medicine – could have the slightest doubt that fermented drinks were items of regular consumption in these societies. The poets never tired of praising the charms of alcohol, and some, like Khayyam, went so far as to reproach God for having created such delights only to forbid them. Medical treatises, written by such dignified doctors and philosophers as al-Razi (d. 932), included chapters on wine's benefits and its place in the humoral economy, without expressing any qualms about its religious status (it was only in recent, modern editions that such chapters were censored).[55] The Hanafi school of jurisprudence recognized the products of certain types and durations of fermentation as legal, justifying this view by reference to the *sunna* of the Prophet.[56]

The legal status and cultural significance of alcohol apart, what do we know of its actual consumption in urban society? It would appear that at least some of the sober bourgeoisie at many points in their history did indulge in the intoxicating joys of wine, and that a whole ritual surrounded such indulgences. Edward Lane, close observer of Cairene society in the early decades of the nineteenth century, relates relevant episodes. Lane, himself an English puritan and strict teetotaller, mixed closely with the bourgeoisie and notables of Cairo, pretending conversion to Islam. He related that 'many of them [Muslims of Egypt], however, habitually indulge in drinking wine with select parties of their acquaintance'.[57] He was referring to the bourgeois notables with whom he associated. Their servants, he continued, know which of their friends are to be admitted to the drinking sessions, and if others should call at these times, then they are told that their masters are either not at home or are in the harem. Lane was clearly one who was not admitted, and his information was based on the accounts of a friend, 'a penitent Muslim wine-bibber',[58] who described to him the procedures and rituals of the wine table, the foods consumed, the jugs and cups utilized and so on. We are left in no doubt that these discreet gatherings were part of an established drinking culture.

The urban bourgeoisie, it would seem, did not drink in public; their revelries were private and discreet. We find similar reports in the social history of the Ottoman bourgeoisie and notables in Turkey, and indeed all that we know about various episodes in the urban history of the Middle East would confirm this as a general picture.[59] We may surmise that members of the ulama, being part of this bourgeoisie, did not always abstain. Folk stories, as well as literary accounts, abound with tales of drinking *qadis* and dissolute muftis. Hashish (cannabis) was another regular item in the cultures of many Middle Eastern regions, and a considerable lore is attached to it. While at times frowned upon by sectors of religious opinion concerned over its effects on social order, it was seldom prohibited. Abraham Marcus, in his social history of Aleppo in the eighteenth century,[60] relates that the mixing of hashish with tobacco for smoking in water pipes was a regular practice, and that people indulged in this pleasure in the coffee houses, in their shops and in other public places. At one point, in response to representations of an unidentified 'group of Muslims', the *qadi* outlawed the practice in public places. But the ban was enforced for only a short time, and then lapsed. From its inception in the sixteenth century, the coffee house in Aleppo and elsewhere played a crucial role as an urban space for public social-izing and pleasure, offering musical and theatrical entertainment to the urban strata, including the bourgeoisie. Efforts to restrict these pleasures by those concerned for social order and morality were always contentious and rarely successful,[61] which indicates the level of powerful support they must have had from sectors of the notables, the bourgeoisie and the rulers.

Asceticism and self-denial

In contrast to the pleasure-loving indulgences we have recounted, there were, of course, many self-denying ascetics (*zuhd*) in Islam, as there were in Christianity. Asceticism is often mentioned in praise of particularly pious and charismatic individuals, including some ulama, with the implication that this is a remarkable and unusual characteristic. For the most part, asceticism was practised by der-vishes and mystics. It is one of the Sufi exercises aimed at achieving ecstatic states and visions. In Weber's terms, it is 'other-worldly asceti-cism', an opposite type to the 'this-worldly asceticism' he attributed to the Protestant ethic. Whatever the rights and wrongs of Weber's characterization of his Protestants, his picture is certainly at great variance with all we know of the Muslim bourgeoisie in a variety of historical and geographical settings.

Where, then, did Gellner get his idea regarding the puritanism of orthodox Muslims? I guess that he got it from the modern reform-ist Muslims. One of the central concerns of reforming Muslims (including modern Islamists), as well as of secular nationalists, is the problematic of backwardness (*takhalluf*). Among the constituent elements of this backwardness are fatalism, superstition and loose sexual practices. These, they were keen to emphasize, are character-istic not of Islam as such, as hostile European observers were apt to surmise, but of historical decadence and corruption – hence their anxiety to restore the original and pure Islam of the scriptures. Like all traditions, this one was selectively constructed. Looking at them-selves through European eyes, these groups were anxious to banish all the negative stereotypes of lascivious sexuality, fanaticism and superstition. Their construction of pure Islam, therefore, underplayed or omitted all the elements in the holy book and the traditions that endorsed or sanctioned such practices. Many of the reformers at the turn of the century, including Abduh, were embarrassed by polygamy, and tried to exclude it on the basis of their own textual interpretations. Rashid Rida (d. 1935) was asked for a fatwa regarding the status of women in Paradise. As we have seen, while believing women can attain Paradise by good deeds, heavenly sexual pleasures seem to be provided only for the men through the services of the virgin *houris*. The questions to Rida were: why do men have this advantage? And how are women to enjoy this aspect of Paradise? His reply was that every woman who enters Paradise must have a husband, and that there is no reason to suppose that *houris* are special beings created only in Paradise, but it is quite possible that the very earthly wives are recast as *houris*![62] There is obvious embarrassment and equivocation in this reply, which would never have been felt by Rida's predecessors in the pre-modern era, for whom the clear words of the Quran on this question would not have constituted an anomaly.

Similarly, the reformers, in their zeal to banish the decadence of popular religion and culture, suppressed any recognition that many of these practices were based on powers and entities attested by the scriptures. It was this orthodox Islam of the modern reformers, looking at their religion and society through critical European eyes, that Gellner took up and generalized to the whole of urban Islam throughout its history.

Tribes and preachers

The combination of tribe and preacher as a threat to a ruler found wanting in piety and justice as prescribed by the Norm is, as we have seen, a basic element in Gellner's Khaldunian model of Muslim society:

> An independent ideology [i.e. independent from the ruler], in the hands of the burghers, and an independent sword-arm of the tribes ...The possibility of these two forces fusing provides a sanction on rulers, encouraging them to enjoin good and suppress evil.[63]

Indeed, this is the combination, according to Gellner, that lies at the root of the decline of one dynasty and the rise of another. What evidence is there for this assertion? Which historical episodes would illustrate it? Gellner seems to have in mind the North African conquests of the Almowahids and Almorawids, as well as, more recently, those of the Mahdiyya, the Sanusiya and, crucially, the Wahhabis. I shall presently discuss the example of the Wahhabis, but let us first look briefly at some of the major dynastic transformations in Muslim history.

The Almowahids (Almohads) (1121–1236) come closest to Gellner's characterization of dynastic transformation, with Ibn Tumart proclaiming an orthodox and scriptural doctrine against the incumbent Almorawid princes, judged decadent and unbelieving, and leading the Masmuda Berbers in a jihad that established his dynasty. The Almorawids had themselves attained power in the previous century through a tribal attack, but with thoroughly heterodox Sufi doctrines. Ibn Khaldun had these and other dynastic transformations in the Maghreb in mind when he put forward his dynamic model.

Dynastic transformations in the Muslim world, whether affected by tribes or not, were often accompanied by religious claims by the challengers (as indeed was often the case in Europe, China and elsewhere), and these were almost invariably of a charismatic and heterodox nature. The orthodox urban preacher leading the tribes is largely a Gellnerian myth. The Fatimids (909–1171), for instance, were a legitimist Shi'i–Isma'ili dynasty in North Africa who eventually established their seat of power in Egypt after defeating the Abbasid governors. Among their armed supporters were tribal federations. The religious claim of the Fatimids was that they were descendants from Ali and Fatima through the line of Ismail, and as such the rightful and infallible Imams of the Muslims. Their *da'is* (missionaries) spread this potent call throughout the Muslim world, and, like other Isma'ili calls, it was considered by other rulers to be the most dangerous of subversive ideas, as it carried much weight among those with widespread Shi'i sympathies: no urban preacher upholding the Norm to the tribes, but a thoroughly heterodox missionary calling for the rule of a charismatic and infallible descendant from a holy lineage. In Gellner's model, this is a typically tribal, personalistic appeal; in this case, however, it was by no means confined to the tribes, but coincided with the aspiration to happiness and justice of most of the urban strata, including the bourgeoisie.

A claim to charismatic Alawid descent was a common legitimation of rebellion, including even the slave revolt in southern Iraq and the Gulf in Abbasid times (Thawrat al-Zunj). The Safavid movement, which triumphed in Iran in 1500 and turned that country to Shi'ism, was similarly based on highly heterodox and charismatic appeal: a mixture of Alawi claims and shamanistic Sufism of the tribes – a far cry from the urban preacher upholding the Norm to the tribes. It was after the establishment of the Safavid state that the first shahs imported Shi'i ulama from Lebanon, because their own religious personnel were for the most part heterodox Sufis. This points to an important function of ulama and Shari'a for centralizing rulers: they are instruments of social control over the tribes and the regions. Gellner seems to be oblivious to this function of the Shari'a – the Norm – as an instrument of rule and social control, rather than a threat to the ruler. Dynasties that come to power on the backs of heterodox and shamanistic movements, once established, then attempt to control the forces that brought them to power by establishing institutions and loyal personnel. The law and the ulama are central planks in this 'routinization of charisma'.

The course of the first Ottoman conquests is shrouded in mythology. Were they militant tribesmen imbued by the spirit of jihad and conquest for the faith, or warrior-peasants vying for supremacy alongside their Greek counterparts?[64] One thing is certain, however: the religion that inspired them was that of Sufis and dervishes, of the *ghazi/akhi* brotherhoods (charismatic warriors), not of ulama and the law. The Seljuq kingdom they displaced in central Anatolia was equally imbued with mysticism, including the later influential Mevlevi order of Mevlana Jalal Eddin Rumi, founded in Konya, the Seljuq capital. Otherwise, their enemies were the Christian Byzantines.

The heterodox Shi'i/Sufi beginnings of dynasties and their tribal supports are almost universal in the history of the Middle East. There

may be examples of Gellner's urban-preacher-militant-tribe combination in North Africa, but he did not elaborate on that. He did seem
to think that Wahhabism was a most significant case of the workings
of his model in recent history. Let us examine this example.

Wahhabism

There is an affinity between Gellner's ideal type of ulama and
Hanbalis: they tend to be literalist in their reading of scriptures,
pedantically legalistic, anti-philosophical, anti-Sufi, and scourges of
heterodoxy of all kinds, especially of the Shi'is. Combine this with
deserts and tribes, and you have a Gellnerian dream come true. Does
Wahhabism, however, corroborate Gellner's model?

Was the founding alliance between Muhammad bin Abdul-
Wahhab and Ibn Saud in the eighteenth century an example of the
'reforming-preacher/tribal fronde alliance'? In the Arabian context,
the distinction between 'tribal' and 'urban' has a different significance than in the civilizational centres of the Middle East. The towns
are tribal in the sense that they are socially organized according to
lineage and descent. Yet, in their own terms, they are distinct from
the nomadic tribes of the desert, to whom they may nevertheless be
related. In this sense, the al-Sauds of Dar'a were urban and tribal.[65]
So was bin Abdel-Wahhab. The urban–tribal boundary, necessary for
Gellner's model, is difficult to establish in this example, and in any
case does not separate preacher and chieftain into urban and tribal,
respectively, since they are both urban–tribal.

Who were the Wahhabis against? What cities were they 'lusting'
for? First and foremost, they were against other dynasties and tribal
federations, their rivals for territorial control. Secondly, they were
against the nominal overlords, the Ottomans, who were in control of
the holy cities of Hijaz and who later backed their dynastic rivals, primarily bani Rashid. Mecca and Medina would have been great prizes
for them (and were briefly taken then lost in 1806), but were not
realistically attainable in the eighteenth and nineteenth centuries, as
they were too important for the power and prestige of the Ottomans
not to be hotly defended. They fell to Ibn Saud only in the context of

the great upheavals of World War I, which toppled the Ottomans and brought in the British as the major players in the region. Until then, the Wahhabis remained only irritants to the Turks, and were firmly defeated by them between 1811 and 1818.

Wahhabism was a movement of religious reform. Who were the primary victims of this reform? Certainly not the rulers and flesh-pots of the cities, whether within Arabia or further afield – except, that is, for the raids on the Shi'i holy cities of southern Iraq in 1801. While the Wahhabis pillaged these cities and inflicted damage and humiliation on their inhabitants and ulama, these attacks remained raids, and the Wahhabis did not settle there. The direct and regular objects of their reforms were the tribesmen and the Bedouins. It was they who worshipped saints, venerated trees and wells, made idols, engaged in magic and so on. So the chieftain–reformer alliance was primarily directed not against the cities, but against the tribesmen, who, rather than being the militant holy warriors of Gellner's model, became the victims of the reforming crusades. Eventually, large sectors of these tribesmen were converted to the cause of reform. At the turn of the twentieth century, the hero of these conversions, who harnessed them to the crusading army, was Abdel-Aziz ibn Saud. To ensure their distance from tribal laxity, he housed them in special settlements – *hujur* – watched over by preachers and enforcers, away from their tribal brethren.[66]

When eventually, during the upheavals of World War I, the al-Sauds did conquer Mecca and Medina, the victims of their reforms were precisely the Shafi'i urban bourgeoisie and their ulama. Their Norm was displaced by the Wahhabi Norm. Can we still spell 'norm' with a capital N?

The context of Wahhabism in the eighteenth and nineteenth centuries was Arabian dynastic politics and the ambitions of al-Saud to rule over the Peninsula, imposing a centralized control over dissident or independent tribesmen. To say this is not to devalue the ideational and religious bases of the reformers, only to point to the political function they fulfilled. This is in line with my earlier observation that the call for purified, legalistic Islam often coincides with the centralizing ambitions of a dynasty or an authority. I am not claiming, however, that this is its only function; it can also function as a clarion call for rebellion, as it does now in some Islamic political currents.

Wahhabism, however, has moved beyond its early context. While it has continued to function in Saudi Arabia as an authoritarian state ideology, it has also spread far and wide in the Muslim world. Its call for purification, for the austerity of the text and the law, coincided with the aspirations and world views of modernizers in every region – the perfect remedy to backwardness, fatalism, superstition and saint-worship. It has fused into the politics of modernity. That is where Gellner found it, and projected its present character back onto its history.

Other Muslim movements of recent history have to be understood in their various socio-political contexts. Sudanese Mahdism, for instance, had the opposite ideological thrust from Wahhabism. It was a charismatic movement of a minor Sufi shaykh who proclaimed himself Mahdi (i.e. a messiah), sent by God and the Prophet to establish a new order.[67] The political context was that Sudanese Islam, dominated as it was by Sufi orders interlinked with tribes and lineages, was under threat from the imposition of a regular, Ottoman-style religious bureaucracy by the Turco-Egyptian regime supported by British colonial masters. Its ultimate military defeat did not hinder its socio-political dominance in Sudanese life, but transformed it into a regular Sufi order with a mass following based on the sanctity of the Mahdi's lineage. The Ansar movement, as it became known, was also established as a political party, playing a central role in independent Sudan. Its British-educated leader, Sadiq al-Mahdi, alternated between high political office and prison or exile under military dictators – the latest being the Islamic military regime fostering its own version of Islamic government and the Shari'a. The descendant of the Messiah is now cast in the role of defending liberal democracy and constitutionalism against the predations of a military dictatorship ruling in the name of Islam.

Variants on a single model of Muslim society? Or a variety of religio-political movements with similar range and diversity to those in any other part of the world?

'Muslim society' and modern Islamic politics

Modernity for Muslims, according to Gellner, has not led to an ero-
sion of their historic essence, but, on the contrary, to its renewal
under new conditions. In this section I shall draw on Gellner's suc-
cinct statement of his position in his later book *Postmodernism, Reason
and Religion*.[68] Unlike other world religions, he argued, Islam has
proved resistant to secularization. He then set out to explain why
this should be so. The social basis of the Low Culture of the tribes
has been eroded with the centralization of state power, urbanization
and the associated processes of modernity. The newly urbanized
– the new bourgeoisie, as it were – identify with the High Islam of
the ulama and the Norm. For them, this is a sign of upward social
mobility, education and learning. Reformed Islam, argues Gellner,
played a role very similar to that played by nationalism elsewhere. It
provided a symbolic focus of national self-identification, transcending the identities and practices of the defunct tribal, local and rural
cultures. It also provided the ideology and leadership for the anti-
colonial struggle.

Within a comparative framework, Islam has the advantage over
other civilizational regions with respect to the suitability of its own
traditions for modernity. The typical dilemma posed for nationalists by the superiority of the West is whether to abandon their own
national traditions and to imitate the Western models to gain in
strength and wealth. Abandoning their traditions is painful and
humiliating. The only example Gellner cited to illustrate this dilemma
was Russia, with its nineteenth-century debate between Westernizers
and Slavophiles.[69] Muslim nationalists are spared this dilemma
because they can happily jettison their legacy of backwardness by
identifying it with popular/folk Islam, and insist on the pure, original
Islam of the Prophet. This is 'rational', legalistic, puritanical, and in
every way coincides with the rules and values required by modernity
(with echoes of 'alternative modernity' – see Introduction). For the
newly urbanized Muslims, this reformed High Islam is progress, as
against what they see as the debased traditions of their backward
rural/tribal ancestors.[70]

Reformed, legal, puritanical Islam coincides with Max Weber's characterization of the Protestant ethic and its suitability for economic enterprise, accumulation and capitalist development. In this respect, too, High Islam coincides with modernity. Gellner goes on to express surprise, therefore, that this characteristic of the faith has not led to economic development and prosperity in the lands of Islam, despite (or because of) petrol wealth.

Gellner recognizes the crucial role played by the Iranian Revolution in the region, and asks why a modern Islamic revolution should occur in a Shi'i country, whose beliefs and traditions are closer to the Low Islam of the peasants and tribesmen: personalistic, charismatic and imbued with ritual. His answer is that Khomeini, while utilizing the traditions of martyrdom to mobilize the populace, at the same time 'shifted Iranian Shi'ism firmly in the direction of a kind of "Sunnification". He took it very close to the puritan version of Sunni High Islam'.[71] He emphasized the centrality of the law. The Hidden Imam, if present, would implement the law, and in his absence this same law had to be enforced. 'It was the law which mattered, not he who implemented it. So the centrality of the law replaced that of the person.'[72] This account shows a profound misunderstanding of Iranian Shi'ism, of Khomeini's doctrine of government and of the nature of the Islamic Republic.

The case of Iran

Let us begin our appraisal of Gellner's characterization of Islamic modernity with the case of Iran. Khomeini may have insisted upon the law, but it is important to realize that his law was not impersonal. The doctrine of Velayet-e-Faqih, the cornerstone of Khomeini's idea of Islamic government, preserves the highly personalistic element of the *ijtihad* tradition in Iranian Shi'ism, while attempting to reduce the traditional pluralism of *mujtahids* to a single authority.[73]

The essential thing to realize about the practice of law in Iranian Shi'ism is that it does not exist in statute books in a codified form, but is made in the reasoning and rulings of *mujtahids*. A *mujtahid* attains his rank by a process of study, then by the patronage of a religious magnate, and ultimately through recognition from the community of ulama. In many respects this is a highly personalistic (as against bureaucratic) process. A *mujtahid* acquires a network of followers (muqallids) who pay him the religious dues of *khums*, and for whom he is the ultimate legal and spiritual authority. He practises law in the sense of arriving at judgements on particular questions posed to him by his followers. In arriving at these judgements he follows canonical sources and conventional forms of reasoning. Different *mujtahids*, however, can arrive at quite different judgements on similar issues, each judgement valid for the followers of the particular *mujtahid*. Although there are ranks of seniority and learning among *mujtahids*, there is no appeal to higher authority: in theory all *ijtihad* emanating from recognized *mujtahids* is valid. The rank of *marja' al-taqlid* (the source of emulation) is one of honorific seniority – perhaps even supremacy – among *mujtahids*. It usually indicates that such a person has a higher level of learning and a wider and more prestigious network of followers. Nevertheless, his authority cannot invalidate the judgement of a colleague towards the followers of that colleague.

Velayet-e Faqih – a system of communal religious authority that remained distinct from the legal authority of the state – was an attempt to centralize and bureaucratize this system, as well as to generalize its authority to judgements on matters of state and society. The system typically applied to communities of believers outside the state. Khomeini implicitly reconceptualized the community as the nation-state, and declared the Just Faqih to be its ultimate guardian. His reasoning proceeded as follows: during the period of Occultation of the Imam of all Time, Muslims must still live a correct life, in accordance with the laws of Islam – and for that reason they need an Islamic government. In the absence of the Imam, however, the person best qualified to deputize for him in ruling the affairs of Muslims is the living Just Faqih, or a council of such *fuqaha* (the plural of *faqih*). This is a crucial point for the argument: Khomeini did not refer the believers and their government to a pre-existing impersonal law, but to the authority of a person. The text of his lectures on Islamic government was entitled *Velayet-e Faqih: The Guardianship/Rule of the Jurist*.[74] Its argument is to establish not just the necessity of Islamic government and the application of Muslim law, but also the central authority of the Faqih or Fuqaha in this matter – a theme pursued on practically every page of the text. The qualifications of the Faqih for rule are: deep learning (not just any learning), justice and leadership qualities. A crucial component of the learning of the leading Just Faqih is that he be able to sift through the multiplicity of sources and traditions; to distinguish the essential from the trivial, the roots from the branches; to clarify ambiguities and contradictions – and through that labour to arrive at the correct decision for the community over which he rules. The Shi'i Faqih has special problems in following sources and traditions. In addition to the Quran, *hadith* and *sunna* of the Prophet (and here the Shi'a discounts many of the Companions, concentrating on Ali), he also has to consider the traditions of the Twelve Imams, and their interpretations of the first sources. Many of the Twelve lived under the rule of hostile and suspicious caliphs, and, as a precaution in such circumstances, practised dissimulation (*taqiya*). One of Khomeini's arguments for the necessity of the guardianship of the Faqih is that, through his extensive learning and thorough familiarity with the lives and thinking of these Imams, he will be able to ascertain their real intent through the mask of this dissimulation, to read the inner meanings of their utterances.[75] This comes close to an esoteric reading aided by inner insights. While Khomeini did not make this claim explicitly, many of his Shi'i readers will have understood it in this way, because there is a Shi'i tradition of gnosticism, of which Khomeini was a known practitioner and teacher. Only the learned and the mature of spirit are allowed to proceed to this form of enlightenment by means of spiritual and ascetic exercises.[76]

In the light of the common Islamist slogan 'The Quran is our constitution', it is interesting to note that the Constitution of the Islamic Republic of Iran is neither the Quran nor the Shari'a, rather, it is the constitution that empowers the Shari'a by declaring it to be the basis of law. Yet it also includes a *majlis* (parliament) elected by universal suffrage, which is charged with legislation. That is to say, it is acknowledged that there is room for legislation beside divine law, providing that the divine law is not infringed or contradicted. Given that the Shari'a is not codified, and that its practice is based on opinion and judgement, the field of legislation and its permissibility becomes an ambiguous one, with room for much political manoeuvring.

The practice of law in the Islamic Republic seems to bring together elements from different legal traditions, including the Shari'a. The civil code is largely inherited from the ancien régime, with obvious minor amendments, such as the deletion of clauses specifying payment of interest (interest is now disguised under other categories). Family law is largely based on Shari'a, which is the practice in most countries in the region whether they call themselves Islamic or not. There are crucial differences, however. One is the legality of *muta'* (temporary marriage), which distinguishes Shi'i practice from its Sunni counterpart, which forbids it.[77] The clerics insisted on retaining this distinguishing Shi'i element, denounced by Sunnis and modernizers as legalized prostitution. We have here an element of Iranian Shi'ism that may be considered an aspect of Low Culture – a practice far from 'puritanism', but which is emphatically affirmed by the Islamic Republic, almost as a symbol of Shi'i distinctiveness. Another is the legislation emanating from parliamentary enactments, under pressure from women members, which is favourable to women and unprecedented in the Shari'a, such as the right of an unjustly divorced woman to back-dated 'wages' for housework she performed in her ex-husband's household.[78] At the same time, women are routinely and arbitrarily harassed and humiliated in public places by Revolutionary Guards and militant vigilantes for trivial infringements of the dress code.

Criminal law is officially declared to follow the Shari'a and the well-known physical punishments it prescribes. The operation of this law, however, seems very uneven. After the initial orgy of judicial violence unleashed by the Revolution, these forms of punishment seem now to be only occasionally employed, usually in relation to politically or morally significant cases. Political cases are often dealt with by Revolutionary Courts, which dispense their own justice based on decree and whim.

There remains the question of constitutional law, and the legal aspects of economic and social policy. In the first decade of the

Islamic Republic, legislation and policymaking were bogged down in debates on whether the measures under consideration conformed to Islamic law, and opinions differed. Legislation on forms of property, land reform, labour and employment practices were stalled by the Council of Guardians, which adopted a conservative interpretation of Islamic law favouring private property and the ultimate rights of owners and employers. That is to say, interpretations of a non-codified law, based on practice and opinion, follow political divisions and struggles. Ultimately, in 1988, Khomeini broke this deadlock by limiting the powers of the Council of Guardians, and transferring authority to the executive – which, being devoted to the interests of the Islamic community as a whole, is empowered to suspend provisions of Islamic law and worship if such interests require it.[79] That is to say, the government, if it wants, can rule by decree or by parliamentary legislation: a far cry from the sanctity of the Norm, and of divine law.

Khomeini succeeded in establishing an Islamic government, but not in centralizing religious authority. Traditional Shi'ism, based on *mujtahids* and their following, appears to have bypassed this government. Khomeini's claim to supreme authority in his lifetime was honoured by wide sectors of political enthusiasts. However, traditional Shi'is – in Iran as well as Iraq, Lebanon, the Gulf, India and Pakistan – continued to follow their chosen *mujtahids*. The most prominent of these, until his death in 1993, was Ayatoallah Kho'i, based in Najaf, Iraq, who was generally accepted as the Marja'. Kho'i was openly critical of Khomeini's doctrine of government, and favoured the traditional separation of religion from politics. His death brought about a rivalry for the succession, with candidates backed by the different political authorities: the Iranian government, the Iraqi government and a third backed by a coalition including Lebanese political Shi'a. Given, however, that there are no institutional means of establishing succession, a successor would have emerged only through recognition and acclaim by important networks of Shi'i ulama and notables in the different countries, and many of these would not follow political nominations. At the time of writing, Ayatollah Sistani, in Iraq, is recognised as successor to

Kho'i's position, enjoying a large Shi'a following in Iraq, Iran and elsewhere. Arab Shi'a 'modernists' tend to follow the Lebanese Fadhlallah. The official Marja' of the Islamic Republic is the current Supreme Leader, Khamene'i – but his following is largely a declaration of political allegiance to the regime, including, for instance, the Lebanese Hizbullah, symbolically attached to Iran.

The account given here demonstrates that the politics and ideology of the Islamic Republic and of modern Shi'ism cannot be encompassed within the terms of a simplistic model of Muslim society and history. Indeed, the elements of this account contradict Gellner's model in crucial respects: Khomeini did not 'Sunnify' Shi'ism – on the contrary, he appealed to specifically Shi'i elements in formulating his doctrine; in this doctrine, the law is not impersonal, but crucially dependent on the interpretation of the particular Faqih(s), who is/are endowed with gnostic enlightenment in addition to their learning; there is no unified system of codified Islamic law operating in the Republic, but a mixture of laws depending on circumstances, politics and personal influence. The executive, with Khomeini's blessing, has in effect granted itself unlimited powers, invoking the overall interests of the Islamic community. In short, Iran is not a variant of a general model of Muslim society, but a particular country with its own politics, sociology and economics.

Where Iran's Islamic claims become important is in their significance for the politics of the region. In this respect, it is very like Russia after the Bolshevik revolution. It is significant, however, that, while this revolution has given a tremendous boost to political Islam in the region, it has not been a model for others in political organization, or even ideology. Indeed, the rise of Shi'i power in Iraq, following the American invasion of 2003, has given rise to highly sectarian, anti-Shi'i sentiment in much of the Sunni world – except, that is, in relation to the Lebanese Hizbullah's involvement in struggles against Israel. Crucially, the ulama have played a secondary and subordinate role in the inspiration and political organization of the Islamic movements in the Arab world and Turkey. Founders and leaders of Islamic movements, such as Hasan al-Banna and Sayid Qutb, did not spring from the religious establishment, but were schoolteachers, and this is typical of the leadership and cadres of these movements, who are for the most part teachers, engineers and functionaries. Militant *'alims*, such as Egypt's Shaykh Kishk, were rare.[80] It is only with the ascendancy of political Islam in their countries that many ulama are now jumping on the bandwagon in an effort to preserve their authority, credibility and claimed guardianship of the Shari'a.[81]

Islamic economics and business

I have argued elsewhere that modern political Islam has become a dominant idiom in the politics and culture of the region.[82] Many different and even contradictory interests, ideas, sentiments and aspirations are expressed in terms of this idiom. In this respect, it has replaced nationalism and socialism/Marxism, which played a similar role in earlier decades. It does not, therefore, represent a unitary ideology or world view, but expresses many different ones. This is also the case in the field of Islamic economics and business.

Gellner, as we have seen, attempted to cast modern Islam in a Weberian mould of rational puritanism favourable to modernity, industrialism and capitalism. In fact, there are many economic enterprises and sectors in most countries in the region that claim Islamic identity – people even speak of Islamic economic sectors in Egypt and elsewhere. Do these conform to the Weberian image? There is a great diversity of economic activities and forms of enterprise in these sectors. Let us examine some of them.

Islamic banking is an important sector in many countries in the region. It involves lending and borrowing without interest, instead using forms of co-investment, profit-sharing or fees paid for a loan. These operations proceed, no more or no less, according to the forms of 'rational' calculation of modern business and accounting practices – just like other financial institutions in the region (see Introduction for an examination of Islamic finance).

There are other, less formal types of non-interest dealings. In Iran (where the official banks give 'prizes' for deposits), there are, reportedly, informal bazaar networks of borrowing and lending without interest that depend on personal confidences, guarantees and reciprocity. In Egypt, a thriving informal sector developed in the 1980s dealing with the foreign exchange savings and transfers of expatriate Egyptians in the petrolic countries. In the middle of the decade, some of these individuals and companies went public, making use of liberalizing measures to invite investments from the public, offering enormous rates of return that were presented as shares in investment profits rather than as interest, and thereby claiming Islamic credentials.[83] After taking a considerable amount in deposits, some of these companies defaulted. There was a public outcry demanding government action to regulate and investigate these activities. It transpired that these companies were paying large returns, not so much from profits, but from the new deposits coming in (so-called Ponzi schemes) – and when these dried up they could not pay. The nature of their contracts and accounting was found to be dubious. The scandals and investigations continued for many years.

These activities provoked wide debates, which focused inevitably on the question of Islamic economics. Some Islamic writers defended these companies on the grounds that they were proceeding in accordance not only with Muslim prohibitions on interest, but also with authentic traditional Egyptian practices of community and village, in which a person with savings would not take them to an alien bank, but to a trusted merchant or landowner and ask for the savings to be invested on his behalf. The logic of this justification is interesting for our discussion, because it flies in the face of Weberian rationality, dependent as it is on personalistic and traditional networks, much like the bazaar practices in Iran already referred to.

The Egyptian Islamic investment companies are just one example among many varied sectors of economic activity. Many of these activities are similar to their secular counterparts. In Turkey, for example, where businessmen's associations proliferate, there is a Muslim business association known as MUSIAD. Its members are engaged in a similar range of businesses as other enterpreneurs (though they tend to be smaller provincial enterprises). Their main distinguishing feature is that with other Muslim enterprises they avoid dealing in interest beyond the rate of inflation. Seeing that most of their dealings are with banks and foreign companies, their abstention from interest dealings is largely theoretical. Otherwise, they are Islamic in that they don't serve wine at their dinners, they pray if their meetings happen to coincide with prayer time and have breakfast parties during Ramadan.

The Muslim sector seems to parallel the secular sectors in terms of business practices. There is a predominance of speculative and non-productive investments and enterprises in many countries – many of them involving bureaucratic corruption (or what critical commentators call 'crony capitalism') – the Islamic sector is not exceptional in this regard. The one distinctive feature that seems to be associated with some Islamic businesses is communal involvement. Some enterprises in Egypt appear to employ personnel from particular religious networks, and make charitable donations through particular mosques and societies, thereby building up communal networks of patronage. Sufi orders in Turkey, when officially prohibited, had organized themselves as *vakif* foundations, some of them with extensive wealth and enterprises.[84] How consistent are these personalistic and communalistic associations with the Weberian model?

Petrol wealth in Saudi Arabia and the Gulf has led to a vast expansion of businesses and enterprises. For the most part, these have depended on government largesse in dispensing subsidies, contracts and commissions. Huge fortunes are made from enterprises that would sink without government subsidy. This culture of government dependency (through kinship and patronage) and of commission seeking has spread far and wide in the region through the ramifications of businesses, investments, remittances and so on. Arabia and the Gulf are impeccably Islamic, as are many of the businesses in the rest of the Arab world that have benefited from the spill-over of petrol wealth. And they are a far cry from the Weberian model.

* * *

We can therefore see that Gellner's characterization of modern Islamic politics and their social contexts is as flawed as the historical model of Muslim society from which it is derived. It appeals to the general (non-specialist) reader first because of its intellectual neatness, and second because it says good things about modern Muslims while, at the same time, keeping them apart and alien. Their peculiar culturally and historically derived social and political forms are conducive to modernity and progress: Islam is a development ideology.

2 Political Modernity in the Middle East

The politics of pre-modern Muslim societies, like those of most pre-modern empires, were those of patrimonialism. Political actors, alliances and struggles were shaped by material interests and the power and influence that sustained them. These, in turn, were structured in accordance with kinship solidarities and associated networks of community and patronage. Was there, then, a specific input from Islam, as ideology or organization, which marked these pre-modern societies as Islamic?

H. A. R. Gibb and Harold Bowen, who entitled their seminal book on the Ottoman Empire *Islamic Society and the West*,[1] at one point appear to be searching for this 'Islamic society', and finding it mainly in the religious institutions. The first chapter in the section on religion opens with the following passage:

> The term 'Islamic Society' applied to the social organization which we are analysing implies that its distinguishing features are related in some way or another to the religion of Islam. Yet of those groups and activities which have been considered up to this point [aspects of government, social and economic life] there is little which can be regarded as specifically Islamic; on the contrary, the organization

of village and industrial life belongs rather to a stage of social evolution which finds close parallels in many non-Islamic regions of Europe and Asia; and that of the Court and the army, though of a more peculiar type, is based upon principles to which such Islamic elements as they display appear to be purely incidental.[2]

They go on to show that institutions and social relations characterized the religious elements of that society. We may follow suit and underline the *materiality* of religion, its social and economic institutions and their inscription in relations of power and authority, and in the shaping of political actors, alliances and conflicts. The churches and their institutions played similar roles in historical European societies. There are also the ideological or discursive elements of religion, in turn related to identity formation. In Europe and the Middle East, religion provided the major vocabularies of legitimation and contest.

The materiality of religion

The social and institutional materialization of religion discussed in the Introduction is an important aspect of pre-modern politics. There are common forms of institutions in most historical Muslim societies, such as the mosques, *madrasas* (seminaries) and *awqaf* (endowments). These, however, had different significance at different times and places. In Ottoman lands, religion, for the most part, was well institutionalized and even bureaucratized. The ulama were organized in ranks and functions divided between education and the practice of law. These, in turn, were related to *madrasas* as educational and qualifying institutions and ranked hierarchically, with commensurate ranks of their diplomas and licenses. There were strict rules as to the level of attainment allowing licensees to assume different ranks within the judiciary, education and the court. These rules, however, were arbitrarily suspended for considerations of kinship and patronage, allowing young men with little or no attainment to take over the ranks of their deceased or retired fathers and uncles.[3]

The *awqaf*

The *awqaf* are crucial elements in the economy and politics of cities and countryside. Vast endowments of agricultural and urban real estate – as well as, in some cases, cash investments and cattle – generated considerable revenues and provided avenues of employment and patronage assumed primarily by the religious classes as administrators, overseers and agents.[4] The Ottoman sultans over the years endowed mosques, *madrasas*, Sufi lodges (mystical brotherhoods), soup kitchens and numerous charities. High-ranking palace officials controlled these revenues (for many years, until the eighteenth century, it was the chief black eunuch, the *kiz aghasi*, who also controlled the *awqaf* of Islam's two holy shrines of Mecca and Medina), but they were disbursed to and through religious institutions and personnel.[5] In Istanbul we have a well-preserved example in the Suleymaniya mosque complex, built and endowed by Suleyman al-Kanuni (the magnificent) in the sixteenth century, with his architect Sinan. It comprised the mosque, a *madrasa*, Sufi lodges and soup kitchens for feeding professors, students (the food portions were double for the former), travellers and the mendicant poor. The revenues and management were controlled by a hierarchy of religious personnel. They were primarily sustained by rents from urban real estate, giving their administrators control over vital sectors of the urban economy. In addition to the royal *awqaf* there were numerous endowments from prominent officials and families, as well as 'private' endowments designed to benefit families and their descendants. As one would expect, these endowments and their administration constituted crucial elements in urban politics and relations of power.[6]

Judicial institutions

The office of *qadi* was one of the edifices of power and patronage in the Ottoman state. Under Shaykhulislam, the top religious rank in the Ottoman court, one of the chief mufti of the Empire, the two following ranks were those of the two *kadi askar*, 'military' judges (*askar* designating the official class) of Rumela and Anatolia. Under them was a whole hierarchy of judges, appointed to each major city and province in the Empire. Each titular *qadi* presided over a hierarchy of deputies and subordinates, carrying out functions of litigation, guardianship over public order and morality, and, crucially, notary functions of sanctioning contracts and transactions, guardianship over *awqaf* and of minors' property – all lucrative functions generating fees, commissions and opportunities for gain, as well as employment and patronage. The titular *qadi*, like provincial governors, was appointed for a limited period of time from the Porte, and was usually foreign to the city or province. He worked through the local judicial hierarchy, who acted as his deputies. For that *qadi*, the position was primarily one of revenue generation for the limited period of his appointment. These institutions, then, constituted another avenue of power, wealth and influence, and were therefore crucial to political functions.[7]

Sufi lodges

Every Ottoman city had – indeed, every Muslim city today has – the shrines of saints as centres of organization for Sufi lodges, pilgrimage and charity. They are typically presided over by a descendant of the founder of the order – the very saint whose shrine is at their centre. They vary greatly in size, wealth and influence, but in most cases constitute important players in urban and regional economies and politics. Typically they are the beneficiaries of endowments, some resulting from the patronage of the mighty: Ottoman sultans and their viziers, and mamluke commanders and other potentates were particularly prone to the appeal and services of the saints and their mystical followers.[8] The shaykhs of the more popular and plebeian orders had their own role in the urban economy and politics, controlling particular trade guilds and associated urban quarters. Some played their part in the political and factional mobilization of the populace at times of trouble.[9] The shaykhs of the major *turuq* sometimes held other religious functions as judges and muftis. The relation between Sufism and the 'orthodox' religious institutions varied with time and context, and while antagonistic and disputatious in certain instances, were for the most part symbiotic and amicable.

The *ashraf*

The *ashraf* (descendant of the Prophet) was an institutionalized religious rank with economic and political privileges. In most cities and regions, the *ashraf* constituted corporate groups, sometimes armed, with tax privileges and access to office. Many of the *mashayikh* (the shaykhs) of the major Sufi orders claimed sharif status, the lineage of the saint being typically traced to the Prophet. The doyen of the Gailani family in Baghdad, for instance – hereditary chief of the Qaderi order and guardian of a major shrine – is traditionally the city's *naqib al-ashraf* (doyen of *ashraf*), and continues to be today.[10]

We see, then, that religion constituted and shaped material factors that occupied the social landscape with its institutions and personnel, as both economic and political spaces and actors. We shall see how these interacted with other political players in historical Muslim societies. But let us first consider the discursive and identity elements within politics.

Discursive and ideological components of religion in politics

Prior to the development of modern secular ideologies regarding political systems (of which more below), the main ideational fields available for political legitimacy and for conducting political contests and struggles were derived from religion, in Europe and in the Middle East. The ruler was the 'defender of the faith', or *amirul-mu'minin*, commander of the faithful, the champion of enlarging the territory of Christianity/Islam and defending it against infidel enemies. Contestation from rival sources for power, or emanating from protests of the lower orders, was also couched in religious terms evoking piety, faith and justice.

For example, having traced the pattern of urban movements in several Arab cities in the nineteenth century, Edmund Burke[11] concludes that riots did not consist of aimless violence, but were indeed directed to particular targets that were the locus of their grievances: 'The burden of the foregoing', he states, 'is that there was indeed a popular ideology of social protest in the Middle Eastern societies which centred upon the application of the Shariʻa by a vigilant Muslim ruler.'[12] He goes on to enumerate the various economic provisions of the Shariʻa whose application was demanded by the protesters, including restrictions on taxation and on debasement of the coinage, and the prohibition of usury.

There is no doubt that the demand for justice and for a just prince was at the centre of popular protest. Notions of justice are inevitably religious and customary (the two not always being distinct in the popular or even learned mind). Indeed, even in inter-elite conflicts, one party would denounce the other as traitors or deviants from religious prescriptions.[13] The language of righteousness and justice was intimately tied to religion, although this is not to say that there was a precise notion of the Shariʻa or of what actually constituted legal and illegal taxes and coinages. From the earliest times, Muslim rulers had levied taxes and other dues dictated by administrative fiat and not according to religious notions, and the ulama and *fuqaha* (jurists) were mostly unaccustomed to raising legal objections. The exceptions were situations of conflict, disorder and crisis in which the weight of fiscal oppression, food prices and plain pillage were regular features, and in which protests – whether by ulama, rival princes or the populace – always laid their claim to justice in religious – that is, Shariʻa – terms. Religion and legality provided a *vocabulary* of demands and contests rather than a determinate notion of alternative political or legal orders. Burke and others have described these forms of contestation and opposition as a 'moral economy'. The argument here is that it is best to regard this economy as a language of contestation rather than as a precise description of an existing or desired system.

Within this ideological sphere of contest, the existing system of rule is taken as given: the object is to make the prince just or to exchange him for a more just ruler. The only form of radical transformation envisaged is that of the end of time. While messianic notions thrived in both Sunni and Shiʻi Islam, they tended to animate rural and tribal rather than urban politics. A notable example was that of the Sudanese Mahdiyya in the latter part of the nineteenth century. This movement was largely a response to Anglo-Egyptian intrusion into Sudan, and the imposition of a colonial order on a country largely characterized by autonomous tribal and religious local rulers. To that extent it contained elements of modernity in its constitution, and addressed a universalist message to a Muslim world. But its messianic ideology and mode of political mobilization of tribal and Sufi religious forces shared much with pre-modern formations.[14] Retrospective accounts from nationalist perspectives (Sudanese, Arab and Muslim) have tried to play down, if not deny, the messianic and tribal nature of the movement to include it in a uniform history of modern nationalism.

The other discursive element of religion in politics was its definition of communal identities in pre-modern societies, in some cases until recent times, which was that they tended to be spatially insulated, largely self-sufficient and self-managing. The primary markers of identity were thus those of locality and kinship. Religious identity tended to be taken for granted ('Of course I am Muslim/Christian! What else? God forbid!'). So this identity only came into political play when religious difference became the site of conflict. Religion then became a communal marker, much like 'Catholic' and 'Protestant' in Northern Ireland and elsewhere. Muslim–Copt relations in parts of Egypt came into political play under certain conditions, such as the Napoleonic invasion and its aftermath at the end of the eighteenth century, which precipitated communal riots against Christians. The communal conflicts and even massacres between Muslims, Christians and Druze in Lebanon and Syria between 1840 and the 1860s are examples of the politicization of religious difference under the impact of the transformations of European power and Ottoman reforms.[15] In other circumstances, bonds of neighbourhood, patronage and clientship took precedence over religious and ethnic affiliations.

The pre-modern Middle Eastern city and its politics

We have already glimpsed the institutional and material religious elements in the political landscape of the historical city. These came into play in relation to the (typically) military and sultanic rulers:

sultans, mamlukes and aghas, with their soldiery and administrative formations. Their main concern in government was revenue and order. Peasants, craftsmen and traders produced wealth; the elites were primarily concerned with appropriating the major part of this production in taxes and rents. Pre-modern politics was primarily about regulating the shares from these revenues between different elite factions. Occasionally – under conditions of crisis and war, when the burden of exploitation intensified – the oppressed populace would protest or even riot.

An Ottoman provincial city, such as Aleppo in the eighteenth century, would be formally governed by a pasha or wali appointed from Istanbul for a limited period – usually one year. He would have to purchase this appointment, and would recoup his investment with profit from the revenues of the province, as would the *qadi* and a host of other functionaries. The pasha would have his own military force, which would coexist with local military forces of janissaries, *sipahis* ('feudal' contingents), mamlukes and sundry others, who were not strictly under his command but took their orders from their own headquarters. There were also non-military groups who bore arms, such as tribesmen and *ashraf* (descendants of the Prophet, organized in corporations), as well as bandits. The appointed governor can only rule effectively through the cooperation of local elites: landowners, merchants and ulama, who were often interrelated in elite families, marriages and functions.[16]

Many of these rich notables were also tax-farmers, and many were involved in provisioning the city from its rural hinterland. The entire populace, including the notables, were liable to tax, with the exception of the official and military classes (*askaris*), including official ulama, who were exempt. Taxes were often levied on corporate and not individual bases: trade guilds, minority religious communities, villages and tribes were such corporate tax-payers, with the communal chiefs apportioning the burden between their members, thus giving them considerable power over members. The common peasants and tradesmen were at the bottom of the pile, and subject to oppressive exactions.[17] Now and again, they would protest and riot. These uprisings, however, were sporadic and confined to particular issues, usually to do with taxes and the price of bread (manipulated by the elites for their profit). What forms did these riots take? And what was the part played by religious elements?

The mosque was the point of assembly and for the expression of grievances for most demonstrations and protests, and the minarets the loci of public calls to action. The crowds almost always took their grievances first to prominent ulama, and attempted to enlist them as leaders and spokesmen for their grievances to the princes. Naturally, this led many observers to suppose that the ulama were the leaders of the urban populace and their representatives before the authorities. This view is strongly challenged by some writers on the subject, most notably for Egypt by Gabriel Baer.[18]

Baer distinguished between the high ulama – the teachers at al-Azhar, the holders of high office and supervisors of large foundations – and the lower ulama – clerks, *maktab* teachers, muezzins and imams at small mosques, and, above all, al-Azhar students.[19] The lower ulama were prominent in leadership and participation in popular movements. But they were regarded by the rulers and the bourgeoisie as part of the lower orders, and not as intermediaries and representatives with access to the ears of authority. These, in particular the students, were prominent in many of the popular movements and events of the end of the eighteenth and early nineteenth centuries, including the uprisings against the French.

As for the high ulama, it is true that the populace first resorted to them when faced with fiscal oppression and famine – particularly to the Shaykh al-Azhar. With few exceptions, however, the responses of the ulama were seldom favourable. They were sometimes coerced by potentially violent crowds into leading processions to the citadel and airing their grievances. André Raymond outlines a typical scenario:[20] the crowd proceeds to the grand mosque, occupies the minarets and calls for resistance, the calls accompanied by the beat of drums. They close the markets and the shops. They assemble in the forecourts and at the gates of the mosque and demand the presence of the shaykhs and their intervention with the authorities regarding their grievances. They participate in a procession, with the ulama at its head 'more dead than alive'. If a favourable response is obtained from the citadel, then the ulama are entrusted as guarantors of its implementation. The people suspect that the ulama are in league with the authorities, and the authorities suspect them of stirring up the people. Naturally, the ulama tried, whenever they could, to avoid this role. Their response was always to try to calm down any potential agitations, and, if they failed, to avoid involvement. They naturally shared with the authorities and bourgeoisie the fear of and contempt for the lowly crowds. In addition, many of the high ulama had close political and economic ties with the princes.

The question of political modernity

The forms of politics described so far can be distinguished as 'pre-modern'. The question then arises as to the nature of political modernity. Michael Walzer characterized it in the following terms:

> A politics of conflict and competition for power, of faction, intrigue and open war is probably universal in human history. Not so a politics of party organisation and methodical activity, opposition and reform, radical ideology and revolution ... The detached appraisal of a going system, the programmatic expression of discontent and aspiration, the organisation of zealous men for sustained political activity: it is surely fair to say that these three together are aspects of the modern, that is, the post-medieval political world.[21]

In *The Revolution of the Saints*, Walzer proceeds to argue that the Calvinists of the English Civil War were the first to develop this form of politics. He goes on, however, to specify general conditions that make such politics: the separation of politics from the household, the appearance of masterless free men, the rational and pragmatic consideration of political methods (as in Machiavelli), and, crucially, the rise of large-scale and inclusive political units, as in the modern state, starting with the absolutist destruction of feudal segmentarity in Europe.[22]

In these terms, the forms of politics described so far are decidedly pre-modern. Inter-elite politics are clearly those of 'conflict and competition for power, of faction, intrigue and open war'. Solidarities are based on personal loyalties and patronage (as in mamluke households), kinship, and, in the case of the popular classes, neighbourhood, guilds, and Sufi *turuq*. Crucial to all these is a strong 'materialism', an orientation to economic interests. The ultimate stakes in practically all political struggles were revenues – and, for the city population, food prices, fiscal oppression and other arbitrary exactions. Popular movements were often spontaneous and short-lived, revolving around immediate grievances. Thus, they were far from 'sustained political activity'. The issues had nothing to do with reform or revolution of a 'system'; such a concept would have been quite alien. Popular aspirations were always for the advent of a just prince who would bring stability and security. It can be argued, then, that pre-modern politics were predominantly 'materialist', and that the ideological elements of religion, kinship and patronage were strongly coloured by these materialist considerations.

To say, however, that such politics are 'pre-modern' may be misleading, for they are universal and have certainly survived into and adapted to modernity. The politics of faction, patronage and kinship have a strong presence in many modern societies, not just Muslim or 'Third World' ones, but also many parts of Europe and America. Modern politics as characterized by Walzer are specific to modernity, but they coexist, in various combinations, with preceding forms.

Episodes in the transition to modernity

Over the course of the 'long' nineteenth century (from the French Revolution to World War I), then the twentieth, Walzer's conditions of political modernity developed at different paces in different parts of the region. They naturally took various forms in different parts following peculiarities of history and society. Let us briefly review some of these conditions.

The transformations resulted mainly from the incorporation of the region within the expanding capitalist markets dominated by the European powers. This was not merely European domination, but represented transformations of economy and society creating new spheres of activity, classes of the population and relations of power. Political, military and administrative reforms were the responses of ruling groups to new situations. The Ottoman reforms started in the late eighteenth century, and, after much turmoil and many set-backs, were consolidated in the Tanzimat and legal reforms through the nineteenth century. This process constituted the formation of the modern state – in fact, in quasi-nation-states – in the Ottoman Empire and Egypt. The centralization of state power was facilitated by the spread of modern means of transport and communication and enhanced military capabilities, not only technical but also organizational and political, such as the bloody abolition of the by then useless and parasitic janissaries in 1826 (see Chapter 1). Many social and economic functions were subsumed under the state bureaucracy – crucially, law and education, which had previously been controlled by religious institutions. The state intruded increasingly into the running and revenues of the *awqaf*, until, by the early twentieth century, they had become largely state institutions. Transport and communication – most importantly, the railways and telegraphy from the mid-nineteenth century – removed the isolation of remote areas and brought them into the spheres of the capitalist economy and under state control, in the process breaking down primary units of production and solidarity.[23]

There were also some crucial conceptual shifts, at least at the elite levels. The concept of 'state' is a case in point. The term now translated as 'state' – *dawla/devlet* – in its pre-modern sense meant the property or patrimony of a dynasty, as in *dawlat bani al-'Abbas*, or, *Bani 'Uthman/Osman*. The sovereign, not a concept of an institution, was the absolute source of power. When Louis XIV uttered his famous claim, *l'état, c'est moi*, it was in the context of affirming a notion that was being contested on the eve of political modernity. In both Muslim and Christian contexts this notion coexisted uneasily with the idea of the absolute sovereignty of God, and many of the religious formulae of power glossed over this ambiguity. Law for the Ottomans, for instance, was, theoretically, the law of God, as promulgated and guarded by the ulama. The fact that so much of the law was statute law, issuing from the will of the sovereign, was justified in various formulae regarding the administration and defence of the interests and powers of Muslims. Ultimately, the law issues from the dual sources of God and king. The conceptual innovation of modernity, as it developed in the Ottoman reforms of the nineteenth century, was to recast the law and its practice as impersonal institutions of 'justice' – *'adalet* – with legislative bodies enacting law, and judges and lawyers, trained in modern law schools, applying codified laws independent from the books of *fiqh* or the statutes of the king: the idea of the 'rule of law', the Rechtstaat.[24] Related to these concepts was that of 'citizenship'. Citizens, as distinct from subjects – *re'aya* – had rights and duties defined by law, were invited to participate in political processes through representation and were equal before the law regardless of religious, tribal or regional affiliation (keeping in mind that these were the concepts, not the practices). Many of the political conflicts and struggles over this period were thus over these issues, grouped under the demand for a constitution, in both the Ottoman Empire and Iran, that would by law limit the power of the king. While most of the reforming Ottoman monarchs of the nineteenth century initiated or supported the reforms, they eventually baulked at the idea of a constitution and parliament that would limit their powers. Sultan Abdul-Hamid II ultimately used Islam as a weapon to abort the constitution and parliament in the latter decades of the nineteenth century, and his ultimate defeat and deposition by the Young Turks (1908/09) was in the name of the constitution. In the processes of political struggles over these issues, Islam was ideologized in modern ways.[25]

Winners and losers

These processes of modernity led to disparities in advantage and loss to different sectors of the population. Local trades and crafts were hit by cheap imports widely distributed through new modes of transport such as the railways.[26] Some agricultural sectors benefited from cash-crop distribution and export, such as cotton in Egypt, but at the same time this led to heightened exploitation and oppression of the peasant. New classes developed: a modern working class in the railways and harbours, for instance, as well as the expanded urban services and administration (see below). Government bureaucracy, as well as new sectors in education and the professions, formed new middle classes with distinct world-views.[27] The religious classes were, for the most part, losers. Their core functions of law and education were being bureaucratized as state functions, performed by personnel trained in modern educational institutions. Some religious figures, mainly from the elites, went along with the reforms and adapted to them, such as Jawdat/Cevdet Pasha, the architect of the Majalla/Mecelle, the codified 'civil law' element of the Shari'a, and the various Egyptian and Syrian modernist ulama who were fascinated by the new world.[28] Other sectors of the ulama, including the lower orders, opposed or attacked the reforms and the processes of modernity in the name of religion and tradition. The weakness of the Empire vis-à-vis the European powers, they argued, was because of the departure from the path commanded by God in his Shari'a, and the imitation of the hostile infidels. Their advocacy found a ready response among the poorer classes who had lost out, as well as some of the old elites consisting of military ranks and landed classes who were also losing ground. These were conservative or reactionary responses.

Another response with religious tinges was that of modernist thinkers and reformers, who opposed not modernity as such, but the autocratic manner in which it was carried out, and the persistence of absolutist power. These included the group, starting in the 1860s, known as the Young Ottomans[29] – intellectuals, poets, journalists and functionaries, widely read in European literature and political theory, who read natural law theory into some construction of an original Islam of the first generation of the Prophet that had been the origin of liberty and law.[30] Liberty, argued Namik Kemal, is not the gift of the sultan to give to his subjects, but was given by God to the Muslims. Those intellectuals, in their ideas and lifestyles, were highly secular, and their appeal was to the new middle classes. One of their demands was for a constitution and parliament to limit the power of the sultan. An associated statesman, Midhat Pasha, was the champion and architect of a constitution and parliament, which came into effect in 1876, only to be suspended a year later by Sultan Abdul-Hamid II.

Abdul-Hamid presided over a much-reduced Empire containing chiefly Turks, Arabs and Kurds, which had lost most of its European territories and had had its Christian populations become almost entirely Muslim. He made an ideological virtue of that by the instrumentalization of Islam against Europe, and at the same time by cultivating conservative Muslim sentiment against the forces calling for democracy and constitutionalism.[31] He cultivated the image of the traditional Muslim absolute ruler enforcing the commands of God and the correct path. At the same time, he continued with the processes of centralization and bureaucratization that etatised previously religious functions, and constituted a form of secularization. In this Abdul-Hamid set the pattern that was to prevail until the present time, of authoritarian rulers resisting opposition or limitations on their power by invoking religion, and casting their opponents as infidels.

Islam was then ideologized and politicized into forms that recur in modern politics: the conservatives, resorting to populism as well as the support of authoritarian rulers; modern reformists reading liberalism into Islam; and, emerging in the early decades of the twentieth century, radical populists such as the Muslim Brothers. At the same time, much of cultural, intellectual and political life was secularized, favouring the emergence and dominance of secular ideologies and political movements.   •

These processes of modernity proceeded in the general context of increasing European penetration – in some cases, as in Egypt, of direct military and political control. This shaped the structure of predominantly urban modern politics into forms of anti-colonial struggle. The models of liberation and of independent government were derived from European ideas and ideologies – first liberal and nationalist, later fascist and socialist. National liberation and nationalism remained central components of all these ideologies and political movements. Islamist ideology also developed in this direction.

On the social level, the processes of economic development and political centralization contributed to the breakdown of primary social unities and solidarities of tribe, village and urban quarter, although this proceeded unevenly in different places. Egyptian guilds were weakened as they lost their monopoly over labour in their particular crafts, becoming redundant by the 1920s;[32] but their Iranian counterparts retained many of their social and political functions in the bazaars until much later in the century.[33] Rural-to-urban migration – a crucial factor in the shaping of the urban economy, society and politics – started in the early twentieth century in Egypt but gathered momentum from the middle of the century, augmented by accelerated population growth. The quarters of central Cairo were transformed, the rural influx leading to the departure of the rich and the middle classes to the more salubrious suburbs, the old quarters becoming impoverished slums. This process weakened the organization and solidarity of the quarters and their function as corporate units.

The expansion of a modernized state and associated public sectors, most notably education, spawned a new, largely secular, intelligentsia. This became the ideological class par excellence, which absorbed and adapted the new reformist, nationalist and revolutionary ideas whose goal was the achievement of national independence and strength and the transformation of state and society in accordance with particular ideological blueprints. From these ranks came Walzer's 'zealous men' organized for 'sustained political activity'.

The overall political and administrative thrust of the Tanzimat was for increasing centralization of government control, and a concomitant expansion in the size, reach and power of the bureaucracy. By the end of the century, it is estimated that there were half a million civil servants[34] who, in addition to mainstream government administration and finance, also administered hospitals, secular schools, agricultural schools and model farms, highways, the telegraph and railroads. Crucially, these were 'modern' functionaries, with institutional positions and powers (as distinct from the personalistic networks that characterized earlier administrations, in which every man had a master). Together with professionals, army officers and some sectors of business people, they constituted the modern middle class and the cadres of modernization and secularization. They supplied the leadership and personnel of the movement of Young

Turks.[35] During the Tanzimat era, this central administration gained in power and control over other power elites. The military reforms, though not a brilliant success in external wars, were instrumental in imposing the central power on the provinces and their elites. The local notables and chieftains, with extensive autonomy until the middle of the eighteenth century, came firmly under the control of the government and its centrally appointed functionaries, although many maintained their local positions as power brokers and tax farmers (a practice that the central government did not succeed in breaking).[36] In the Kurdish and Arab provinces, the nomadic tribes were firmly subordinated by the new military forces and by the extension of transport and communications. This was an important step in pacifying these provinces and enhancing the security and productivity of the settled agricultural populations.

The expansion of government service; employment in the expanding private sectors of commerce, transport and communication; the growth of educational institutions and the professions – all these developments led to a large expansion in the numbers and significance of the modern educated middle classes, as well as the beginnings of a modern working class. These literate strata constituted a market for print products: newspapers, magazines, novels and plays (many translated from French, and there was a special fascination for Jules Verne and other science fiction),[37] and books on science and discovery. Government censorship and control stifled political news and analyses, and discourses on European government, parliaments and revolutions. But newspapers and magazines filled their pages with news of scientific discoveries, biographies of prominent men, travel stories, practical tips on health and domestic organization and so on.[38] Many people read, and the illiterate listened to others reading aloud. The effect of print media on the secularization of culture is in the way it presents an alternative universe to that of traditional, limited horizons and ranges of interest. These printed works were sources of knowledge and models of living quite outside the world of religion, custom and authority. This also has a profound political effect: Juan Cole pointed out (in relation to contemporary Egypt) that the accessibility of news of government and politics, and evaluations of events and actions in the press, engender in people the frame of mind of participants in events, having their own opinions and interests, as opposed to being passive subjects of the decisions and policies of rulers and ulama – the traditional *ahlu al-hall wal-aqd*, those who bind and loosen.[39] The café played an important part in political dissemination, argument and intrigue in many Middle Eastern cities in the nineteenth and twentieth centuries – to the present day, some traditional cafés in Turkish cities are called *kirathane* (*qira'at-khane*), reading rooms, indicating the function of reading newspapers and pamphlets, perhaps aloud (they are now mostly games rooms). These constituted an important element of the emerging 'public sphere' in those cities. Under the Abdul-Hamid regime at the onset of the twentieth century, police spies were ever vigilant in monitoring the coffee houses.

Gabriel Baer contrasted the social and ideological composition of the popular movements in Egypt first at the time of the Urabi revolt in 1882, then in 1919 in the nationalist demonstration led by Sa'ad Zaghloul against the British occupation.[40] The first was led by junior ulama and al-Azhar students, with slogans against the infidel Christians, whether Europeans or Egyptian Copts – thus expressing 'traditional' communalist sentiments. By 1919 the leaders were teachers and students from the modern schools and universities, and the slogans urged national unity (between Muslims and Copts), independence and liberty. Zaghloul's famous slogan was '*Al-dinu lil-lah wal-watanu lil-jami''* – 'Religion is for God and the fatherland (*watan*) is for all its members'. That is not to say, of course, that communalist sentiments were transcended: we know from the history of the region that these sentiments were frequently and effectively evoked by interested parties to combat opponents. Communalism as a political weapon was to recur in Egypt until the present time, with various Islamists playing on antagonism to Copts to gain support and revenue in Upper Egypt and elsewhere. The difference now, however, is that communalism, while popular, is stigmatized by respectable political activists and theorists of all hues, including mainstream Islamists. This is much like populist racism in Europe, denied by all respectable parties but always tempting for politicians seeking cheap popularity. This shift in the politics of communalism comes after more than a century of modern politics, mostly secular and nationalist.

The period of political modernity in Iran

Iran presents us with a political history distinct from that of the Ottoman lands. The Qajar state was decentralized, with much power in the hands of local elites. It did not have a significant standing army, and relied on tribal forces for its wars (with disastrous consequences). The religious institutions and personnel enjoyed considerable autonomy from the state, forming parts of the decentralized power elites of landlords, merchants and clerics, many with private militias. The clerics controlled wide networks of merchants, guilds and the popular classes. The tentative steps towards modernity and the increasing power and influence of Britain and Russia led to waves of discontent and protest, often directed by the clerics and culminating in the agitations for the Constitution in the opening years of the twentieth century, and then the Constitutional Revolution of 1906.[41] The campaign for the Constitution was initiated and supported by a number of diverse constituencies, both traditional and modern. The ideas were those of modern, educated intellectuals of the upper classes. They were supported by some clerics, though for motives of their own. Some traditional clerics saw in the Constitution and parliament a way of limiting the now threatening power of the shah and his European financiers and backers, which made them liable to taxation. Others, notably Mirza Mohammad Hosein Na'ini, became articulate advocates of the Constitution, providing a religious rationale for its implementation.[42] A third constituency were bazaar merchants fed up with arbitrary rule and taxation and allied to some of the ulama. Few of the clerics understood the meaning and implications of the Constitution. Na'ini supported it with a theological treatise; Fazlallah Noori, a conservative, opposed it as un-Islamic. These two understood it well and took sides accordingly, but most of the clerics who supported the Revolution saw only its practical effects in limiting the power of the shah in their favour in the new representative system.[43] The Revolution was followed by much conflict, reaction and war, in which Britain and, particularly, Russia played decisive parts. The situation finally stabilized with the accession to power in 1926 of Reza Shah – a modernizing dictator, who admired his Turkish contemporary, Ataturk, and aspired to similar reforms, including the secularization of Iranian society by curbing the powers and privileges of the clerics. Political modernity and its particular forms of organization and mobilization came to Iran in those years and those that followed, operating side by side with the 'traditional' forms of allegiance and action. Intense political struggles taking these different forms developed in the years during and following World War II.[44] A consideration of this period is instructive for our discussion of political modernity.

Ervand Abrahamian analysed the transformations in crowd behaviour between the events of the Constitutional Revolution and the political struggles surrounding the Mossadegh government in the early 1950s.[45] Modern political organization, both nationalist and socialist, developed and grew during the 1920s. In particular, the Tudeh (communist) Party became an important political force that played a crucial role in subsequent events. The leading sections of the various parties, as might have been expected, consisted of educated middle-class professionals, particularly students and teachers, but they also included elements of the new working classes in the oil refineries, railways and the few modern factories, as well as some traditional artisans and bazaar workers. The Tudeh Party became dominant in trade union organization and militancy. Until Reza Shah's removal in 1941, these activities proceeded clandestinely and were subjected to violent repression. Reza Shah's deposition by the Allies inaugurated a more tolerant, though by no means liberal, regime, which allowed more open political activity and organization, and under which first the Tudeh Party and then the National Front came to prominence. This period ultimately culminated in the premiership of Mossadegh, his nationalization of Iranian oil and his struggle against the monarchy and its allies. Mossadegh's stormy rule was ended in 1953 by a US-instigated military coup that returned Reza Shah to absolute power, and resulted in harsh political repression.[46]

The Tudeh Party and the trade unions associated with it assumed commanding positions in popular organization and mobilization. In 1945 the Central Council of United Trade Unions had a total membership of 400,000.[47] In addition to workers in modern industries, it included the syndicates of teachers, lawyers, engineers and doctors. One public meeting in 1946 was attended by 15,000. On May Day 1946, the union parade in Abadan brought out 81,000 demonstrators. The union pursued militant demands in the oil industry, and the company's attempt to break a strike led to violent riots in Abadan and Ahwaz.[48]

Mossadegh came to national prominence as a nationalist leader in 1945, and immediately attracted mass support, particularly from the bazaar and from students. The National Front, a coalition of nationalist parties, organized this support, and the Tudeh Party joined in, though the alliance was often uneasy because of serious differences within the Front over communism and the Soviet Union. The ulama were notable for the minor role they played in these events – apart from one prominent cleric, Ayatollah Kashani, who initially supported Mossadegh, then turned against him. While, no doubt, the mullahs continued to enjoy the allegiance of some popular sectors, these sectors were not politically significant at this point. New sectors of the urban populace were affiliated to the new politics, and now liberated from the earlier hegemony and affiliations of bazaar and ulama.[49]

In July 1952, Mossadegh, faced by hostile manoeuvres by the shah and his supporters, resigned tactically, succeeding in eliciting a revolt in Tehran. As soon as news of his resignation reached the bazaar, traders and craftsmen fought the security forces to make their way to parliament. The National Front deputies called for a general strike, and the Tudeh joined in. The bazaar closed down entirely, and there were strikes in all the sectors controlled by the Tudeh and the unions. After attempts at violent suppression, the government capitulated. The heaviest fighting took place in the bazaar; in the working-class industrial districts and the railway repair shops; on the route between the university and parliament; and in Parliament Square. Students, of course, were prominent in these events. The worst slum districts of southern Tehran were quiet. The centres of popular activism had shifted.[50]

There were marked differences between Cairo and the Iranian cities in the first half of the twentieth century. Cairo underwent a basic dislocation of its old urban structure of quarter organization, guild and *tariqa*, caused both by the impact of colonial penetration and incorporation into world markets, including wide-ranging rural development, leading, eventually, to mass migration to the city. Egypt also underwent a significant level of industrialization. Through bazaar associations and their coordination, Iranian cities maintained important sectors of autonomous urban organization. Modern politics and ideologies of nationalism, liberalism and communism developed and thrived for the most part in the new social spaces of university, school, workshop and coffee house. At the same time, they were only effective in urban mass mobilization through articulation with the structures and interests of the bazaar. These, in turn, were transformed by the forces and processes of modernity, but were never displaced as centres of urban autonomy. The bazaar was to be the hub of organization, finance and coordination in all the political upheavals of the century, and, crucially, during the Islamic Revolution of 1978–79.

Given the secularization of the political field in the middle decades of the twentieth century, why was the 1979 Revolution led by a cleric and why did it lead to the establishment of the Islamic Republic? The years between the Mossadegh government and the Revolution were a time of severe repression of all non-regime politics. The next episode of challenge to the regime and subsequent confrontation came between 1961 and 1963, this time from religious sources in Qum; this was the first appearance of Ruhullah Khomeini as a clerical challenger. The occasion was the religious agitations against land reforms by the shah. Khomeini broadened the challenge to the arbitrary powers of the shah and his disregard for religion and its upholders. It was the culmination of a simmering resentment by the religious classes and their supporters against the secularizing regime of Reza Shah, followed by that of his son. Khomeini's forthright denunciation of the shah and his policies agitated religious students and elements of the bazaar in Qum and Tehran, where his agents had been organizing support. This elicited forceful and violent repression by the authorities, and ultimately the arrest and then exile of Khomeini – first to Turkey, then to Iraq.[51] On that occasion, the secular opposition of the nationalists and the left stood aside, showing a characteristic distaste for what they considered reactionary religious forces, dubbed 'black reaction' (a reference to the black garments of the clerics) by the regime.

The shah attempted to control all centres of social and political autonomy, and ultimately to subsume any civil association under his Rastakhiz Party, in imitation of the nationalist one-party states of the Third World. The social and economic upheavals inaugurated by the oil revenue boom of the early 1970s included high levels of rural migration, high inflation, economic dislocations and disappointment of the expectations of wide sectors of the population. The educated middle classes – beneficiaries of the shah's generous educational measures and lucrative employment – were frustrated by the continuing repression and by their exclusion from political participation. All these factors led to a crisis of legitimacy and mounting discontent, which was to break out in the revolutionary events of 1977–79.[52] When, for a variety of reasons – not least pressure from an uneasy US administration under the comparatively liberal Carter presidency – the shah loosened his grip, a variety of political and cultural forces stirred. These, for the most part, lacked organization and resources, and mostly acquiesced in the Islamic leadership, which offered both. This acquiescence was facilitated by the anti-imperialist and seemingly liberationist slogans of Khomeini and his followers, calling for a 'Republic', denouncing monarchy and *taghut* (godless tyranny), championing the *mustazefin* (oppressed) and, above all, chanting 'death to America'. There were also hints about democracy. Political anti-imperialism of the left also carried with it a Third Worldist and populist cultural nationalism, and Islam (in its modern phase) was seen as an expression of a national essence and as the creed of 'the people'.[53] It therefore provided a nativist and populist idiom for a revolution; that is to say, the remnants of secular modern politics accepted religious leadership that seemed to adopt their own ideological motifs in an Islamic idiom. The Islamic politics and ideology of the Iranian Revolution fell mostly within the paradigm of modern politics as characterized above, and worked through ideological mobilization of 'the people'. At the same time, sectors of the urban popular classes were mobilized for the Revolution through reconstructed traditional channels of the bazaar, guild and religious networks of patronage and allegiance, as well as the familiar religious slogans and symbols of faith and the cult of the martyrs.[54]

The repressive and authoritarian regime established by the clerics of the Islamic government was equally modern: a clique capturing the commanding heights of a petrolic state and using its resources for consolidating power and wealth. The Islamic institutions and ideologies of this regime then lost their garb of piety, and were seen by the ruled population for what they were: politicians clinging to power and wealth. Yet the popular Revolution was not just a change of government. The mobilization of wide sectors of the Iranian population, prominently including women, shook the foundations of authority. New attitudes and expectations made it difficult for the clerics to eradicate opposition, despite repression that was at times severe. This loosening of controls was aided by the rise of rival centres of power within the government, and within religious and economic institutions. No single dictator – no Saddam or Mubarak – was to emerge and monopolize power. Reversing the general trend towards piety in the region, Iranians, whenever given the opportunity, displayed their rejection of religious rule. From the 1997 election of Khatami to the presidency, then the parliamentary elections of 1999, Iranians supported reform, and were bitterly critical of the failed reformers. Ultimately, the conservative clerics had to resort to further transparent acts of repression and falsification in order to retain control. The election of the populist hardliner Ahmadinejad to the presidency in 2005, which was the result of such manipulation, added to the disillusionment of the masses with failed reforms and continuing economic hardships and disparities. His re-election in 2009, widely believed to be fraudulent, led to widespread movements of protest led by students and the modern intelligentsia, but elicited even wider popular support. The violent repression unleashed against the protest movement by the regime has highlighted the enhanced role and power of the security forces, notably the Pasdaran (Revolutionary Guards), now enjoying control over many government functions as well as economic enterprises. This repressive turn has led observers to speak of a new style of security state, nearer in form to the neighbouring Arab dictatorships. Despite its continuing Islamic rhetoric, the balance of power is shifting towards the military and security forces. Yet the plurality of elites with some hold on centres of power – including conservatives, reformers and radicals – has not been eliminated. An important element in the armoury of the opposition is now the internet resources of bloggers and organizers of protest, opposition and the dissemination of information.[55]

Iraqi cities, like their Iranian counterparts, maintained strong elements of quarter identity and solidarity. In the first half of the twentieth century, migration to Baghdad was confined to specific areas adjacent to the city. Urban identities in Baghdad were reinforced by the religious and ethnic divisions of the city. The suburb of al-Kadhimayn, for instance, housed the holy shrine and pilgrimage centre of the Shi'i Imam al-Kadhim. Across the river was al-A'zamiyya, named after the shrine of Abu Hanifa (known as al-Imam al-A'zam) located there, and therefore a Sunni centre. Other districts were predominantly Jewish or Kurdish. In the political and ideological struggles of the twentieth century, these quarters did not function according to their sectarian identities, but mostly as centres of the various modern political forces. The Iraqi Communist Party organized wide popular constituencies among the intelligentsia and the workers, and in the middle decades of the century also had a wide following among the urban poor. Their rivals and antagonists in opposition politics were various strands of Arab nationalists. In the 1940s and 1950s, the Shi'i and Kurdish quarters were strong bastions of communism, while some of the Sunni quarters were centres of Arabism. Here we have another example of modern political organization and ideology being articulated through urban identities and solidarities.[56]

The long decades of Ba'thist rule (1968–2003) suppressed all forms of politics outside its control – traditional or modern – with brutal and indiscriminate violence. In addition, the decades of destructive wars and the sanctions regime from 1991 resulted in great hardship and dislocation in the populace at large, and pushed people increasingly into the embrace of reconstituted communal and tribal solidarities and allegiances.[57] These were to be the most prominent players in the political chaos following the removal of the regime, and the main 'parties' in the first elections of 2005. The realignment of forces since then, and in the elections of 2010, while differentiating the components of the sectarian blocs, has not succeeded in enfeebling sectarianism as such.

The modern political fields and their components

The modern nation-state, following on in some cases from the colonial state and inheriting many of its features, established the parameters of the new political fields. In the first half of the twentieth century these states followed the colonial model of constitutional and 'democratic' institutions – with parliaments, multiple parties, elections and in some cases constitutional monarchies. Many of these states, such as Egypt and Iraq, continued to be dominated by British interests during that period. Political pluralism was partly maintained by these interests, which sought to play one party against another. In Egypt, historians have noted the tripartite centres of power, divided between the monarchy, parliament/government (often controlled by sectors of the Wafd) and the British High Commission. Political liberties were precarious, with episodes of suspension of legal protections and imposition of martial law, and the permanent banning of parties considered subversive, such as the Communist Party and the Muslim Brotherhood.

In the 1950s and 1960s a series of coups d'état in many of the region's countries transformed government and politics. Most notable and influential was the Nasirist transformation of Egypt. These were nationalist regimes (Egypt, Iraq, Algeria, Yemen, Libya) that finally escaped dependence on the colonial powers and established independent states. This was made possible by the context of the Cold War, which assured Soviet support for the new regimes. In turn, these regimes modelled themselves, to various degrees, on the Soviet example of state socialism – the one-party populist state – but with a military elite at the top. The states pursued programmes of land reform, nationalization of major economic enterprises and a welfare-state system. Other countries – chiefly the monarchies of Saudi Arabia, the Gulf states, Jordan and Iran – remained in the Western camp, but with equally authoritarian and repressive regimes, aided by oil wealth in gaining the acquiescence, if not the support, of their populations through welfare perks and the provision of economic opportunity.

Another important factor in the politics of the area was the creation of Israel in 1948, and the subsequent wars with the Arab countries and the Palestinian population. The Arab–Israeli conflict remained a powerful source of political themes and symbols, religious and secular, in the whole region up to the present day.

A third phase of government regimes, starting in Egypt in the early 1970s and spreading to other countries, may be called the *infitah* era. The 'socialist' model had essentially failed, weighed down by cumbersome bureaucracy and corruption. The Soviet connection was no longer so attractive, compared to the more tempting benefits of association with the USA and the connection to oil-rich Saudi Arabia. Sadat of Egypt started the new wave in the 1970s by expelling the Soviets, aligning with America and Saudi Arabia, liberalizing the economy (within severe limits of bureaucracy and corruption) and introducing some measure of political freedom and pluralism, while retaining the dominance of the ruling party. This was accompanied by a peace treaty with Israel, ushering in a chequered history of relations with that state. The collapse of communism, starting in 1989, cut the final connections of some of the nationalist states, primarily Syria, to that camp, and led to the triumph of the American connection – the only game in town. The most prominent exception to this process was Islamic Iran.

Styles of politics

The two styles of politics noted above – the modern politics of ideology and organization, and the universal politics of faction, kinship and patronage – coexist to the present time, with authoritarian governments trying to use the former to their advantage through the mobilization of the populace behind the government, while in practice fostering the latter by suppressing political pluralism and encouraging particularistic allegiances as a form of social control.

Egypt's Wafd Party, for example – in the first 'liberal' era – was an ideological party aiming at national independence and a democratic constitution, and fought battles – with the British, with the monarchy – to this end. The party enjoyed support from the ideologically motivated modern strata of educated middle classes of functionaries, professionals, teachers and students, as well as from sectors of the new working class. These were mobilized in demonstrations, strikes and electoral campaigns, although apparently the party never instituted a system of membership, and branch offices only operated for elections.[58] At the same time, the main electoral support for party candidates came from peasants and the poorer classes, who were in dependent relations of authority and patronage with the class of rich notables who supplied the party candidates. Peasants, for instance, were bound to vote for their landlord. Some parties, such as the currently ruling National Democratic Party in Egypt, get their support entirely from interested groups seeking jobs, positions, contracts and benefits for particular regions. I should point out that this 'spoils system' of electoral politics is not peculiar to the region – in fact, the term comes from the USA, where much party support comes from interested constituencies.[59]

The Nasirist state was strongly ideological, pushing the symbols of pan-Arab nationalism and socialism under the one party and the one leader. It borrowed the communist rhetoric against (false) bourgeois liberties and pluralist democracy in favour of national unity and independence, and economic development and prosperity. Through land reforms and welfare measures it mobilized the population in apparent support for the party and its leader. The nationalization of the Suez Canal in 1956, and the subsequent war from which Nasir seemed to emerge victorious, gave him tremendous credit and popularity with the Egyptian and Arab public. His portraits were hung, with genuine enthusiasm, in offices, cafés and homes, not just to avoid trouble. At the same time, the authoritarian state established by Nasir, and its parallels elsewhere, spawned new systems of patronage and particularistic politics. An effect of land reform and nationalization was to eliminate autonomous social centres of power based on property. This also had the effect of blocking the processes of 'class struggle' that would generate ideological political organization and solidarity[60] – which were, in any case, banned and suppressed: civil organizations, trade unions and professional associations were either prohibited or incorporated into the state or its sole party. People were then deprived of avenues of organization and association to further their interests, ideologies and social presence, and individuals and groups were thus pushed into informal and personalistic networks of kinship and patronage, linking them to government bureaucracy and to nodes of the 'black economy' from which they could benefit. Diane Singerman,[61] among others, has argued that the common people in Egypt do participate actively in politics, but particular types of politics – those of family, neighbourhood, the informal economy and of their connection to state bureaucracy through patronage and mutual favours. Which sounds very much like the 'pre-modern' and universal politics of personal salvation through allegiance to family, community and patrons, and distinct from the modern politics of ideology and organization.[62]

The demise of ideological parties was given another boost with the collapse of communism in the late 1980s, making leftist ideologies and models less viable. It also removed the Soviet camp as a source of inspiration and support to the secular left. This, together with the suppression or restriction of other parties and civil associations in most countries, opened the field for Islamic political activism. Although Islamic political parties or associations, such as the Muslim Brotherhood, were also banned, their associations and networks could operate through various avenues of religion and charity, as well as banks and businesses, aided by connections to the oil-rich centres of Salafi Islam in Saudi Arabia and the Gulf. These became particularly prominent in the *infitah* period, from the mid-1970s. From that time, spurred by the Iranian Revolution, Islamic politics became the dominant genre and idiom in the region. Let us consider these politics in the light of the concepts of politics developed above.

The diversity of modern Islamic politics

There is a tendency in public and media discourses in the West and elsewhere to assume Islamic politics to be unitary, entirely subsumed under the label of 'fundamentalism'; if any distinction is made, then it is only that between 'moderates' and 'extremists'. These labels hide a wide diversity of ideas and movements. We should note that, for the majority of Muslims in the world, Islam is not about politics, but about faith and observance. Politics may come into it when religious identity comes to define social groups or forces in conflict, much as with 'Catholics' and 'Protestants' in Northern Ireland. What we see in the 'Islamic revival' of the late twentieth century is the rise of political movements drawing on Islam for identities and ideologies. This ideologization of Islam is not new, but has, as we have seen, been a feature of politics since the inception of modernity in the nineteenth century. For most of the twentieth century, however, with the secularization of society and politics, Islamic politics as such constituted one, often minor, element among other, mostly secular, ideologies. I shall survey this history in what follows.

For the present, we should note that current Islamic movements and ideologies are diverse. We may see Islam as an *idiom* in terms of which many social groups and political interests express their aspirations and frustrations, and in which ruling elites claim legitimacy; and we may distinguish a number of types of orientations in the Islamic politics of recent decades.

Three broad and overlapping types of Islamic political orientation may be discerned across the countries in the region. First, conservative or Salafi Islam (*salaf* means ancestors, so for its adherents it is the correct religion of the first Muslims), is the orientation dominant in the Saudi establishment, but has a strong presence throughout the

Muslim world. Its main emphasis is on authority, hierarchy, property, meticulous observance of ritual and correct conduct – including segregation of the sexes and the covering up of women, and other strictures of family morality and propriety. Its general thrust with respect to rights is repressive, with a strong tendency towards the censorship of opinions and expressions. This orientation is political in that it seeks to influence government and policy towards the application and enforcement of religious law and morality, and towards regulation and censorship of the media and of art and cultural products. This orientation is typical of the 'pious bourgeois' businessmen, professionals, and many clerics. There are some interesting parallels between this orientation and that of the Christian evangelical right in the USA, which is also concerned to pressure government into the enforcement of religious observance and moral conduct. They share the desire to censor intellectual and cultural products judged contrary to religious teaching. They are both, for instance, opposed to the teaching of Darwinian evolution in schools. We see here an instance of affinities across supposed civilizational boundaries: it is a clash within, not between, civilizations.

The second type of orientation is radical and militant, typically pursued by young students and other sectors of alienated youth. It differs from that of the conservatives not so much in its objectives, but in its methods. While the conservatives seek Islamization through influence over government and control over levers of power and communication, the radicals tend towards direct, often violent, action. They take the religious injunction to enjoin the good and forbid evildoing as a mandate to every Muslim to intervene forcefully in implementing religious precepts. This direct action applies especially to government and authority, which are seen as culpable for their neglect of the law, and for their corruption and laxity. The leading ideological influence on this orientation is the thought of Sayyid Qutb, an Egyptian militant executed in 1966 on an accusation of armed sedition. He argued that any state that ruled by man-made law and not by what God had decreed was an infidel authority, however much it might pretend to be Islam. A society governed by laws other than those of God is equally errant. Thus, the governments and societies of the Muslim world were not truly Muslim, but lived in a *jahiliya*, a term used to describe the state of ignorance and barbarism that preceded Islam. It is the duty of true Muslims, then, to insulate themselves from this barbarism, recruit followers, entrench their strength in faith and in military training, and, in time, come out to wage jihad against the infidel government and the non-believers, re-conquering the world for Islam in imitation of the Prophet and his generation. This has been the dominant creed of the militants throughout the region.[63]

The third type of orientation is reformist and modernist, typical of some intellectuals, professionals and modern businessmen. It seeks to Islamize government and society, but in the context of economic development, social reform and political democratization. That is to say, it espouses politics that go beyond the moral and ritual agendas of the others. In some respects its cadres seek to continue the national projects of the previous nationalists and leftists, with an emphasis on economic and social programmes. This is the trend that is most concerned with questions of rights and democracy, and comes to the fore wherever Islamism becomes part of a genuinely pluralist electoral politics – primarily in Turkey, and in another form in Iran.[64]

The violent militants, with their outrages and massacres, dominated the headlines in the 1980s in Egypt and the 1990s in Algeria. In Egypt, a wide-ranging and intensely repressive campaign by the authorities decimated the militants, killing, imprisoning and torturing many of them alongside members of their families and neighbourhoods. By the mid-1990s their imprisoned leadership declared an end to hostilities. In Algeria the militants waged a civil war, which included massacres of whole villages and other outrages rivalled only by state security forces. They, too, were suppressed in the end. It should be noted that the decline or demise of the militants, while directly effected by government repression, was also aided by the fear and loathing of most sectors of the population faced with atrocity and disruption. In Egypt, for instance, by attacking foreign tourists they threatened the livelihoods of the many Egyptians dependent on that industry. The conservative, pious bourgeoisie and their clerics, while supporting the militants when they were attacking and assassinating secular intellectuals and artists, drew the line at the disruption of social order.[65]

Islamic politics in the twentieth century, then, were divided between many different orientations – conservative, reformist, liberal and radical. These combined in different articulations with the secular ideologies that dominated much twentieth-century politics. Outright secularism in the Turkish Republic subordinated religion to a nationalist state, and created unique combinations of religion and nationalism. Egypt, where religion was much more prominent in public life, saw many tendencies towards and patterns of Islamic activism. The Muslim Brotherhood, a modern Islamist political movement, emerged there in 1928, and has continued to feature in Egyptian political fields to the present time. Its policies and programmes have fluctuated with the times, from the nationalist, anti-colonial struggles of the first half of the century, to strands of 'Islamic socialism' in the 1950s and 1960s. It spawned radical and violent movements, which split from the mainstream from the 1970s. It has now evolved into a party containing all the tendencies reviewed above, but with a dominant leadership advocating civil Islam and democracy.[66]

By the turn of the twenty-first century, most Islamists had given up on the installation of an Islamic state by force or revolution.[67] Faced with repression and persecution by authoritarian governments, they have increasingly opted for campaigns for democracy and political participation. The Egyptian Muslim Brotherhood, for instance, now calls for political liberalization and pluralism, apparently accepting other, non-Islamic political parties and forces as legitimate. The Turkish Islamic parties have long participated in elections and entered into coalition governments with other parties, based on political realism rather than ideological affinity. Their opponents, however, have questioned their democratic credentials, accusing them of using democracy to gain power that, once gained, will be used to subvert that democracy. The fact is, that although many people in the region now speak the language of democracy, including presidents, kings and shaykhs, there are few democrats in action. This is because democracy comes not from ideological pronouncements, but from political institutions and processes that force parties into it.

The politics of global Islam

Recent decades have been marked by the emergence of 'transnational' and 'global' phenomena. In relation to Islam and politics, these have two distinct manifestations: global jihadism (the 'Afghan phenomenon') and transnational networks of migration. What they both have in common is an abstract notion of a global Islamic Umma, superimposed on actual politics and social relations.

Global jihadism emerged from protracted conflicts in Afghanistan from the 1980s. With American and Saudi organization and finance, large numbers of Arab, Pakistani and other Muslim jihadis were recruited and trained to fight the Soviets in Afghanistan. The departure of the Soviets in 1989 and the subsequent collapse of the communist regime set the different jihadi groups fighting among themselves, destroying Kabul and other Afghan cities in the process. In the mid-1990s, the Taliban – this time with Pakistani and covert American support – emerged as the rulers of the country. The Arab jihadis' camps continued to recruit and train, and after the defeat of the Soviets a traffic in both personnel and ideas developed between these camps and the countries of the region, with the jihadis organizing violent attacks in various countries. The most notable and protracted episode in this backwash from Afghanistan was the civil war in Algeria, but it also had important manifestations in Egypt and elsewhere. The Iraq–Kuwait War of 1990–91 provided another focus for jihadism. American and other international forces (including those from Arab states) invaded the Gulf region to expel Iraqi forces from Kuwait. American bases were established on the Arabian Peninsula, notably in Saudi Arabia: infidels in the home of the holy cities of Islam. The jihadists then focused their ire on the Americans and the Saudis, who had together been responsible for their creation. This was particularly important in Saudi Arabia, which espoused as its official ideology Wahhabi Islam – which also provided the inspiration for the jihadists, who pointed to the laxity and corruption of the Saudi rulers and their subservience to the American infidels, now cast as the global enemy of Islam, and the allies and backers of the Israelis. A global battle was then postulated between the theoretical Islamic

Umma and the Christian (Crusader) and Jewish enemies, but also against Hindus and Sikhs in relation to Kashmir. From these events emerged the phenomenon of al-Qaʻida – not a coherent organization, but a loose association of jihadists, many trained in Afghanistan but then freelancing in various cells all over the world. The battle culminated in the 9/11 attacks in the USA and the subsequent 'war on terror', including the invasions of Afghanistan and then Iraq by the Americans and their allies. The postulated global battle between Islam and the rest seemed to the jihadists and many other Muslims to have been fully joined. These events, and the politics and ideologies they engendered, have had profound repercussions for the other aspect of globalized Islam: the transnational communities.[68]

Transnational communities are a product of extended migrations in the latter decades of the past century. Its most interesting aspect for our discussion is the settlement of Muslims in European and American cities. There is now extensive literature on Islam in Europe and the West. These Muslim individuals and groups are diverse by ethnicity (Pakistanis, Bangladeshis, Turks, Maghrebis, Africans, Arabs and so on), class and occupation, and religious and political orientations. There is no uniform 'Muslim community', although communal leaders and some politicians would like to pretend that there is, so that they can speak on its behalf. Some of those Muslims, though, partake in the notion of the universal Umma, and this perception was strengthened by the events following 9/11 – especially the 'war on terror', which has created threats and difficulties for many Muslims in the West. Prior to these events, the results of many polls and studies in the various countries of Western Europe showed that about 70 per cent of Muslims were largely secularized, much like other Europeans, with some becoming 'cultural' Muslims, confining their observance to celebrating festivals and observing rites of passage. Of the observing 30 per cent, most were engaged in private piety, and were not political Muslims. Those who were politically active as Muslims constituted a small minority, but a vocal one that attracted sensational media attention. Following 9/11, these orientations have undergone various mutations.[69] Many more Muslims in Europe have developed religious sentiments and orientations towards the virtual universal Umma. There is a sense of Muslim solidarity in the face of a threatening world. A survey in the British *Guardian* newspaper found that 46 per cent of Muslim men, and as many as 68 per cent of Muslim women, reported that they prayed every day – though, of course, it is difficult to know how much of such self-reporting of piety is for media consumption.

Most Muslims in Europe remain politically inactive. Those active vary in their orientation to the politics of their country of origin (retention of which is especially marked among Turks) and of their country of residence. Many Pakistanis and Bangladeshis in Britain have become active in mainstream party politics, with leading figures standing for public office, as have many Turks in Germany. Their concerns are mainly practical, relating to the distribution of public goods – of education, housing and policing, for instance. But an important role has been played by ideological issues – notably that of the *hijab* in France. Questions of foreign policy have also come to the fore in recent years, especially following the military interventions in Afghanistan and Iraq. With numbers reaching upwards of 5 million Muslims in France and 3 million in Britain, Muslims have become an important item in electoral calculations for parties.

A majority of European Muslims are disadvantaged, occupying the lower rungs of the ladder in terms of employment and pay, and are disproportionately represented among the unemployed. This reinforces a sense of alienation from mainstream society, especially on the part of the young, who also suffer from racism and the hostility to Muslims following 9/11. France is where such youths, living in the slum suburbs (*banlieu*) of Paris and the main cities, rioted violently in 2005, causing a national crisis. It is significant that the grievances of those rioters were framed in terms of economic and social demands, voicing particular objections to repressive policing, rather than in terms of religious ideologies or solidarities. The International Crisis Group's (ICG) 2006 report on these events, in the context of the transformation of the politics of Muslims in France, concluded that, following the political surges of the 1980s and 1990s, a process of depoliticization among Muslims was now taking place, of which the riots were one manifestation. Political and religious associations, some encouraged by the French government as official interlocutors, had become ever more distant from ordinary Muslims, and especially from the young. Political Islam, mostly led by offshoots of the Muslim Brotherhood, became more integrated into official institutional structures, winning respectability and recognition from the state as interlocutors on Islam.

The ICG report distinguishes a number of orientations of Muslims who had moved in a depoliticized direction. It highlights two strands of Salafism: 'shaykhist' and jihadist. The first is a pietistic orientation emphasizing observance and ritual, fostered by Wahhabi clerics from Saudi Arabia with their funds and mosques. It discourages political participation in favour of individualized piety. Jihadism, as we have seen, is the violent face of Salafism, equally emphasizing observance and distance from non-believers, but incorporating active hostility to the latter as enemies of Islam. Riots are forms of spontaneous and apolitical response. These two orientations are distinct from the communal and ethnic Islam of earlier generations, and the political Islam of the 1990s. Some Muslims are receptive to the appeal of jihadist Salafism, and the idea of a universal confrontation between Islam and the West. Much of this receptivity remains at the level of sentiment, and only few progress into organization and action; radical and jihadi groups recruit from within this minority. However, an interesting phenomenon is that they are also successful among converts to Islam – especially those from other disadvantaged groups, notably Afro-Caribbean youth in Britain. The young radicals of immigrant origin are mostly second- and third-generation immigrants. As such, they are culturally integrated into the life of the host community, having been through the education system and having a native speaker's knowledge of the local language. They are mostly alienated from the ethnic cultures of their parents. The radical Islam they embrace is not that of their parents, but a de-ethnicized, de-territorialized Islam containing Salafi or Qutbist ideas and motifs. Equally, many educated middle-class Muslims – to the extent that they believe and practice – embrace a modernist, reformed Islam with universalistic tendencies, distinct from the ethnic Islam of their parents. It is important to note, then, that Islamic affiliations – whether radical or liberal – are typically modern and individualized, and distinct from the conservative and communitarian Islam of previous generations, which tends towards traditional ethnic orientations. These modern forms of Islam do not represent a 'clash of civilizations' with the West, but in fact constitute part of the West's ideological diversity.[70]

3 Shifting Social Boundaries and Identities in the Modern Middle East

The Middle East is 'middle' from the geographical perspective of north-west Europe. A definition of the region, then, must be relative to how that part of Europe defined itself and its others. That 'other' of the Middle East also contended with diverse definitions of identities and boundaries.

The frontiers of Europe and its identity are clear on maps and in geography textbooks, but not so clear in the realms of ideology and symbol. The privileged sites of enunciation as to what constitutes Europe have come from the dominant centres of its north-western countries, where the idea of Europe was developed and elaborated, particularly in the intellectual and political milieux of France, Britain and Germany. In the discourses on Europe – romantic, literary and political – 'Europe' is given an honorific identification as the centre of civilization, then the dynamic motor of modernity, characterized by a spirit of rationality, liberty and justice. This is conventionally contrasted to the 'Orient', or Asia – the realm of despotism, fanaticism and historical fixity. These stereotypes were of course regularly contested within the diversity of European thought, which always included strands of subtlety and ambivalence. They can be observed in characterizations of the contrasts between Charles-Louis de Secondat, Baron de Montesquieu, Voltaire, Georg Wilhelm Friedrich Hegel, Maine de Biran and Karl Marx, all of whom had concepts of what is 'Asiatic', yet with diverse evaluations.[1]

More interestingly, this honorific notion of Europe rarely included the whole of geographic Europe, within which northern Europeans were always drawing boundaries. English nationalists contended that 'Wogs begin at Calais'! Klemens Wenzel, Prince von Metternich, is reported to have stood on a balcony in Vienna to declare: 'Here begins Asia', and the English derogatory term for the Germans during the twentieth century's world wars was 'Hun'. Russia and the East were always problematically European, verging on the Asiatic. Even more problematic were the Balkans, known until the later nineteenth century as 'European Turkey', and considered typically 'Oriental' though within geographic Europe. Greece posed a particular problem: seen by romantics as the cradle and origin of Europe, it always disappointed them when they were confronted with the reality of nineteenth-century Greece, which was a backwater and, despite independence from the Ottomans, still characteristically 'Oriental'. Italy and Spain both displayed a clear division between their (European) north and (Mediterranean/African) south. The Mediterranean itself is an area of ambiguity as regards Europe. Until the first half of the twentieth century we can discern many cultural and social traits in common between the urban and peasant realms on both shores, north and south. The urban cultures of Tunisia, say, and Aegean Turkey had much in common with southern European cities. Consider modes of dress: women in southern Europe, especially married women, always covered their heads and sported styles of clothing that paralleled those of their counterparts on the southern shores (I hesitate to call the southern shores 'Muslim', because many of their inhabitants have been Christians and, earlier, Jews). Ideas on family, 'honour' and group solidarities were also shared, not to mention food and music. They were not the same in all these territories, but they shared 'family resemblances'. What happened in the course of the twentieth century is that the south of the European countries was increasingly absorbed into the north and became 'European', while the 'Muslim' shores were increasingly peasantized, with massive migrations from the interior into the coastal cities. The cities lost their *citadinité* – their sense of urban identity and pride – and were swallowed up in the tide of migrating peasants and by the high rate of natural population growth.[2] So, the distinction and difference between the European and the 'Muslim' Mediterranean is largely one that does not represent a deep and essential cultural cleavage, but one that is produced by the socio-economic and cultural processes of the twentieth century, in which the formation of the European Union played an important role in integrating the European south into the north.

The closest and most important 'other' for Europe in modern history was the 'Muslim world', and in particular the Ottoman Empire and its successor states. What was the self-perception of this world? Like that of Europe, self-definitions were diverse and shifting, with boundaries drawn in accordance with context and circumstance. An inclusive self-definition of Islam – and one that was reciprocated by Europeans – relied upon its distinction from Christendom. Within that opposition grew the 'problematic of decline': why was the world of Islam declining in relation to a dominant Christian Europe? Was it, as the conservatives argued, because Muslims had abandoned their faith and adopted other gods? Or was it, as their reformist opponents argued, because of the decadence of religion and society, and the need for a renaissance modelled on the modern European world? I shall return to this question presently. First, however, let us consider the vocabulary of designations of self and other within the Ottoman world.

The common designation of Ottomans and Muslims by Europeans was that of 'Turk' – a label that became synonymous with 'Muslim'. We have seen that even the Christian domains of the Balkans were designated 'Turkish Europe'. Ottomans did not favour the label 'Turk', which for them referred to rough country and tribal peoples, and not to the polished urbanites who furnished Ottomans with their own self-identity. Similar distinctions were made in the Arab world, where until the rise of Arab nationalism in the nineteenth and twentieth centuries the term 'Arab' commonly designated a Bedouin or a peasant – and this persisted as common usage in casual talk until recent times. One self-designation used by the inhabitants of geographical Turkey was 'Rum' – Roman. Earlier in Muslim history, Muslims had designated their Byzantine antagonists, constituting the Eastern Roman Empire, as Rum. Their country, Constantinople and Anatolia, was thus known in Arabic as Bilad al-Rum, 'the country of the Romans'. In time, inhabitants of that country would be referred to as Rum, even though some were Muslims. The dynasty of the Seljuqs of Anatolia (1077–1307) was designated Rum Seljuqs, to distinguish it from the earlier eastern Seljuq empire. The notable medieval poet and mystic of Konya (central Anatolia) was Jalal-u-ddin al-Rumi (1207–73), for instance. The Ottoman inhabitants of that country referred to themselves in certain contexts as Rum.[3] We find Iraqi Bedouins in the early twentieth century referring to the Turks as 'Rouam' – an Arabic plural form for Rum. Common designations by Iraqi writers of their two powerful neighbours were Rum and ''Ajam' (Persians). But there was an ambiguity in this designation of Rum, because Greeks were Rum, and their church and *millet* were so designated. (To this day, the Arabic designation of Greek Orthodox is Al-Rum al-Orthodox.) To the Muslims, European Christians were divided into 'Franj' (Franks) and Rum. The first were northern European and Catholic (later of all denominations): the Crusaders were Franj, and the Crusades, to the Muslims, were the wars of the Franj; the term *salibiyun*, so commonly used now with hostile connotations, only came into use in the later nineteenth century. Rum were the Orthodox of Anatolia, the Arab provinces, Greece and the Balkans.

With the rise of Turkish – as against Ottoman – nationalism from the nineteenth century, the designation 'Turk' became honourable and patriotic. 'Rum' acquired other connotations in the contests between the strident secularism of the Kemalist state and the many (underground) quarters of Muslim resistance. The pious populations of provincial Anatolia viewed the secular and Europeanized Istanbul and Ankara bourgeoisie with hostility, and considered them alien to the true Turkey, which was Muslim. They were therefore designated

Rum, as opposed to the true Muslim Turks of the interior. Thus there has been a shifting play on these designations and their opposites.

Greek self-designation is particularly interesting. The modern Greek nationalist movement, emerging in the eighteenth century and continuing into the nineteenth, was heavily influenced by northern European romantic ideas about ancient Greece as the cradle of Europe. In accordance with this notion, independent Greece defined itself as 'Hellenic'. In fact, the territory of independent Greece was by then a backwater of the Ottoman Empire, and the flourishing of Greek culture, as well as the bulk of Greek populations, were elsewhere. Constantinople was the spiritual home of Greeks, and its loss the great historic catastrophe. The Greeks of Constantinople in Ottoman times still constituted an elite, and their own elites, notably the Phanariots (families of rich notables who acted as diplomats and financiers for the Ottomans) were the patricians of the Greek world. They continued in their Ottoman functions even after Greek independence. The patriarchate of Constantinople, like those of Antioch and Jerusalem, was opposed to Greek independence, arguing that the sultan was chosen by God, and that the *ra'aya* (subjects) had a religious duty of obedience.[4] In fact, they thoroughly disapproved of the Enlightenment and French Revolutionary ideas and practices behind modern nationalism, and rightly considered it a threat to their authority over the faithful, entrusted to them by the sultan. Indeed, the modern Greek state had to establish its own church hierarchy, parallel to that of Constantinople.

Greek communities flourished on the shores of the Black Sea from ancient times. In modern times they became part of the Ottoman lands around the basin of that sea, and of Russia (particularly Odessa). All those Greeks considered themselves Rum, and their unifying reference was their church, heir to Byzantium. The Greek language was spoken in widely varying dialects, and some of the Black Sea Greeks spoke Turkish, which they wrote in the Greek script.[5] It was ultimately the system of nation-states that reconstituted Greek identity as an Hellenic 'diaspora' from an original territory of Athens and the Greek nation-state. However, Constantinople continued to be a dream of Greek nationalism, until that dream was dashed by the events following World War I, which led to the tragic exchange of populations between Turkey and Greece. It is interesting that in that exchange Turkish-speaking Christians were defined as Greek, and Greek-speaking Muslims (mostly from Crete) were defined as Turkish. Thus, the secular Turkish Republic was born with a homogeneous Muslim population. A piece of oral history: Yucel Terzibasoglu, interviewing a Turkish peasant in the Aegean region in the 1990s, was told that the 'local Greeks' (*yerli rum*) had been expelled, but that then they got 'foreign Greeks' (*yabanci rum*) – meaning Muslim migrants from Crete![6]

Arabs, Turks and Europeans: the problematic of 'backwardness'

In the Ottoman world on the eve of modernity – from the late eighteenth century – there was a sense of decline. For the elites this was embodied in the series of military defeats and losses of territory to European powers, as well as subordination of their finance and commerce to European interests. There was an accompanying general diminution of revenues and the corruption and disorganization involved in their collection. Groups of common people suffered from similar processes: competition for local products from cheap imports, the break-up of the guilds, the burden of taxation (accompanied by its increasing complexity and efficiency) and so on. But there were also benefits in the expansion of certain sectors in agriculture and crafts and new fields of employment, facilitated by improved transport and communications – with roads and railways developing from the mid-nineteenth century – as well as the expansion of employment in the growing spheres of bureaucracy and the professions, and urban growth in general. The senses of decline and economic hardship were dramatically illustrated for many people throughout the nineteenth century by the waves of Muslim refugees arriving in Anatolia from the lost territories of the Balkans and the Caucasus. Interestingly, for the Russians and Austrians, all Muslim populations (Bosnians, Circassians, Crimeans) were classified as 'Turkish'.[7]

The most common framework within which these conflicts were

perceived was that of the opposition between Islam and Christendom. Conservatives asserted that decline and defeat were consequences of a departure from the true faith, and resisted reforms and modernity, in what proved a losing battle. Many, however – especially among the elites – saw reform according to European models as inevitable for recovery, beginning with military reforms, but in turn depending on administrative, fiscal, legal and educational reforms. These reforms were also pressed by the dominant European powers. Did they, then, represent an abandonment of traditional cultural and religious heritages and an imitation of Europe? That is how the conservatives presented them. Reformers argued that they were necessary for the preservation of the Empire, and therefore of Islam. The most interesting view, however, was that of Islamic modernists, who accepted the reforms but conceived them in a novel Islamic framework.

The Young Ottomans of the 1860s and 1870s were men educated in European languages and ideas – some of them aristocrats, some from Istanbul's prestigious School of Translation. They opposed the autocratic nature of the reforms and the alarming dependence of the Empire, financially and militarily, on European powers and banks. They rejected the idea underlying the reforms that law and justice were granted by the sultan. They argued that the original Islam of the Prophet and his Companions, when purified from subsequent corruption and accretions, contained all the finest principles and procedures upon which European civilization and law were based. They demanded a constitution that enshrined those liberties and limited sovereign power. These modes of argument were further elaborated by the Islamic reformers of the late nineteenth and early twentieth centuries, who were mainstream ulama and presented the arguments in the language of theology and jurisprudence. The most notable and often-cited of these reformers were Jamaleddin Al-Afghani (d. 1897) (who we shall encounter in Chapter 4 as a cosmopolitan wandering between India, Iran, Egypt and Turkey) and his Egyptian disciple Abduh (d. 1905), who became mufti of Egypt. Their ideas are particularly interesting for our discussion.[8]

The religious reforms were part of a general 'renaissance' (*nahdha*), as it was conceived by its practitioners. It proceeded not only in religion but also in science, literature, language, law and in general intellectual and cultural outlooks. The men of this renaissance (and they were predominantly men) shared a view of their society as one that had suffered a decline, and had over the centuries become 'backward' and corrupt – hence the need for a renaissance. But 'renaissance' implies the rebirth of an essence that was there in the past – and that was indeed the assumption. The reformers had internalized the European gaze upon their societies, which read these societies as backward, corrupt, fatalistic, fanatical, libidinal, irrational and so on – all the 'Orientalist' stereotypes of Muslim society. At the core of these negative traits was religion – Islam itself, which was seen by European commentators as having generated all these handicaps. The reformers' response was to implicitly accept that these were aspects of the backwardness of their societies, but they declared emphatically that these were not the product of Islam, but of the corruption of that religion. The original Islam of the first ancestors, they argued, contained all the noblest elements of modern civilization in embryo: democracy and constitutionalism were to be seen in the principles and procedures of the first Muslim society inaugurated by the Prophet in Medina. Rationality and science were also enshrined in these Islamic principles. All that distinguished the best of European modernity was original to Islam, long before it came to Europe. The present backwardness and decline were due not to Islam, but to corruptions and accretions – the products of centuries of political tyranny and obscurantist outlooks. The reforms that were now due, they argued, would be based on a restored and purified Islam, and would be fully compatible with modernity. In effect, these reformers were advocating or approving the adoption of European models of government, law, education and culture, though giving them an Islamic ancestry, thus preserving cultural authenticity while fully integrating into the modern world.[9]

The question of *who* is to blame for the decline is an interesting one for our purposes. With nationalism and the formation of nation-states, various writers presented arguments placing the blame for backwardness on Middle Eastern nationalities other than their own. Arab intellectuals – notably Rashid Rida (d. 1935), Islamic reformer and disciple of Abduh – partially blamed the Turks for the corruption and decline of Islam. Secular intellectuals tended to look to the pre-Islamic heritage of their countries for progressive and civilized essences – the Egyptian heritage of the Pharaohs, or Hellenism, or the roots of Persian civilization, or the traditions of the Turkish peoples of the steppe. One particularly interesting argument in this context was that advanced by the great Egyptian writer and educationalist, Taha Hussein, in his book *Mustaqbal al-Thaqafa fi Misr* (The Future of Culture in Egypt), published in 1937. He argued that medieval Islamic civilization and thought had developed in parallel with those of Europe. Indeed, Islam had the priority in rationality and logic, in that it was Muslim intellectuals who had first discovered Hellenic philosophy, transmitting it to Europe. Christian Europe had progressed through the rationality that came from integrating Greek philosophy into religious thought, and Islam was progressing in a similar direction. The progress of Islam in general and of Egypt in particular was arrested by the Turkish conquest, which imposed political and cultural controls, leading to the corruption and backwardness of subsequent centuries. Now, in the twentieth century, Egypt had to resume the progress that had been interrupted, and look to the Mediterranean and Europe for its inspiration without departing from its true heritage, which was to be found in Islam and Hellenism. Needless to say, the book was highly controversial and widely attacked by traditionalists. Hussein later wrote on Islamic history and the life of the Prophet, but in a vein that presented that history as a precursor of modernity and progress.[10]

We should note in passing that Hussein's historical narrative relating to the Ottomans – what may be called 'the Ottoman interregnum' story – is common to many Arab and Balkan nationalist narratives. National history and progress (Arab, Egyptian, Greek, Serbian and so on) was proceeding apace when interrupted by the imposition of the 'Turkish yoke' of oppression and backwardness, thrown off thanks to heroic struggles, and now the nation can resume its glory and progress. The long Ottoman centuries are thus bracketed out of the historical narrative.

The Turks reciprocated with their own intellectual endeavours to separate their heritage from those of Arabs and Persians. Turkish nationalism culminated in the Young Turks (Committee of Union and Progress) movement of the early twentieth century, followed after defeat in World War I by Kemalism and the Republic. One key intellectual of that nationalist movement was Zia Gokalp, who was influenced by the sociology of Emile Durkheim as well as by German nationalist thought, adopting the German distinction between 'culture' and 'civilization'. Turkish culture was anchored in the ancient Turkish peoples, and had its own distinctive heritage of equality and rationality. At one point in its history it was articulated with Islamic civilization, with which it flourished for a period. However, this articulation with Islamic civilization was no longer progressive, and Turkish culture now had to benefit from a re-articulation with European civilization. Turkey's destiny, then, was with Europe, and detached from 'Oriental' associations, now understood as backward and archaic.[11] Islam is retained by Gokalp as a moral system and an element of social cohesion, à la Durkheim, but not as a civilizational project. This orientation to Europe was taken up by Mustapha Kemal, and became enshrined in the ideology and culture of the Turkish Republic and its Kemalist ideology. One interesting area was that of music: the Republic declared that true Turkish music was that of rural Anatolia, played on the typical *saz* instrument. Its project (aided by the Hungarian composer Béla Bartók) was to discover the rules and modes of this music, which, it was argued, was akin to European folk music and distinct from Oriental music with Arab and Persian associations. Only this pure Turkish music was to be broadcast on national radio. A popular response to this broadcasting policy was for listeners to switch to radio Cairo![12]

More recent Islamist ideologies have insisted on the unity of the Muslim community, and asserted that it was European and Western imperialism and its followers that cultivated the divisions between Muslim nations. Modern Islamists, including Arabs, have argued that Arab nationalism against the Ottomans was part of a European conspiracy against Islamic unity and the Ottoman caliphate.[13]

In the history of early modernity in the Middle East, then, we see an ambivalence towards Europe. The conservatives, who lost out, rejected Europe and modernity; the reformers, many of them keen to maintain cultural authenticity, but at the same time convinced that only progress along European lines would rescue their societies, adopted these models but asserted that their features had their origins in their own history and religion. It was later generations of nationalists and Islamists, for whom the reforms and modernity were taken for granted, who then embarked on a rejection of Europe and the West, and an insistence on the unique distinctiveness of their culture from the West.

Post-Ottoman identities

The aftermath of the 'long' nineteenth century and World War I saw cataclysmic movements of populations and formations of new polities and identities, with innovations in vocabularies and symbols. Modern Turkey was born as a republic, and a secular republic at that, after the demise, then active rejection, of empire, sultanate and caliphate. Also rejected were the pluralist world of imperial ethnicities and religions, the *millets* and the multiplicity of corporate units recognized under the Empire. This process started in the course of the nineteenth century with the loss of most of the European and Christian territories of the Empire – its wealthiest, revenue-rich lands in the Balkans and south-east Europe. These were transformed from *millet* to nation, with religion forming a central element of both institutions and identities. In Greece, Serbia and the Balkan countries, there was always a contention between church authority, with its specific Orthodox–national identity, and the modern nationalists with Enlightenment and French Revolutionary models of nation and citizenship. The tension continues to the present day in Greece and Serbia. National independence in these states, as well as in Russia, and Austrian rule in other former territories of the Ottomans, culminated in massive expulsions and migrations of Muslim populations from these territories: Caucasians, Bosnians, Albanians and others, who streamed into the remaining, predominantly Muslim parts of the Empire, and added to the poverty, land disputes and ethnic tensions in those areas.[14] These refugees, of diverse ethnicities and languages, were classified by their European persecutors as 'Turks'. 'Turk' became equivalent to 'Muslim'.

This ethnic cleansing was reciprocated in geographic Turkey during World War I and the years leading up to it: the large Armenian population of Anatolia was massacred or expelled, as were the smaller Christian denominations in the south. With the loss of European Christian territories, the remaining populations of the Empire of Turks, Arabs and Kurds were predominantly Muslim. Sultan Abdul-Hamid II (r. 1876–1909) then emphasized Islam as the identity and the solidarity of the Empire. Christian populations, some inspired by the independence of their co-religionists, inclined towards the European powers as their saviours. They became the enemy within. The ultimate result after World War I and the debacle of the war with Greece, followed by the exchange of populations, was that the Turkish Republic emerged as a secular state with a largely Muslim population. Sunni Islam of the Hanafi *madhhab* (one of the four Sunni law schools, which was followed by the Ottomans) became the ideal identity of Turkish citizenship.[15] Unlike neighbouring Arab states, Turkey had very few non-Muslim inhabitants who could be classified as ethnically Turkish, such as Arab Christians and Jews. The Islamic identity of Alevis, for example, who constitute a sizable population in the south-east of Turkey, has been disputed by the Sunni majority, who have considered them heretics. Their full citizenship is thus implicitly challenged.[16]

The Shi'a and Arab identity

The Shi'i population of Ottoman Iraq constituted an anomaly in the Sunni identity of the Empire. It was complicated by the affinity of that religion to neighbouring Iran, which, from Safavid times at the start of the sixteenth century, became the centre of Shi'ism and the antagonist of the Sunni Ottomans. Over the centuries Iraq constituted a battleground. The shrine cities of Najaf and Karbala, while under Ottoman rule and taxation, retained a large measure of autonomy under the rule of rival *mujtahids* and local power elites into the twentieth century.[17] This posed a particular problem for the

Hamidian regime (1876–1909), which laid increasing emphasis on Islamic solidarity as the basis of Ottoman nationalism. While the earlier nineteenth-century conception of Ottomanism ('Osmanlilik') was an attempt to create Ottoman citizens of all constituent religions and ethnicities, the Hamidian conception emphasized Sunni Islam. Rival Islamic adherence, whether Wahhabi or Shi'i, was conceived as a subversive threat to the uniformity and solidarity of the Empire. The regime embarked on feeble attempts to convert the Shi'a, including one idea – never realized – of appointing Hanafi missionaries, to be titled *da'i-l-hak misyoner* ('guide to the truth', missionary)![18] Local Sunni ulama were entrusted with the task of propagating the correct Muslim faith, but with no success. Above all, Iraqi Shi'a were always suspected of affiliation with or allegiance to the antagonist Iran – a theme that persists to the present day.

Within Iran, Shi'ism is closely associated with Iranian national identity, even among the many secular Iranians. This is not only a function of the historical association since the sixteenth century, but also the intermingling of Shi'i themes and rituals with Iranian popular and high cultures and institutions. The boundary is reasonably clear between Iran and the Arab and Turkish worlds. The situation is much more complex for the Arab Shi'a, especially in Iraq.

Naturally, the Iraqi Shi'a have many associations with neighbouring Iran. Clerics of Iranian origin and language are often to be found resident in the shrine cities of Najaf, Karbala and Kadhemiya (a suburb of Baghdad), and many clerical families have branches in both countries. This is also true for some merchants. Under favourable conditions there is a constant traffic of pilgrims and students from Iran into these locations, and a trade of burials of the pious dead in the sacred soil. Nevertheless, Iraqi Shi'a remain distinct from their Iranian co-religionists.

The Iraqi Shi'a are predominantly Arab: from earliest times, Iraq was the main home of Shi'ism, and its inhabitants were Arabized at an early stage of Muslim rule, while the Bedouin tribes of the south were converted to Shi'ism in the early nineteenth century. In response to the Wahhabi raids and the devastation of the shrine cities in 1802, the leading clerics set about converting the tribes as a military force against further raids. As a result, Iraqi Shi'ism acquired a considerable tribal and Bedouin population, with its own composition and religious flavour, quite distinct from the urban dominance characteristic of Iran. Even though the Shi'i merchant class was prominent and important in Iraq, it was not so intimately related to the clerical classes as was the bazaar in Iran. In the course of the twentieth century, the Shi'a of the two countries drifted apart as the institutions of the two nation-states were formed, with their distinct educational systems and political fields and identities. Some commentators have argued that during the Iran–Iraq War (1980–88) the predominantly Shi'i soldiery of Iraq fought with patriotic commitment.[19]

At the same time, the dominant Sunni ideology, combined (as in Iraq) with pan-Arab nationalism, always cast doubt on the Arab identity of the Shi'a, and hinted at their ultimate allegiance to their Iranian co-religionists. These themes were heightened in times of conflict and strife, such as the anti-Saddam intifada following the Iraq–Kuwait War of 1990–91, and indeed the present situation following the 2003 invasion. An institutional addition to this situation is the strange Iraqi nationality law. With the emergence of post-Ottoman independent Iraq, the new Iraqi nationality was confined to previously Ottoman subjects. Many of the Shi'a in late Ottoman times claimed Iranian nationality to avoid military service, and to enjoy some of the capitulatory privileges of foreign subjects. These constituted ambiguous citizens of the new Iraq, described as *taba'iya iraniya*, 'Iranian affiliation'. This status continued to be inherited by their descendants to the end of the Ba'thist regime in 2003. Some Jewish families were also included in this classification. These ambiguities allowed the Ba'thist regime to expel hundreds of thousands of Shi'a at various points in the 1970s and 1980s, including large numbers of Fayli (Shi'i) Kurds, but also the Shi'i merchant elites, allowing the regime and its personnel to appropriate their wealth.[20]

The Arab Sunnis constitute a minority within Iraq, but are part of a large majority in the Arab world. Many Arab Sunnis, of course, did not participate in these sectarian conceptions, nor did their Shi'i counterparts. Both – as well as Christians, Kurds and Jews – participated in common political and cultural pursuits in parties and associations of leftist and liberal character. Sectarianism, however, was a potent force utilized and mobilized by successive regimes, and most persistently by the Ba'th, which depended on a narrow sectarian and tribal base.[21] From the earliest period of the Iraqi state, politicians and ideologues pursued an Arabist agenda that entailed casting doubt on the Arabness of the Shi'a.

An interesting episode in Iraqi history illustrates these issues. Muhammad Mahdi al-Jawahiri (1903–97) was the poet of Iraq in the twentieth century.[22] He marked the events and features of Iraqi history and society with his poems, which were memorized and recited by many. Jawahiri was from a Shi'i Najafi family of ulama and *udaba* (literati). As a young man and budding poet and writer, he applied for a job as a schoolteacher in Baghdad in 1927. His appointment became an issue between the Shi'i education minister and the director of education, who was none other than Sati' al-Hussri, the famous theoretician of pan-Arab nationalism. Al-Hussri had previously been an Ottoman official, from a Syrian family, and he had followed Faysal I to Iraq and high office. Hussri and his officials put many obstacles in the way of the appointment, including questioning al-Jawahiri's nationality status, resorting to the doctrine of Iranian *taba'iya*. The 1927 interview with Hussri is reported differently in the respective memoirs of the two men. Hussri claims that when he questioned Jawahiri about his nationality, Jawahiri responded that he was Iranian, and argued that if the director of education can be a Syrian and Turk, then why not an Iranian teacher? This version of events was drawn to Jawahiri's attention by friends who had read a study of Hussri by a Canadian academic, and Jawahiri responded to it in his more recent memoirs. His account is that he replied to Hussri's questions with scorn, asking how a Syrian Turk who spoke Arabic with a thick accent and needed an interpreter could question the Arabness of a descendant of the flower of Arabic letters, himself one of their budding practitioners.[23] Regardless of the respective truth of these accounts, the episode illustrates the play on ambiguities of identity and boundaries in the cultural and political fields.

The question of the Arab allegiance of the Shi'a has been raised sharply in relation to the current events in Iraq. It is clear that a majority of Shi'a and their leadership were happy with the downfall of Saddam Hussein's regime, but not necessarily with the American occupation and its aftermath. Nevertheless, the Shi'a and the Kurds, for the most part, set about trying to establish some kind of settlement and stability, with a political process that would ensure their representation in future government. The insurgency is directed primarily from Sunni Arab quarters (though these are not representative of the totality of Sunnis), and reflects a convergence of Ba'thist sentiments with Islamic jihadism. Both of these wings of the insurgency have strong feelings against the Shi'a, judged by the Salafis to be *rafida* (deniers of true faith and authority) and heretics, and as the national enemy with Iranian connections by the pan-Arabists. Violence is increasingly directed at sectarian targets. The jihadists are explicit in targeting the Shi'a, but many Arab nationalists are circumspect about sectarian sentiments, though they hint at both Iranian connections (references to 'Iranian mercenaries') and 'collaboration' with the invaders! What these charges have in common is that they exclude the Shi'a from the Arab fold as aliens, thereby supposedly explaining their perfidy.

4 Cosmopolitans, Nationalists and Fundamentalists in the Modern Middle East

In the last two or three decades of the twentieth century, with the rise of 'identity politics' in many regions, and specifically of Islamic political advocacy in the Middle East, the public mind has viewed this region as having religion as its essence. This association has been strengthened after 9/11 and other violent attacks. The impression has been created that the societies in this region have always had religion as their essence, and their history is being read backwards. In this chapter I shall offer a different history that comprises lively and varied social and cultural formations in which religion is only one element – and one that, for most of the twentieth century, was not dominant.

Cosmopolitanism

'Cosmopolitanism' is not a precise concept: it slips between different discourses and associations. It is embroiled in ideological contests: construed by some as designating inauthenticity, rootlessness and moral corruption; for others connoting desirable diversity, tolerance and sophistication, as well as 'fun'. In recent decades, in various corners of the Middle East, it has been the stuff of nostalgia: with the rise of Islamic ideologies and regimes in the region, intellectuals, liberals and revellers have engaged in nostalgic trips to a romanticized past of cosmopolitan and Bohemian spaces and sociabilities. Istanbul, Alexandria and Beirut, facing an influx of rural and provincial migrations, and with these of narrower cultures and outlooks, well laced with religious disciplines, hark back to this golden past of cultural vitality, diversity and tolerance. Is it, then, the nationalists and fundamentalists who have stolen this past? Let us delve into aspects of relevant histories to respond to this question.[1]

Empires

The phenomena of cosmopolitanism are the products of empires. They bring diverse peoples together into their urban centres who are engaged in various relationships, economic and political. The association of cosmopolitans with imperialism is one reason nationalists and fundamentalists have found for denouncing it. The two pertinent empires for the modern history of the Middle East (since the mid-nineteenth century) are the Ottoman and the British, which had important inputs both from French language and culture and from German nationalism.

The Ottoman Empire is sometimes described as 'cosmopolitan' in that it brought together diverse peoples, ethnicities and religions, which, for the most part, coexisted peacefully. The '*millet* system' is cited as a model of tolerance and harmony, however the non-Muslim *millets* (and non-Sunni Muslims, not classified as separate *millets*) were always legally inferior and burdened with restrictions on residence, dress and comportment, and worship. They were subject to extortion by rapacious governors and mamlukes (slave dynasties that ruled in Egypt, Syria and Iraq intermittently). The Egyptian chronicler al-Jabarti tells us that, at one point in the late eighteenth century, a mamluke prince proclaimed that Jews and Christians were henceforth prohibited from carrying the personal names of prophets.

Given that the Quran celebrates all Jewish and Christian prophets and biblical kings, it meant that people with the names of Abraham, David or Joseph had to change their names! Of course this was only a ruse to extort money, and a suitable sum was agreed after strenuous bargaining.[2] In any case, the co-presence of diverse peoples does not necessarily entail social and cultural mixing. For the most part, individuals were confined within their own social boundaries, and often the topographical locations of their communities, under the authority of their religious chiefs, who were in turn supported by the power of the sultan. Even when diverse peoples are free, under a liberal regime, the coexistence of different ethnicities and cultures does not constitute what is meant or connoted by 'cosmopolitanism'. For example, on my first visit to the Canadian city of Toronto in the mid-1970s, the wide range of ethnicities and nationalities in its population impressed me. Hungarians, Portuguese, Chinese, Indians, with their own colourful districts and markets. Yet this was not 'cosmopolitan': people from all over the world brought their families to this place of prosperity and security, and were enclosed within their homes and communities, having little to do with others except in the marketplace. This, of course, was generally the case with migrants everywhere, including in centres like Paris or New York. What makes those cities (and perhaps also Toronto in later decades) 'cosmopolitan' is the presence of particular milieux of social and cultural mixing and hybridity across communal boundaries, and indeed the permeability of these boundaries.

Cosmopolitanism as social promiscuity

It was only during the course of the nineteenth century and into the twentieth – with a combination of the processes of modernity and capitalism under the increasing hegemony of the European powers, especially Britain, and the responses of Ottoman reforms – that communal barriers became more permeable, especially in the main centres of power, commerce and culture. The new print media, the creation of 'public opinion', the spread of literacy and reading to wider sectors of society, and attractive European models of public and cultural life – all of these combined to bring about new strata and associations, many of which cut across communal barriers, at least for some of the elites. The ideas and aspirations of the Enlightenment stimulated intellectuals from the *millet* to reject 'backward' religious and communal authority. This was further stimulated for the Christian *millets* by the attractions of the Anglo-Saxon Protestant missions and their educational and cultural activities.[3] These missions played an important part in the revival of Arabic language and culture in Syria and Lebanon, and are credited with stimulating the beginnings of Arab nationalism among Christian Arabs. The Alliance Israélite Universelle played a similar role for the Jewish communities of the Empire. The products of these educational institutions cultivated notions of citizenship and active participation in public life, which was partly satisfied by the emergence of the modern sectors of state bureaucracy, education and commerce. The railways and telegraphy were crucial not only in facilitating the opening up of isolated regions and integrating them into the capitalist market, but also in providing employment for the literate.[4]

Cosmopolitan milieux

Istanbul, Cairo, Alexandria and Beirut became the locations where economic and cultural modernity flourished from the latter part of the nineteenth century. While some new intellectuals and statesmen were ideologically attached to Islamic and Ottoman roots, most had adopted new lifestyles and associations, and explored new horizons, stimulated partly by the painful realization of European superiority in wealth and arms. One enclave of cultural as well as political endeavours was that of the Young Ottomans, a group of intellectuals versed in European languages and ideas, but seeking a renaissance of Islamic/Ottoman civilization.[5] Their prominent member Namik Kemal (1840–88), a poet, essayist and liberal political philosopher, was deeply influenced by European currents: he translated Charles de Secondat, Baron de Montesquieu, debated Voltaire and Nicolas de Condorcet, followed the nationalist models of Giuseppe Garibaldi and Giuseppe Mazzini (the Young Ottomans had personal and political connections with Italian nationalists and the Carbonari societies). Kemal and many of the others spent periods of exile in Paris, London and Geneva, where they published the journals that were prohibited in Istanbul, intriguing with patrons and factions in and out of government. Intellectually and politically, these were 'cosmopolitans'. Yet Kemal was firmly attached to the idea that a revived Islam must form the basis of society and government. He tried to find Islamic idioms for expressing the main ideas and concepts of the Enlightenment – those of Jean-Jacques Rousseau, Montesquieu and the natural law tradition. He was highly critical of the ruling functionaries of the Porte for their blind imitation of Europe. The Tanzimat was denounced, not for its reforms, but for failing to institute a liberal constitution empowering the people as citizens – ensuring liberties supposedly granted by God, as against reforms imposed from above by an autocratic government. For these intellectuals and reformers, Islam became an ideology of national authenticity rather than of ritual observance and their disciplines – a kind of cultural nationalism that persists.[6]

Freemasonry

Many of the members of the Ottoman elites, including politicians and high functionaries, and some Young Ottomans, became members of Masonic lodges first started by Europeans with their own rival lodges, in which political and personal factions and intrigues, as well as the interests of European powers, were pursued. A similar situation prevailed in Egypt in the nineteenth and twentieth centuries. The most renowned Muslim reformer of the time, Jamaleddin al-Afghani (Asadabadi to the Iranians) (1838–97), was a member (by some reports a master) of such a lodge in Egypt. We have in the figure of al-Afghani a remarkable cosmopolitan.

Freemasonry featured prominently in the cultural and political life of the Ottoman world in the nineteenth and early twentieth centuries, and constituted an important aspect of the cosmopolitan milieu.[7] Branches of British, then French and other continental lodges were established in Istanbul from the early nineteenth century, often by diplomats, including ambassadors from these countries. Initially their membership was confined to Europeans, officials and merchants, and then open to non-Muslim Ottomans; but from the 1860s it was fully opened to Muslim Ottomans, statesmen, intellectuals and other public figures. Istanbul, Izmir, Salonica, Cairo and Alexandria were prominent centres for Masonic lodges, but they also spread to Syrian and even Iraqi cities.

Masons included some of the main reformers and intellectuals, including Reshid Pasha (1800–1858) and Midhat Pasha (1822–84), and the previously discussed writer and intellectual Namik Kemal. Masonic lodges, especially the French ones, came to foster Ottoman reforms, liberalism and constitutionalism.[8] Sultan Murad V, who ruled briefly in 1876 before being deposed and imprisoned by his brother Abdul-Hamid II, was a patron of the liberal constitutionalists, as well as a Freemason himself.[9] A failed conspiracy to liberate and restore Murad emerged from Masonic networks, which incurred the wrath of Abdul-Hamid.[10] The long reign of Sultan Abdul-Hamid II (r. 1876–1909), was one of reaction against liberalism, the suspension of the nascent constitution, and the exile of prominent reformers and liberals, notably Midhat and Kemal. Abdul-Hamid's reign was marked by repressive measures, censorship and strict regulation of associative life. Freemason lodges came under scrutiny and occasional interdiction. The sultan, it transpired, was correct in distrusting the lodges, as the Young Turk conspiracy that deposed him in 1908 was partly hatched in an Italian lodge in Salonica.

Not all Freemasonry, however, harboured liberals. There was a parting of the ways between the British lodges, more conservative and cautious, and the French Grand Orient network, animated by the spirit of the Revolution. A crucial split came in 1877, when the French jettisoned what had been a founding clause in the Masonic constitution specifying a belief in the Supreme Being and the immortality of the soul as conditions of Masonic affiliation. This formulation was aimed at religious universalism, thus opening up membership to people of diverse religions. But an unspecified religious belief of some kind was a condition of membership, until its termination in the French lodges. This became a clear issue of controversy between the British and the French, with implications for Ottoman membership. The main avant-garde lodge that welcomed

Ottoman membership was *i Prodos* (Greek for 'Progress'), an offshoot of the Grand Orient, founded in 1868. It was there that the liberal intelligentsia, including Namik and Midhat, were affiliated. It soon introduced rituals and proceedings in Turkish.[11] It is interesting that most of the Ottoman intelligentsia who were Freemasons continued to adhere to the French and Italian lodges, despite, or maybe because of, their more secular stance, deemed 'atheist' by their detractors. Indeed, some Muslim clerics were affiliated to those lodges, including, in the later period of the Young Turk coup d'état, no less a figure than Shaykhulislam Musa Kazim.[12]

Salonica at the turn of the twentieth century presents interesting examples of the paradoxes of multi-ethnicity and cosmopolitanism. It was home to a bewildering variety of ethnicities and religions: Jews, Donmeh,[13] Greeks, Bulgarians, Albanians and Ottoman Muslims (a diverse category of ethnicities ranging from Circassians to Sudanese, many Turkish speaking).[14] In many respects this diversity constituted a 'mosaic' society of distinct communities, which were closed in on themselves and had little to do with one another. The rise of Balkan nationalisms in the nineteenth century contributed to this insulation, and indeed generated fierce hostilities, especially between Greeks and Bulgarians fighting over the national identity of Macedonia. Yet, in the associations and events of the Young Turk Revolution of 1908, we see an episode of enthusiastic common participation by individuals from the various communities, in a rare political and cultural identification with Ottomanism in what promised to be its liberal constitutional evolution. The Masonic lodges played a prominent part in the plotting of the revolution and in the cosmopolitan surge that accompanied it.[15] The Salonica branch of the Committee of Union and Progress was the main mover of the revolution, with its military members manoeuvring the Third Army in a coup d'état against Abdul-Hamid's autocratic regime in favour of restoring the constitution and parliament. Its initial ideology was one of liberal Ottomanism, embracing all the ethnic and confessional elements of the population in an attempt to preserve the shaky Empire. The plotting for the revolution was carried out largely in the Italian Masonic lodge Macedonia Risorta, which followed the Italian Grand

Orient and shared the liberal and secular ideology of its French counterpart.[16] The lodges afforded the conspirators secrecy, as well as the protection of foreign connections, immune under the capitulations[17] from Abdul-Hamid's vigilant intelligence networks, which were active in Salonica but frustrated by the immunities of foreigners sheltering the plotters. Officers and civil servants who subsequently became prominent statesmen included Talat Beyand Enver Bey (later pashas). They cultivated Greek notables to help in their plans, and involved some notable Jews who became public figures, including the journalist Nissim Rousso and the politician Nissim Mazliah, as well as the Donmeh Mehmed Javid Bey. A prominent figure was the president of Macedonia Risorta, Emmanuel Carasso, an Italian Jew.[18] The involvement of Jewish individuals in these Masonic contexts elicited, even at that stage, accusations of Zionist conspiracies, which have more recently become prevalent, as we shall see presently. In fact, the Jews in question were not sympathetic to Zionism, seeing it as incompatible with the Ottomanist patriotism that was their basic ideology, as well as that of the Young Turks.[19]

The ideological cosmopolitanism of the Young Turks – embodied in their Ottomanism, which embraced all elements of the Ottoman population – was soon to be assailed by catastrophic wars and strident nationalisms, both in the Balkans and in the Turkish heartlands.[20] Already, in 1909 a 'national' Masonic lodge had been founded – the Ottoman Grand Orient, which embraced the main actors in the Committee of Union and Progress,[21] but maintained affiliation with the Grand Orient of France. The Balkan War of 1912 spelled disaster for the Empire, with the combined forces of Greece, Serbia and Bulgaria displacing the Ottomans from almost all their European territories, and at one stage threatening Istanbul itself.[22] The dominant ideology and policy of the Young Turks in government turned towards Turkish nationalism, confronting the ethno-national movements combining to assail the Empire. World War I brought defeat and ruin, the flight of the remaining Young Turk leaders and the ultimate dissolution of the Empire – then, after the war of liberation from the occupying Allies, the rise of a highly nationalist Turkish Republic. Freemasonry, along with many other forms of associational life, was banned by the Ataturk regime, but licensed again in 1948, though with little political or ideological effect.

Egypt in the later nineteenth century, and into the twentieth, had a strong Masonic presence. The British Grand Orient was the first and main lodge, and recruited many of the prominent public figures of the time, including at one point Khedive Tawfiq, who served as its honorary president. It also included many intellectuals and states-men, including Boutrus Ghali, the scion of a major Coptic family and a prominent jurist; Sa'ad Zaghloul, a prominent nationalist who led the al-Wafd independence movement in 1919; Lutfi al-Sayed, another prominent nationalist intellectual; and many of the ruling circle and army officers. Most interesting, however, was the active membership of the most prominent Islamic reformers of the time, Jamaleddin al-Afghani and Muhammad Abduh.[23] Ali al-Wardi cites al-Afghani's letter of application to join the Grand Lodge in 1875,[24] in which he addresses the Masons as Ikhwan al-Safa ('brothers of purity'), the title of a group of rationalist intellectuals in early Islam. He was admitted, and proceeded to the rank of president of one of the lodges in 1878. Many of his disciples were also Freemasons, including Muhammad Abduh. Al-Afghani also counted among his disciples the Christian Adib Ishaq (1856–85) and the Jew James Sanua (1839–1912),[25] which indicates the wide cosmopolitan milieu of which they formed a part, and the attraction of Freemasonry in offering a tolerant congruence between religions and ethnicities. Al-Afghani, while charismatic and charming, was also a sharp polemicist who made many enemies. He clashed with the authorities of the Grand Orient over his politiciza-tion of Freemasonry in opposition to Khedive Ismail, then to his successor Tawfiq (a Freemason). It is not clear whether he left that lodge or was expelled, but he soon founded another under the tute-lage of the Grand Orient of France.[26] Al-Wardi cites extracts from his letter of reproach to the British Masons, in which he denounced their 'cowardice' and refusal to pursue the Masonic ideals of liberty, equality and fraternity against oppression and corruption, for the benefit of the whole of mankind. Subsequently, in the aftermath of the failure of the Urabi military revolt of 1882, Abduh and other disciples were exiled from Egypt for complicity in the revolt, and eventually found refuge in Beirut, where they were welcomed and assisted by the lodges of that city.[27]

Al-Afghani was a maverick character, who dissimulated his ideas and his identity to achieve maximum influence in different contexts. Though almost certainly of Iranian Shi'ite birth and formation, he assumed the identity of an Afghani Sunni, dressing in the manner of Sunni ulama from that country when he was in Turkey and Egypt, but dressing as a Shi'ite cleric when in Iran, and even assuming Arab dress in Hijaz. His main designation was al-Afghani, but at times also called himself al-Husseini (the title of descent from the Prophet through Imam Hussein) when in Shi'i Iran, and even Istanbuli, depending on his target audience. His Islamic adherence was challenged by many of his adversaries, but also by scholars and historians – notably Elie Kedourie who argued that he and Abduh were positivist rationalists, if not atheists, and pretended a belief in Islam for political reasons. Al-Afghani's Islamic modernism certainly favoured reconciling religion with science and rationality, but he was not consistent. In India he denounced Sayid Ahmad Khan, the religious reformer and modernist – though he espoused similar views to those al-Afghani held himself – because Ahmad Khan adopted a conciliatory attitude to British colonialism, seeing it as a progressive stage in the advance of Indians and Muslims into modernity. In Istanbul al-Afghani was denounced by the orthodox clerics for lecturing on the congruence of religion with rational philosophy.[28]

Like that of the Young Ottomans, al-Afghani's pan-Islamism was aimed at the restoration of Islam to its pristine origins, which would then make it superior to European creeds in political order and civilization. The intended reforms, however, would result in polity, law and society looking remarkably like idealized European models. Politically, his objective was a pan-Islamic unity that, armed with a reformed religion, society and polity, would stand up to European domination and revive the strength and glory of historical Islam. Like all reformers of his time, he sought to influence elites – primarily the princes and kings of Islam. These welcomed him at first, flattered by his attentions, but soon realized the import of his advocacy and sought to get rid of him – at which point he turned to dissident intellectuals and constitutionalists to propagate his ideas, which landed him in exile.

The cosmopolitanism of al-Afghani spanned not only the boundaries between Islam and Europe, but also those between different Muslim cultures. He operated between British India, Iran, Egypt and Turkey, as well as from the European capitals. He worked in Persian, Turkish and Arabic, and knew English and French. He debated with the Indian Muslim reformers and the Arab clerics, and his best-known work was a polemic with the French writer Ernest Renan. In this later work, al-Afghani advanced a rationalist explanation of the formation and history of religion and of its social functions – arguments that led to accusations of 'atheism' by opponents in the Muslim world (who had access to the French publication), and by European commentators who sought to detract from his reformist project.[29] His cosmopolitanism extended to aspects of culture and lifestyle: apart from his membership of Masonic lodges, he was also known to frequent cafés and clubs, to be fond of cognac and was rumoured to have illicit sexual encounters. Recent Arab historians who have written on these aspects of his life – especially his Freemasonry – have been attacked by orthodox Muslims who still claim him as an early advocate of their reforms.

We may now ask what the attractions of Freemasonry were for the elites of the Ottoman lands in the nineteenth and early twentieth centuries. First, Freemasonry offered clear instrumental advantages: contacts, networking and mutual aid in relation to positions, promotions and business dealings. Secondly, the lodges offered the means of secrecy and dissimulation for political planning and campaigning, as well as plots and conspiracies – as we saw in the case of the Young Turks and al-Afghani's clique. Foreign involvement in Salonica also afforded protection for the Young Turk conspirators. Apart from these instrumental benefits, however, there were clearly ideological and aesthetic attractions. Thierry Zarcone argues that the mode of sociability of Masonic lodges – as secret brotherhoods, with their elaborate rituals and hierarchies of initiation and promotion – had close affinities with Sufi orders and lodges as a form of sociability and brotherhood. In particular, the interdiction, and then clandestine

flourishing, of the Bektashi orders after the destruction of the janissaries in 1824, generated forms of secret organizations that attracted
intellectuals who combined modern enlightenment with heterodox
mysticism, distinguished by its adherents as 'enlightened Sufism' – a
combination we may also observe in the case of Iranian secret societies of the time. Zarcone further argues that there was an overlap of
personnel, institutions and ideas between the two forms of association. He shows that many of the people involved in the politics of the
Young Turk period and after were adepts of both Sufi orders (mainly
Bektashi and Melami) and Masonic lodges.[30]

Zarcone devotes one section of his book to the life and work
of Riza Tevfik – a prominent intellectual, philosopher, teacher and
politician of the Young Turk era, who wrote, among other things, a
dictionary of philosophy. Tevfik declared himself a follower of both
Ibn Arabi, the source of much Sufi philosophy and mysticism, and
of Herbert Spencer, the English evolutionist philosopher and social
theorist. The link that Tevfik forged between the two philosophies
was, from our point of view, tenuous, and to do with a scepticism
that he identified in them both, in relation to the theory of knowledge; the elaborate arguments he put forward need not concern us
here. What is interesting, however, is Tevfik's 'mentality' or outlook,
which was not uncommon among modernist Turkish and Iranian
intellectuals of the nineteenth and early twentieth centuries who
subscribed to European Enlightenment currents that were mainly
positivist, rationalist, evolutionist and sceptical of religious verities,
as well as to mystical philosophies with a Muslim and Greek heritage.
They were also liable to form and affiliate to secret societies, including Freemasonry. What these diverse currents seemed to share was
a rejection of the verities and disciplines of orthodox Islam and the
authority of its ulama and institutions. Above all, it was the idea of
the Shari'a as the basis of social order – buttressed by the authority
of ulama and *mujtahids* and enforced by absolute rulers – that was
rejected and seen as the cause and hallmark of the stagnation and
backwardness of their societies and polities. Further, that orthodoxy
had forbidden free philosophical enquiry, in which the modern intellectuals were finding exciting truths and programmes for renewed

conceptions of social and political life. Montesquieu, Rousseau, Spencer, Charles Darwin and John Stuart Mill were the prophets of this Enlightenment, and the inspiration for a dreamt modernity of liberty and rationality. Many of the intellectuals of that generation stopped at that; rejecting the religious baggage of their Ottoman heritage, they embraced unencumbered positivism and scientism. Many others, however, attempted to find a link between the European Enlightenment and elements of their philosophical heritage, linked to mostly heterodox Sufism, which metamorphosed in nineteenth-century intellectual and political contexts into Bektashism. And these currents, or torrents, of ideas and programmes were socially embedded in the secret societies and rituals of Freemasonry and Sufi lodges – with, according to Zarcone, a healthy traffic between them.

We may speculate that a crucial element of the appeal of Freemasonry to those intellectual and political elites was the *imaginaire* of participation in a milieu of the civilized world (*medeniyat*), a regular theme in the discourse of modernity and reform at the time. The 'brotherhood' with similar elites in the 'civilized' world, participating in their spheres of sociability and in their discourses and intrigues, and the universalism of their world – these were powerful draws, taking the form of an active cosmopolitanism.

Freemasonry, along with other cosmopolitan and liberationist currents in the Middle East, was to gradually dwindle in the course of the twentieth century, confronting ever more strident nationalisms and ethno-religious movements, and the authoritarian regimes that fostered them. In these contexts, secret societies were always suspect, perhaps rightly, as the locations of conspiracies. Added to that were the cosmopolitan dimensions of Freemasonry, emphasising human communalities and the basic unity of all religion – a basic universalism – as the exclusive claims for the allegiance of both orthodox religion and nationalist regimes. That, after all, was why Pope Clement II had declared his ban on Freemasonry in 1738, soon after its foundation: its secrecy and universalism were a threat to the exclusive allegiance of the faithful to their mother Church.[31] As we have seen, Ataturk banned and dissolved Masonic lodges, which were revived after his death. We should note, however, that after that charismatic period of intellectual and political effervescence in the late nineteenth and early twentieth centuries, Freemasonry, where it survived, appears to have been 'routinized' into its predominant form in the modern world – as merely an instrumental medium for promoting its members' interests in business and in public life, with its intellectual and spiritual dimensions reduced to formulaic affirmations. Even so, its secrecy and refusal to be supervised by the monitors of the authoritarian regimes resulted in its being interdicted in most Middle Eastern countries. Nasir's Egypt banned and dissolved Masonic lodges in 1964, ostensibly because the lodges refused supervision and regulation by the Ministry of Social Affairs.[32] Freemasonry was banned in Syria the following year, but survived in the more liberal and bourgeois Lebanon. Everywhere, 'Masonry' and 'Zionism' became twin evils, weaving imperialist conspiracies against the Arab and Muslim nations. In Iraq, after the 1958 revolution that toppled the monarchic regime, the show trials of the luminaries of that regime included indictments for Masonry, famously against Fadhil al-Jamali, a statesman of the ancien régime and actually a Mason. In his interrogation by the revolutionary judge, al-Jamali defended Masonry as a universalist humanism, respectful of national interests and innocent of complicity with Zionism.[33] Under Saddam Hussein, being a Mason became one of many capital offences, and accusations of Masonry were flung at members of the old bourgeoisie who were disliked by the regime.

Drinking cultures

Masonic lodges, cafés and salons were among the milieux of cosmopolitanism, but in nineteenth-century Istanbul, these also included taverns and a drinking culture. The prohibition of alcohol is iconic for orthodox and political Islam as a marker of authenticity and distinction from the dissolute other – i.e. 'the West'. It has also contributed to the intrigue and romance of drink throughout the history of Middle Eastern societies: in poetry, Sufism (mysticism) and *belles lettres*. Drinking cultures were high and low: the sumptuous wine tables of the rich and the taverns of the soldiery and *awbash* (rabble).

The janissary corps, the military mainstay of the Ottomans, who as we saw were intertwined with the Bektashi order, were well known drinkers, and many of their entertainments, as well as intrigues and conspiracies, were conducted in taverns. Dancing boys, dressed as girls and offering sexual favours, were a regular item of entertainment.[34] The disorders and violence perpetrated by the janissaries in their years of decadence in the late eighteenth century, and until their destruction in 1826, were fuelled by drink. Soldiers and the lower orders, however, were not the only patrons of taverns. One Nihali, a sixteenth-century *qadi* of Galata and a celebrated poet with the nom de plume Jaafar, boasted of his frequenting the taverns of that part of Istanbul, which was 'cosmopolitan' even then.[35] For the most part, however, the respectable classes drank in private, with their own circles of companions. In some Middle Eastern cities in the nineteenth and twentieth centuries, public male drinking cultures became respectable and open – a sign of modernity and *medeniyat*. Alcohol thus became an issue in contests of identity and authenticity.

François Georgeon has written a fascinating account of the symbolic significance of alcohol for notions of modernity and civilization in Turkey from the nineteenth century.[36] Sultan Mahmud II (r. 1808–39) was the first reforming ruler who made a serious impact. He modelled himself on other European rulers, and included alcohol as a feature of public occasions such as official dinners and receptions. Champagne, which was not new to the Ottoman court, then came out in public. Over the course of the century, and among the modern elites and the official classes, drink came to be associated with being modern and with civilization (*medeniyat*). Husrev Pasha, *serasker* (army chief),

> [would drink] champagne with an influential European [even though he did not like it and preferred water], to show how he had shed completely the prejudices of the old Turkey: he knows full well that the fact will be noted in a newspaper article.[37]

Georgeon adds that the disappearance of the janissaries and their association with alcohol from the public scene after 1826 'permitted a shift to civilian, and by extension "civilised" consumption of alcohol'. Later in the century, the state class of the expanded reform bureaucracy became the vanguard of the drinking classes. To cater for them, a new type of refined and opulent tavern or *meyhane* came into existence, with a professional guild of tavern keepers and their assistants trained in the arts of serving drink and its accompaniment of mezze, and in the skills of nursing a *narguila* (water pipe). Among the consumers, a new *adab* – etiquette and lore of drink – determined a kind of *savoir boire*.

Much of this new culture of drinking revolved around the newly fashionable *rakı/arak*, displacing wine as the favoured drink. It became an identity marker as a specifically native drink, in contrast to the more cosmopolitan and European wine.[38] It acquired the honorific description of *arslan sutu* (lion's milk), and in Arabic (at least in Iraq) of *halib sha'* (lion's milk). It became the drink of choice in the cafés, clubs and salons of intellectuals and reformers, which included the poet Kemal and the statesman Midhat. Later in the century, under the more religious and authoritarian reign of Abdul-Hamid II (r. 1876–1909) there was a backlash against this drinking culture, both religious and medical, but with little effect. *Rakı* was to feature again as part of the culture of the Turkish Republic under Ataturk, himself a noted devotee of the beverage. It is said that old Kemalist stalwarts were still to be seen until recent times at the bar in Sirkeci railway station at sunset raising a glass to the memory of their hero, accompanied by the classic and austere mezze preferred by the pasha: the *beyaz maza* (white table) of white cheese, melon, and yoghurt and cucumber.

Alcohol and drinking culture became an issue concerning authenticity and identity. In the aftermath of municipal elections that brought the Islamic Refah Partisi to power in Istanbul in 1994, one of the first issues that arose between the Islamic mayors and the Kemalist bourgeoisie was that of drink. The bars and restaurants of Beyoglu, the cosmopolitan centre of the city, were targeted by the mayor, who did not dare to ban alcohol but made rules restricting its visibility: establishments were requested not to allow drinking on terraces and at street tables, and to hide their drinkers behind curtains. An outcry from the modern bourgeoisie, with demonstra-tions of street drinking, soon forced the withdrawal of the order. On a more recent visit to Istanbul I came across two new bars in Beyoglu: one named Victor Cohen Sheraphanesi (wine bar), the other going by the equally typical Greek name of Stavros Sheraphanesi. On inquiry, it seemed that both were run by Turkish Muslim entrepre-neurs who had acquired the old names to recreate the atmosphere and associations of the old 'cosmopolitan' Beyoglu. Another disco bar in that quarter had the potentially blasphemous name of Abdul-JabBAR (Abdul-Jabbar being a reference to one of the attributes of God). More recent reports, however, indicate that in the more con-servative parts of Istanbul and other cities, especially in Anatolia, authorities from the ruling pro-Muslim AK Party (successor to the Refah Partisi of the 1990s) are banning or pressuring establishments serving alcohol in areas under their control. Alcohol consumption in today's Turkey has become a potent identity marker in the political and cultural struggles between secularism and religiosity. The mod-ern bourgeoisie of Istanbul stands in contrast to the vast Anatolian territory of conservative mores and religious sensibility, now fully present in the city and seen by the bourgeoisie as representing the threatening barbarians at the gates. The contrast is illustrated in the following anecdote:

> [T]wo Turkish women, one veiled, the other not, encountered one another in front of the Ayasofya museum in the old quarter of Istanbul. The short-haired woman, dressed in a skirt to her knees, a trimly fit blouse, and a short coat, asked the other woman who was wearing a black veil, whether this was the line for tickets to the museum. The veiled woman was surprised. 'You speak Turkish?' she asked in amazement. 'Yes, I am Turkish!' asserted the short-haired woman, put off by the question. 'Oh! You don't look Turkish. You look like a Westerner,' said the veiled woman. 'You don't look Turkish either,' said the other. 'I thought you were an Arab.' 'Oh!' said the veiled woman, 'thanks to God, we are Turkish and Muslim.' 'Well, we are too,' said the short-haired woman.[39]

Egyptian cosmopolitanism

Much of the nostalgia for cosmopolitan milieux in the Middle East relates to Egypt, and in particular to Alexandria. The transformations of the Egyptian economy and society of the nineteenth century, culminating in the British occupation from 1882, brought many migrants and entrepreneurs from Europe and the Levant, who formed a diverse and colourful society: not only opportunists and adventurers, but also Greek shopkeepers and Italian stevedores – a glimpse of which can be seen in the highly romanticized fiction of Lawrence Durrell's *Alexandria Quartet*. There are many things to be said about this society, but let me pick out a contrast between two facets of cosmopolitanism at that point.[40]

The subsequent nostalgia for this golden age conveniently forgets its imperial context. Cosmopolitan Alexandria, for instance, included a rigorous system of exclusions for native Egyptians, including segregation or exclusion on buses and trams, and certainly from clubs, some bars and cafés, and many social milieux. Native Egyptian society provided servants, functionaries and prostitutes for the cosmopolitan milieu. They were inferiorized and despised. It was no coincidence, then, that the Muslim Brotherhood was founded in 1928 in Ismailiya, in the Canal Zone, and had as its founding programme the rescue of Muslim youth from the corruption of European dominance – drink and prostitution; it is no wonder that it found an echo in Egyptian society.

On the other hand, Egypt in the first half of the twentieth century witnessed a flourishing of intellectual and artistic movements and milieux (as well as religious and nativist reactions against them). The new Egyptian university, a lively press, the film industry, an artistic and musical renaissance and intellectual opening – all looked to the wider world for inspiration and innovation. Taha Hussein, a prominent figure in Egyptian letters, declared the Pharaonic and Hellenistic roots of Egyptian culture: it was to the Mediterranean world that it must look for its future.[41] The 1932 Congress of Arab Music in Cairo, attended by musicians and theorists from the Arab world, but also by major European figures such as the composers

Béla Bartók and Paul Hindemith, debated the links between tradition and modernity, particularism and universality.[42] Paradoxically, it was Bartók who defended traditional music against the Arab modernists who proclaimed the decadence of the old, and the necessity of innovating and evolving in line with the general progress of society and the opening to universal trends and values. The British anthropologist Edward E. Evans-Pritchard was giving his seminal lectures on primitive religion at the Egyptian University.[43] Films portrayed a universe of romance and music in social settings contrasting the old and the new, the popular quarters and the Europeanized suburbs. This cultural mix and excitement was cosmopolitan in a much more profound sense than the celebrated European–Levantine milieu of Alexandria.

These milieux and ideas ended with the Nasirist transformation of the country, with the expulsion of most foreigners and Jews following the 1956 tripartite invasion of Egypt. Subsequently, Egypt became a bastion of Arab nationalism, modelled on a Soviet-style command economy. Its internationalism became that of intergovernmental cooperation.

Let us now turn to aspects of nationalism and Islamism.

Paradoxes of nationalism and Islamism

The Istanbul bourgeoisie, nostalgic for past cosmopolitanism, are ideologically and socially products of the sternest Turkish nationalism – that of Kemalism. The paradox of Kemalism is that it sought to assert a particularism of Turks – as distinct from Arabs, Persians, Ottomans and traditional Islam – by orienting itself to Europe and modernity. Its official ethos might appear 'cosmopolitan' in relation to the styles it adopted: the dress code, from turbans and fez to hats and formal European dress, as well as prohibition of the *hijab* and religious garb; the change of script from Arabic to Roman; lifestyles, including Ataturk's insistence on European-style festivities, including balls and ballroom dancing for official occasions; the culture of drink, especially the national *rakı*; and so on. But the actual policies and processes in the establishment of the Turkish Republic brought about the homogenization of the Turkish population and culture: ethnic cleansing of Greek and Armenian populations, then the enforced Turkicization of Muslim minorities, Kurds and Circassians.[44] The ideal citizen of the new secular Republic was a Sunni Muslim of the Hanafi *madhhab* (as opposed to the Shafi'i Kurds and the 'heretical' Alevis). That is why, in spite of the bitter antagonisms between Islamic and secular Turkey, there remains a basic affinity between different groups. Kemalist identification with European modernity was at the same time explicitly opposed to the culture of cosmopolitanism. Like all nationalist ideologies, Kemalism rejected cosmopolitans as inauthentic and lacking in moral rectitude. Its aim was a unitary and homogeneous nation.

German Romantic nationalism (which was the ideological underpinning of many Arab and Middle Eastern nationalisms) was explicitly anti-cosmopolitan. In the opposition between culture and civilization, it was culture – rooted in the *volk*, in the blood and soil – that was the positive, desirable element. Civilization was a superficial veneer – artificial, seductive to the weak and fashionable – that undermined the natural rootedness of *volk* culture. For Johann Gottfried Herder, it was French civilization against German culture. Yet for Herder and his followers this nationalism was part of a universalist commitment: he was not against other nationalities and cultures, but against mixing, hybridity and dilution; the ideal was for every people to conform to its own culture and roots and be true to its nature, which would fulfil a universal harmony. Cosmopolitanism was hybrid, superficial and immoral – psychologically, and even biologically, debilitating.[45] Kemalists and Arab nationalists incorporated these notions, often explicitly, into their ideologies and programmes.

Islamism, the cosmopolitan and the transnational

We have seen how the leading Muslim modernist reformers were in many senses 'cosmopolitan'. They formed part of the elite circles of intellectuals, aristocrats and politicians, and focused their efforts mostly within these elites. A subsequent generation of Muslim leaders turned to populism and mass mobilization, deploying a much more puritanical and nativist Islam – notably the Muslim Brotherhood in Egypt under Hassan al-Banna, which emerged in 1928; these were the 'fundamentalists'. Their ideology was one of a return to the purity of early Islam and the first generations – hence 'Salafi' (*salaf* means 'ancestors'); but their politics were essentially those of modern populist mass mobilization.[46] Their appeal was largely that of national liberation from foreign rule, but also, essentially, from foreign customs and lifestyles; they rejected not only the Europeans, but also those of their compatriots and co-religionists who adopted European ways, and precisely those forms and styles considered 'cosmopolitan'. In this respect they shared the nationalist quest for authenticity. Indeed, at the present time we see an explicit convergence between forms of Islamism and Arab nationalism (though there is diversity within both) in rejecting 'the West', seen as the aggressor against all Muslims and Arabs.[47] An essential part of this perceived Western invasion is the cultural component – *al-ghazw al-fikri* – of alien ideas and corrupt lifestyles.

This convergence between nationalists and Islamists on the cultural front is illustrated by the example of the trials of homosexuals in Egypt, the *Queen Boat* episode.[48] This boat was one of the many entertainment venues on the Nile in Cairo suspected of being a gay venue. It was raided by the police and all those present were arrested, some subsequently tried – reportedly after the usual police performance of beatings and maltreatment. This highly publicized episode occasioned public outrage against the victims. The thrust of the press campaign was that homosexuality was a Western corruption, alien to Egypt and Islam. One lawyer beseeched the judge to acquit his client to prove to the world that there was no homosexuality in Egypt. While homoeroticism of various forms has been common and unremarked upon throughout the region (see Introduction), these particular groups become a target because of their style and culture: they are engaged in a lifestyle and forms of sociability associated with modern social libertarians – with 'gay' culture – and they are thus seen as alien and threatening; they are, in our parlance, 'cosmopolitan'.

What of Islamic cosmopolitanism? After all, Islamic ideologies are directed at a world community of Muslims, and at proselytizing universally. Indeed, many Islamists have denounced nationalism as being divisive of the universal Muslim Umma. The prominence of Arab Christians in the leadership and ideology of Arab nationalism, from Ottoman times, has prompted many Islamists to denounce Arab nationalism as a Christian conspiracy with the West aimed at the destruction of the Ottoman caliphate and Muslim unity. In practice, however, Islamic politics had been oriented towards particular countries and regions, not the world community. Even the Sufi orders, which had generated widespread networks in the past, had become nationalized within state boundaries. This has changed in recent decades, first with the internationalization of Islamism through the Afghan wars (courtesy of the Americans and the Saudis), then through the spread in migrant and transnational communities and networks. This is a complex phenomenon demanding extensive treatment to do it justice. For the present, let me say that transnationalism is distinct from the thrust and connotation of 'cosmopolitanism'. Transnational networks and ideologies are often directed at social particularism and exclusiveness. While nation-states in the Middle East and many other parts have engaged throughout the twentieth century in attempts to homogenize their populations through ethnic cleansing and the suppression of minority cultures, the cities of the West have undergone the opposite process – one of increasing diversification, fusion and hybridity. Within these spaces develop transnational networks with diverse ideologies and cultures. But one prominent element in this mix is what has been called 'long-distance nationalism', including exclusivist religious networks. Muslim groups, communities and associations in the West are diverse, and most are secular. There are also Euro-Muslims – those who want their religion to be recognized alongside the other major religions in European society. But the most vocal and publicized are the Salafi, 'fundamentalist' groups who, while content with a transnational presence, insist on exclusiveness and distance from others.

Cosmopolitanism in the new age

Our own time is marked by the most profound technical revolution in global communications, transcending national and cultural boundaries. At the level of the common people, television soaps from Hollywood, Mumbai and South America are beamed into every home and followed with passion. This is accompanied by international patterns of mass consumption, with global brand names that have become iconic (Levi's jeans, McDonald's and Coca-Cola being the most prominent). At the technical and institutional levels, the internet is conquering ever more frontiers: even the most repressive and isolationist Middle Eastern states are connected, but always looking for means of control and censorship. Add to that the enormous explosion in tourism, travel, commerce, international media and the translation and publishing industries, and impressive cross-cultural transactions and mixes are achieved.

Side by side with this cultural globalization, we have the most xenophobic and intolerant manifestations of narrow nationalisms and religious revivals, of which political Islam is the most prominent in the Middle East.

Does cultural globalization represent heightened cosmopolitanism? And is the xenophobia of political Islam a reaction? I would argue that manifestations of cultural globalism have transcended the problematic of cosmopolitanism. The context of the cosmopolitanisms of the first half of the twentieth century were networks and milieux of intellectuals, artists, dilettantes and flaneurs in urban centres – deracinated, transcending recently impermeable communal and religious boundaries, daring and experimenting. Or, at least, that was the projected image, one that defined identities and outlooks. These kinds of networks and milieux persist, and are probably more extensive than ever before. In the age of cultural globalism, however, they have been 'routinized', and have lost their special identities and charismatic images. At the same time, global means of communication in the form of television, the internet and other media do not necessarily breach communal and particularistic boundaries and spaces. People receive foreign soap operas in their own homes or neighbourhood cafes, dubbed into their own language. They consume them in terms of their own constructions of meanings and life-worlds.

In another global context, international business creates its own uniform milieux, with its executives and personnel travelling the world and residing in diverse centres, but always in the 'same' hotel rooms or apartments, served by Filipino maids, and the same networks of sociability of colleagues and associates.[49] Tourism similarly creates its own milieux: at the cheaper levels, resorts, hotels, entertainments and food that strive for standardization, from Benidorm to Bodrum. Upmarket tourists pay for a touch of exoticism and local colour, often constructed within the safe and hygienic confines of their hotels: witness the constructions of popular cafés and souks in the Cairo Nile Hilton – complete with Ramadan nights if you happen to stay during the blessed month. What is intriguing is that these constructions are not just for tourists, but attract the native prosperous classes, who also like to engage in ersatz exoticism without rubbing shoulders with their poor compatriots.

In conclusion, we can say that cosmopolitanism in the Middle East – in the old-fashioned sense of communally deracinated and culturally promiscuous groups and milieux – continues to exist in particular corners of urban space. These, however, are submerged by the two major forces of the metropolis: the urbanized masses and their transformation of the city and its politics; and the forces of international capital of business and tourism, and their towering hotels and offices, their media and the consumption of goods and images that cater to them.

Mass higher education produces a proletarianized, poorly educated intelligentsia, lacking in wealth and resentful, directing its 'ressentiment' against the Westernized elites, seen as the agents of cultural invasion. These are the main cadres of nationalist and religious xenophobia, currently so powerful in the region.

While some degree of liberalization has benefited cultural production in Egypt and elsewhere in recent decades, these limited gains have been very insecure, especially now that they are threatened by religious censorship and intimidation, which also extend to the urban spaces, such as cafés and bars, that form the social milieux of intellectuals and artists. It is not surprising, therefore, that the main cultural flourishing of Middle Eastern cosmopolitanism now occurs in London and Paris.

5

The Public and the Private in Middle Eastern History and Society

The theme of public versus private has been widely discussed and debated in social theory, as well as in feminist literature. The distinctions between the two spheres are often found problematic. The notion of the 'public sphere', introduced by Jürgen Habermas with regard to its postulated emergence in relation to bourgeois modernity in Europe, has proved popular in many sociological and ideological contexts, and thus has been 'hijacked' from the very specific history stipulated by its author.[1] A consideration of the debates relating to that theme would not be directly pertinent to my task, which is to explore the shifting and problematic public–private distinction in various contexts in Middle Eastern histories and societies. It is pertinent, however, to note some of the defensive responses from writers on the 'Islamic world' anxious to demonstrate that the public sphere was indeed equally present in historic Islamic societies. *The Public Sphere in Muslim Societies*,[2] discussed in the Introduction, is a collection of essays devoted to this subject, demonstrating the vitality of public institutions over a long span of historical time and over the vast geographical scope of 'Muslim society'. The public sphere is defined as the institutions and practices between the private/domestic and the official/ruling bodies. Such a sphere, however specified, is of course a feature of all urban societies, which are parts of complex polities. The quote from the Introduction to *Public Sphere in Muslim Societies* cited on p. 14 presents a highly utopian image of this public sphere and the society it served, characterized by harmony and order. The institutions of this public sphere are all religious: Shari'a courts, *madrasas*, *awqaf*, Sufi lodges, and a public opinion led by the ulama. Markets, coffee houses, bath houses, venues for the performance of poetry and music, including the salons of the notables – all important public spaces, but 'secular' – are largely absent from the list.

But does this constitute a public sphere in the Habermasian sense? Habermas's public sphere is the product of the emergence of a bourgeoisie in Europe (soon overtaken by the further and more repressive development of capitalism) – one of communication between equal interlocutors in free and largely secular media and venues, of the coffee house and the newspaper. This is quite distinct from the previous sense of 'public', which denoted the authority of princes and the church hierarchy. The religious public sphere presented in *The Public Sphere in Muslim Societies*[3] is analogous to the European religious sphere of church institutions, universities, monasteries, religious property and charity and canonical courts, as well as the institutions linking the church and the state. All complex historical societies featured equivalent spheres. In the Middle East, the Habermasian public sphere of autonomous and equal interlocutors only emerged (hesitantly and always encumbered by authority) with modernity, starting with the Ottoman reforms (see Chapters 1 and 2). Having clarified these definitional issues, the discussion that follows is not encumbered with the Habermasian problematic, or the defensive reactions to it.

Let me first introduce an important general point on 'spheres'. Historically, both in Europe and the Middle East, we find 'segmented' publics, as we shall see. They are segmented in the sense of spaces and spheres isolated from one another: different elites; elites and masses; regions; religious and ethnic communities; distinct urban quarters and spaces. Modernity and modern media bring a common public space to which various actors and speakers address their discourses and advocacies, as we shall see.

Boundaries of public and private in social and spatial locations

Historically, in Middle Eastern societies the boundaries were drawn in many spheres. The domestic sphere, for instance, is normally considered the private par excellence. Yet the houses of notables were themselves divided between the *hareem* (private) and the *salamlik* (public). The latter was a sphere of the exercise of power and influence, and of maintaining networks. These spheres, of course, had parallels in the European nobility and notability. They also survive today in the institutions of *mudhif* and *diwaniya* in Arabia and the Gulf. These are public in a different sense, and with a different social composition from those of government offices, mosques, churches and coffee houses, in that they are the public portions of private homes. These different locations with their boundaries between public and private were for the most part particular to specific groups and communities, with varying boundaries between them, such as urban quarters and religious communities. Others, such as guilds, would in some instances cut across these boundaries, but impose their own.

Another public sphere is that of the marketplace. In addition to their core functions of exchange, markets have also been spheres of sociability, gossip and public opinion, guild organization and religious fraternities. Shops and stalls are foci of sociability, as well as of transactions. People sit around to drink tea, smoke a *narguila*, pass the time of day, and do business. Smoking hashish in *narguilas* was one of the vices that the *qadi* of Aleppo in the eighteenth century was keen to regulate, if not prohibit. Secret or discreet drinking was carried out at the back of grocers' shops, only among select and known associates. In many cities market guilds were important organisms, not just in organizing work, but also for social networks, charities and political mobilization. Iranian cities are where these organizations and activities have survived (guilds in Egypt and Turkey were destroyed in the early twentieth century by cheap imports). Guilds in Egypt and Iran were associated with religious organizations: in Egypt with Sufi *turuq* (orders), in Iran with *hey'a* (committees), some of which were nuclei of popular organization for the 1979 revolution.

But are markets public spaces? It depends which market, and under what circumstances. As buying and selling venues, the main markets of the large cities were public in the sense of being universally accessible – though not in their networks, guilds and fraternities. Many urban markets were identified with particular quarters, guilds and sometimes Sufi orders. To the extent that the quarters were restricted, often walled and gated (the first 'gated communities'), access to markets may have been restricted. We know, for instance, that until recently (and perhaps up to the present) it was perfectly respectable for women to shop on their own in particular venues, confined to their neighbourhood shops and markets, but not elsewhere. In a sense, the quarter and the market were seen as extensions of a private, almost domestic space. We get a (fictional) glimpse of these arrangements in some of the novels of Naguib Mahfouz (*Malhamat al-Harafish* and *Awlad Haretna*).[4] There, the *shaykh al-hara* (chief of the quarter) is also *shaykh al-tariqa* (shaykh of the Sufi order), sharing authority with the chief of the *futuwa* (militia) of the quarter, enforcing the shaykh's authority and imposing rules on the inhabitants (even arranging marriages), as well as defending them from external threats.

Similar considerations apply to mosques. In the major cities, *al-masjid al-jami'* is the cathedral mosque, open to all Muslims, and a universal public space and one which enshrines sovereign political authority in the Friday prayers and sermons. It is not only the locus for prayer and ritual, but also a refuge for travellers, a space for study and discussion, and a locus of public meetings, and, on occasion, protests against the authorities. The Suleymaniya in Istanbul is an example of a mosque complex, featuring the main prayer area, the *turba* (cemetery), a *madrasa* and library and a soup kitchen (*imaret*). Many mosques also contained the shrines and tombs of saints (such as the Eyup shrine in Istanbul) and *zawiyas* or *tekyas* (lodges) for Sufi orders. These spaces in the complex were accessible through membership and networks. Soup kitchens[5] fed sundry types, but mostly served students and teachers of the *madrasa* (the portions were specified: teachers ate double the students' portions) and travellers of Sufi or ulama rank; they would have been unable to feed all the poor supplicants, so there must have been 'registered' poor. Smaller mosques could be private or attached to particular neighbourhoods or fraternities, where strangers would be discouraged. These religious, charitable and educational formations were typically instituted as *awqaf* (endowments), the prevalent legal forms for many public bodies. *Awqaf* dominated the spatial and economic landscapes of Middle Eastern cities, and constituted the arenas for economic and political contest between different elites and individuals benefiting from their revenues and powers. They were a dominant form in which religion was 'materialized' in society, similar in that respect to the institutions and properties of churches and monasteries in Europe.

Turbas are another space used today and in the past for segmented public functions. On specified feast or holy days, families take picnics to cemeteries where their departed are buried, where they engage in rituals (Quran readings by professionals) and spend some hours in family sociability. It is a public space in which the public consists of 'private' families and neighbourhoods. On the eve of modernity, in the eighteenth century, cemeteries in part of Syria may have been locations for gatherings of a more generalized public, providing public spaces free of political control and religious censure, groups of dissident 'intellectuals' and sectarians were able to meet.

Let us now turn to the less respectable and more subversive public spaces. Chief among these was the coffee house – the *gahwa*. Today these are largely innocuous and uncontroversial (they serve a lot more tea than coffee, and are also commonly called *chaykhana* – tea houses). However, at the introduction of coffee and the inception of coffee houses in the sixteenth and seventeenth centuries they aroused controversy and censure in many Middle Eastern locations. The coffee houses, and even more so the (mostly clandestine) taverns, were areas of potential social disorder – insofar as they were not closely controllable by religious and political authorities. Ralph Hattox has narrated this story of coffee in the fifteenth and sixteenth centuries, and the debates and prohibitions it elicited from the religious authorities.[6] One thing is clear from these accounts: the debate over whether coffee was a prohibited intoxicant akin to wine[7] had a subtext, which was the potential of the coffee house for uncontrolled public sociability. These considerations of social control continued to feature in urban conflicts in the following centuries. There is an interesting description of the phenomenon in eighteenth-century Aleppo in the work of Abraham Marcus.[8] The legality of coffee drinking, and of tobacco and hashish smoking, continued to be debated and frowned upon by the moral censors, and occasionally prohibited – as it was under Sultan Murad in 1630 (himself notorious for drunkenness), when he tried in vain to eradicate these habits throughout the Empire; things returned to normal after a few years. There were persistent complaints by moralists that these establishments, which stayed open late into the night, were venues for drinking, prostitution and pederasty. *Qadis* and governors would crack down occasionally. But the authorities were also irritated by the entertainments that took place in these establishments: music, song and shadow theatre (*qaraqoz*), as well as storytelling – especially during the nights of Ramadan, when many cafés operated well into the night, as they continue to do. The objections were not only against music – deplored by the pious but ever popular with a passionate public of all classes and confessions – but to the shadow theatre and some of the storytelling, which, of course, often alluded to current events and personalities in satirical and mocking tones. The janissaries were mocked in Aleppo cafés after their disgrace in the Russian campaign of 1768. We also find a vivid narrative of the subversive character of coffee houses in Orhan Pamuk's *My Name is Red*,[9] in a café that was the haunt of artists and storytellers, of drink and satire – especially against jealous religious censors, who ultimately have their revenge in the sacking of the café and the murder of its main figures. It can be argued that, in this respect, coffee houses came closest to the modern notion of the public sphere insofar as they escaped authoritarian control and constituted venues for the formation and expression of public opinion.

Women were not entirely excluded from public sociability; their venue was the bath house, the *hammam*:

The public bath houses also doubled as places of amusement and socializing, again especially for women, and a rich lore of popular sayings and stories centered on this social institution ... Parties of women and children brought food and entertainers along with them to the baths, and spent the day socializing in the relaxed atmosphere, their excited voices reaching the streets ... Wary of the excesses of such revelry, the Christian clergy issued periodic regulations prohibiting women from feasting in the baths.[10]

Such bath entertainments for women continued throughout the region into the twentieth century, and episodes are recounted in many anecdotes and memoirs.

The tavern

The tavern is celebrated in poetry and literature – the *khammara* in Abu Nawas's Abbasid eighth-century poetry, the *meykhaneh* or *meykadeh* of the Persian poets (Khayyam, Sa'di, Hafez). It is claimed that the use of this word for tavern is a mystical metaphor for something other than imbibing, which may be true in some cases, but it certainly meant real drinking for the poets mentioned. Stories of taverns and drink are also common in literary and historical narratives, such as the tenth-century *maqamat* (narratives) of Hamadhani, and of Hariri in the eleventh and twelfth centuries, and the essays of notables such as Tanukhi on Baghdad in the eleventh century. In more recent times, the *meykhaneh* (*meyhane* in modern Turkish) features in tales, poetry and history. How much of a public venue was the tavern? The fact that it was periodically interdicted by the authorities would indicate that it continued to function for most of the time, more or less publicly. In Ottoman locations, the soldiers – especially the janissaries – were known for their drinking in taverns that had diverse entertainments, notably dancing boys and gambling.[11] In the nineteenth century, with the Ottoman reforms and the self-conscious integration of the Ottoman elite into the world of progress and civilization (*medeniyet*), drinking culture became public and respectable.

Drinking venues and cultures, then, discussed in Chapter 4,

constituted important elements in the public culture at various points in the history of Middle Eastern cities, and with varied significance.

Censor and *hisba*

In past centuries, Muslim societies always contained some form of censor who was responsible for both public and private spheres of conduct. The office of *muhtasib* is precisely such a source of censorship on public life, mainly markets. It is based, however, on the concept of *hisba* – literally, accountability (before God). The *qadi* was also empowered to control the social conduct of private individuals, relating, for example, to drink and loose sexuality within a neighbourhood – but only in response to complaints. Yet the forbidden use of drink and music, as well as pederasty and other forms of illicit sex, was not only widespread throughout Muslim history, but also celebrated in poetry, song and mysticism, as well as theorized, as we saw in the case of alcohol. Books of philosophy and mathematics theorized music, medical treatises discoursed on the benefits of wine and the 'mirrors of princes' genre offered advice on the comparative benefits of copulating with boys or girls. The courts of the princes and the houses of elites revelled in all these vices, as did many Sufi lodges, enriched with religious mysticism. Yet the scholars advanced elaborate treatises on their prohibition and prevention – sometimes the very same scholars and jurists who practised them in their *majalis* (plural of *majlis*), gatherings and lodges.[12] Could it be that these contradictory strands of thought and literature only coexisted so easily because they were only 'public' to segmented elites (who were paradoxically known as *al-khassa*, the 'private' or special, as distinct from *al-'amma*, the 'public' or common people). Separate and discrete circles of the literate elite were the authors and consumers of these materials. Jurists fulminated against philosophy, yet *fiqh* and philosophy coexisted for the most part – except when a philosopher brought his rationality into *fiqh*, like Ibn Rushd in twelfth-century Spain. What distinguishes modernity is precisely the common exposure of these spheres to a common literacy and a 'public'. This point is illustrated by *kitab manfi' al-aghdhiya wa-daf' madhrriha* (The Book of the Benefits of Nutrients and How to Avoid Their Harm), by al-Razi (d. 932),[13] a book of medicine and diet which contained a chapter on wine and its benefits. 'Asim 'Aytani, in his introduction to the 1985 Beirut edition, reproached al-Razi for writing on forbidden wine and excised the chapter, lest the reader should fall into doubt regarding the matter of forbidden drink.[14]

The law, the public and the private

Let us now turn to law and religion in social life, and in particular to the question of privacy. How is the private sphere conceived and protected from public exposure? A basic thrust in the Muslim religion – indeed, in all religions – is communitarian and authoritarian. Religious observances and moral rules are not left to the discretion of the individual and his or her relation to God and the afterlife, but enforced here and now, and this constitutes much of the sphere of Shari'a. In Islam, the injunction of *al-amr bil-ma'ruf wal-nhy 'an al-munkar* (to command virtue and forbid vice) is apparently binding on every Muslim, who must correct errant behaviour when he or she encounters it. There is much debate on whether this is an individual responsibility or that of the authorities as *uwly al-amr* (guardians), and under what conditions. There are also many Quranic injunctions to Muslims to care for and watch over one another. These can be interpreted either as egalitarian and participatory, or as authoritarian – restricting individual autonomy and liberty, subordinated to communal censorship (officially personified in the office of *muhtasib*). In fact, the legal scholars over the ages were concerned with the question of privacy, as narrated by Michael Cook in his *Forbidding Wrong in Islam*.[15] A common point of view is expressed by Ibn Taimiya: 'Manifest wrongs must be acted against, in contrast to hidden ones, the punishment of which [i.e. divine punishment] afflicts only the perpetrator'.[16] This is a common distinction: sins are only combated when manifest (for example, when relating to the use of music and liquor). Scholars who advocated respect for privacy cited the anecdote about 'Umar ibn al-Khattab, the second caliph, who entered a man's house by climbing over the wall and caught him engaged in wrongdoing. The man protested that, whereas he had sinned once, 'Umar had sinned three times: he had spied when God had prohibited spying; he had entered through the roof, against the command to enter the house by its door; and he had failed to greet the inhabitants when entering the house, as God had commanded.'Umar let the man be, ordering him to repent.[17] Another theme is the injunction not to expose a respectable Muslim, advocated by many scholars, including Gahzzali (d. IIII). Indeed, it is the duty of a Muslim to hide (*satr*) the shame of another from public gaze. If you discover sin committed in private, then you may admonish the sinner, but not expose him to public gaze.

These sensibilities of scholars and jurists were not always observed in practice. We have notable examples in the modern world – in both Saudi Arabia and Iran – of zealous incursions into the domestic and private domains by public authorities in the name of commanding the good and forbidding sin. In this context, Azar Nafisi reflected on the Western feminist slogan 'the personal is political', and found it problematic in the Iranian context, where women – and men – would rather that the political did not infringe on the personal.[18] This is precisely what the clerics and their supporters are arguing and practising: personal autonomy and privacy are subjected to collective political goals dictated by authorities in the name of obedience to God's commands. The private is subordinated to the public – but 'public' in the sense of authority and command, or of communal authoritarianism, not in the sense of the give-and-take of 'public opinion' and the 'public sphere'.

Modernity and the public sphere

The transformations of modernity include a more general and integrated 'public', which starts with the modern elites and middle classes (functionaries, officers, professionals, modern businesspeople), then integrates further sectors of the population. These developments take place in the context of increased transport and communication (railways, telegraphy, intensified commerce, expanding bureaucracies), as well as spreading literacy in new educational systems. The new figure of the 'public intellectual' comes on the scene, whose role is defined by addressing this new public. The new media of press and books are, above all, the lubricants of this new process. Benedict Anderson's notion of the nation as 'imagined community' fits this picture.[19] The boundaries between insulated communities become more porous, and individuals are recruited into this no-man's-land of the 'public', aided by the emerging 'print capitalism'. Anderson postulates a historical imagination, preceding the nation, of a universal religious community of Christendom or the Umma of Islam, which remain theoretical, alongside a reality of bound and insulated communities with limited perspectives. The imagination of the nation is facilitated, above all, by common education systems and this print capitalism (in the context of expanding and enveloping general capitalism). Karl Mannheim advanced a relevant picture for emerging modernity in post-medieval Europe, and the rise of what he called 'free-floating intellectuals'.[20] They are free-floating in that they are released from communal and caste moorings, and thrust into the emerging field of universal public discourse. Their predecessors were the schoolmen, a caste of church clerics and theologians bound, like a guild, to limited thought systems of Aristotelian philosophy and church dogma, and to a 'truth regime' of reasoning from authority and precedent – the wisdom of the elders.

A crucial aspect of this emerging modernity is secularization. That is not to say 'secularism', which refers to an ideology calling for the separation of religion from government, or even a rejection of religious belief. 'Secularization' is a socio-cultural process, regardless of the piety or unbelief of individuals, by which spheres of society, politics and culture are separated from religious discourse and authority – largely as they become irrelevant to it, as we see in the experience of Iran under the Islamic Republic. Science, technology, bureaucracy and administration – the workings of modern economic forms – are not against religion, but indifferent to it, except in making religion irrelevant to so much of life. The processes of capitalism and the emergence of modern state practices are the components of this process. Even spheres previously intrinsic to religious authority, such as law and education, are withdrawn from it and taken into the modern state sphere, and into public space.

Ottoman intellectuals of the nineteenth century, such as the Young Ottomans, while defending Islam as the principle of their identity and civilization, were at the same time engaged in activities that subverted it, such as the translation and dissemination of modern European philosophy and literature. A new public of educated middle classes, consisting of functionaries and intellectuals, was absorbed through translated novels, the science fiction of Jules Verne, and the adventures of Alexandre Dumas (serialized in weekly instalments by enterprising publishers), as well as news of scientific discoveries and technical wonders and the biographies of great men.[21] While, in the closing decades of the nineteenth century, the Sultan-Caliph Abdul Hamid II instituted a regime of repression and censorship against any politically or religiously subversive materials, these genres – apparently neutral, but in reality deeply subversive – continued to thrive.

This 'public' also brings about new forms of language. The archaic forms of writing, designed for the limited circle of the literate, adorned with rhyming sentences in which sense and comprehension were sacrificed, give way to more direct prose – clear, lucid and communicable to the expanding literate public. Namik Kemal, the leading Young Ottoman (see Chapter 4) was a pioneer of the new writing.

The inclusion of expanding sectors of the population in this 'public' involves a process of democratization, as well as universalization. Cole relates how political newspapers in the latter part of the nineteenth century altered the attitudes of common people towards authority in Cairo.[22] A literate person, usually a schoolboy, would read aloud news and (critical) commentaries to a largely illiterate audience in a café or market gathering. This had the effect of an imagined popular inclusion and empowerment, not only in partaking in the news of current affairs, but also in participating in the criticism, and even satire, against powerful figures of *khedives*, princes and politicians. The idea of participating in an 'imagined community' of the incipient nation is thereby formed. These, for Cole, are some of the preludes to the first popular nationalist revolt in Egypt in 1882 – the Urabi revolt.

Religion itself is transformed by these processes. Religious reformers partake in this creation of the public and its space, and address it as new intellectuals. A significant development at this point is in the pronouncing of fatwas. The fatwa takes the form of an answer to a question posed by a private individual on a matter of faith and ritual, by a judge on a point of law, or by a prince on a matter of policy. A qualified mufti responds, typically with a brief one-sentence answer, written or oral; it is a private and circumscribed exchange. From the late nineteenth century, the religious reformer as public intellectual used the fatwa to pronounce on a range of social and religious issues, in elaborate reasoning addressed to a public often in the process of contest and debate. Muhammad Abduh, Rashid Rida and their successors addressed their fatwas to the public, and published them in newspapers. Rida had his own influential magazine, *al-Manar*, that carried these fatwas, as well as an array of religious, social and political discourses and debates. This process contributes to secularization, in that it places religion alongside other forms of discourse and communication in a public, profane space. Religion is removed from its sacred location and unitary authority, and placed into the fray of public discourse, competing with secular ideologies and forms of knowledge.[23]

The twentieth century

These processes of the formation of the modern state and political fields, of public spaces and the sites of enunciation within them, all continued into maturity in most countries in the region throughout the twentieth century. The new forms of media and entertainment – particularly the cinema, then television and finally the internet – were added to the innovations in this area. Egypt was and remains the main home of the Arab cinema, which captured the imagination and the passions of Arab publics. More than any other element in public space, it was a democratic form that attracted wide audiences from the urban poor and common people. Taxi drivers and market porters, as well as students and teachers, could afford the entrance fees. Popular films (Bollywood-style, with song, dance, romance and adventure) would attract faithful audiences of people re-viewing them frequently, until they had memorized the songs and the dialogue and could join in on subsequent viewings, thus carrying over habits from traditional storytelling. Film stars, singers and dancers – Abdul-Wahhab, Um Kathum, Asmahan, Farid al-Atrash and many others – created a sphere of celebrity, glamour and intrigue, feeding romance and gossip in the many newspaper and magazine pages devoted to that world. This sphere of celebrity has been enhanced in more recent times by television, video clips and the internet. It is intriguing to see how academic writing on the 'public sphere' is largely devoted to religious fields, and mostly silent on these aspects of popular culture, which are the subject of a different literature.[24]

The political struggles of the twentieth century were mostly fought with secular ideologies, reflecting political formations of nationalism, socialism, fascism and even liberalism. Politicized religion, such as that of the Muslim Brotherhood, was only one tendency among many, with ebbs and flows of fortune depending on context. In Egypt and much of the Arab world, Nasirism became a popular ideology that entranced the masses from the 1950s to the 1970s. In Iraq, Iran and the Sudan, communism, though clandestine, dominated the opposi-tional political scene in those middle decades, and rulers encouraged Islamic currents to combat the left. These currents only started to gather momentum in the later 1970s, and took off after the spectacle of the Iranian Revolution of 1979.

Islamic currents and the public sphere

This emerging public sphere and its physical spaces largely escaped religious authority and censure. Religious authority in most coun-tries was on the retreat from the nineteenth century. The ulama lost control over law and education, as well as endowments as sources of revenue. Only when secularist or liberal writers or artists encroached on their own religious terrain did they react. Literature, the arts, entertainment, music, cinema, universities, the press – all went ahead with limited reference to religion, often only honorific. It was in the later decades of the twentieth century, starting in the 1970s, that a new form of religious movement, that of political Islam, attempted to impose religious authority over these spheres. The Islamic Republic in Iran was the most comprehensive of these movements in its extension of religious authority, deploying a combination of traditional clerics and a modern 'cultural revolution' within all aspects of social and cultural life. Egypt, the leading country in cultural modernity from the nineteenth century, witnessed a wave of religious activism and sentiment, comprising political agitation for Islamic law, some of it violent, as well as pietistic and moralistic preaching and direct religious intervention in many spheres. At first these currents emanated primarily from outside the religious establishment and its personnel, and its leaders were drawn predominantly from other spheres, including many doctors and engineers. Later, religious institutions and personnel jumped on the bandwagon. Al-Azhar committees took on the functions of censorship of cultural products; Islamic lawyers took to litigation against writers, artists and film-makers for religious or moral impropriety; threats and intimidation restricted the range of cultural production; there were campaigns for the segregation of the sexes in public places and institutions. We therefore see, first, the prominence of religious advocacy of various kinds in the public sphere, 'staging virtue' to wide audiences from the mosques to television and the press. These same agents then attempt to control, censor and moralize public spaces. The moral campaigns also enter private lives with pressures for religious observance and moral conduct. The rulers and their agents are vigilant in suppressing any manifestation of political opposition or disruption from Islamic or other sources, but tolerant and even complicit in pious and moral campaigns of social and cultural control – avenues of control that are attractive to authoritarian rulers.[25]

We have seen that a central plank in Islamic political advocacy is the call for the application of the Shari'a; and it is in the name of the Shari'a, presented as God's commands, that many of the authoritarian measures are conducted. The issue of the Shari'a poses compelling questions about the distinction between public and private spheres.

Iran is the most interesting example in this respect. The Islamic Republic was explicitly committed to legislating the Shari'a systematically as modern state law. Asghar Schirazi has argued that the great difficulty that arose in attempting to derive public law from the Shari'a was a consequence of the Shari'a being, in its history, a body of largely *private* law of the 'mercantile, agricultural and nomadic society' to which the historical Shari'a was addressed.[26] As a result, Schirazi argues, the bulk of the legislation in the Majles (parliament) of the Islamic Republic is irrelevant to the Shari'a. He calculated that 1,022 bills had been approved by the Revolutionary Council, and 1,385 passed by successive parliaments up to 1995. The Guardian Council, with few exceptions, did not establish any relationship between the bills and the Shari'a.

> The absence of the shari'a from much legislation was felt by some leading clergy to be an embarrassment which had to be addressed. Ayatollah Montazari declared that these provisions followed the shar' injunction 'Regulate your affairs', and in so far as these regulations are approved by the Guardian Council, then they become Islamic. In effect, legislation by the Islamic government becomes by definition Islamic![27]

Are these trends reversing the processes of secularization that started in the nineteenth century and matured through the twentieth? Ostensibly yes, but let us dig deeper. Three decades of the Islamic Republic in Iran have produced a thoroughly secularized society. All the indications are that the majority of a predominantly young population (70 per cent of the population are under 30) strongly resent Islamic government and its controls over their social and cultural lives. They use every opportunity to subvert these controls through their music, football, dress, courtship and sexuality. In the cultural sphere the censors were, until recently, subverted by elements within the ministries that produced the remarkable renaissance in Iranian cinema. Reformist and innovative newspapers, magazines and books were suppressed and banned, only for others to emerge. At the time of writing, the 'security state' of the Ahmadinejad regime has clamped down on these outlets through more authoritarian repression. In the religious sphere itself, the ruling clerics have succumbed to pragmatic considerations, and while maintaining the Islamic rhetoric have introduced many policies and measures that have abrogated their original specifications. The enhanced role of the Revolutionary Guards in state, society and economy under the Ahmadinejad regime, while retaining and reinforcing authoritarian religious discourse, is encroaching increasingly on the power of the clerics. In effect, the process of secularization continues. What remains of Islam is its vocabulary and personnel. This, in turn, has reinforced the cynicism of the people: these are now merely politicians, clinging to authoritarian rule by religious formulae. On the other hand, there are new and innovative sources of religious spirituality in the old spaces and institutions, such as the seminaries of Qom and Najaf, defying the legalistic formulae of the rulers.

Egypt apparently represents an opposite case, where an ever-pious public takes oppositional stances towards an authoritarian regime that has ambiguous religious credentials, is apparently friendly to the USA and at peace with Israel. Islam, for many, has become the idiom of opposition and the expression of frustrations. Would a dose of Islamic government lead to similar results as in Iran? There are many indications that, underneath the symbols of piety, the 'economy of desire' envelops many spheres, especially for the young. Young women wearing the *hijab* still walk hand-in-hand with their boyfriends on the Nile Corniche, and play ball in university precincts – at least in Cairo. Shopping malls, apart from being temples of consumption of fashion, food and music – all mostly in the styles of the vilified West – are springing up in ever-greater profusion. They are the venues for much entertainment, for the mixing of the sexes, for courtship and display – especially for the young.[28] *Urfi* (common law) marriage is vociferously denounced by the moralists and the sensational press. Though, the public censors were silent when this form of religiously sanctioned but socially ambiguous marriage was contracted by rich Saudis with poor Egyptian girls. Now, however, *urfi* marriage is also being used by young students away from home as a way of cohabiting without parental knowledge or consent, and without the expensive paraphernalia of weddings.

Religiosity in some Islamic lands, then, is a modern political and cultural wave with varying significance across time and place. It is not peculiar to Islam: we see the retreat from universalist ideologies, whether liberalist or Marxist, in many parts of the world, such as Eastern Europe and the Balkans, and the salience of ethnic and religious boundaries. This is an integral part of an increasingly globalized and secularized world. Weber's 'disenchantment of the world' is now at its peak, and we witness individual and collective attempts to re-enchant the world. When this attempted re-enchantment culminates in social and political authoritarianism, however, the economy of desire and its capitalist underpinning re-emerge and subvert the enchanted sphere.

6

Islam and Nationalism

Continuities and Contradictions

Islamic advocates in politics have often proclaimed that the Muslim's nationality is his faith. Many such Muslims have denounced nationalism for dividing the Muslim community, the Umma, into fragmentary units, contributing to its weakness in the face of its religious and civilizational opponents. Sayyid Qutb, the founding ideologue of modern radical Islam, responded as follows to the prosecutor's questioning of his patriotism in the trial that culminated in his execution in 1966:

> I believe that the bonds of ideology and belief are more sturdy than those of patriotism based upon region and that this false distinction among Muslims on a regional basis is but one consequence of crusading and Zionist imperialism which must be eradicated.[1]

Such proclamations reinforced the view of some Western commentators, including Ernest Gellner, that the Islamic idea of the religious community as the political unit is incompatible with the territorial nation-state. Nationalists, on the other side, have exalted the nation as a cultural and territorial unit as the ultimate basis for unity and solidarity. Few nationalists are actually hostile to religion and faith as the cement of social solidarity. Faced, however, with religious divisions within territorial nations, many secular nationalists have advocated a separation between religious faith and national solidarity, exemplified in the slogan of the early Egyptian nationalist leader Sa'ad Zaghloul (1857–1927), 'Religion is for God, and the fatherland is for all its members'. Arab nationalists have often considered Islam as a most valuable part of the heritage, *turath*, of the Arab nation, alongside language. In some contexts this assertion has the effect of devaluing its specifically religious content and its claim to be a basis for a political unit in the form of Islamic government.

We may discern three overlapping bases for conceiving the political unit in the Middle East: (1) the territorial nation-state, such as Egypt, Iraq or Turkey; (2) pan-Arab nationalism (for the Arabs); and (3) Islam. In practice, nationalist as well as Islamic discourses have moved between and combined these principles in response to the problems and situations at hand. Few Islamists have followed the logic of Islamic community as against the nation, and few nationalists have not accorded religion a place of honour in the attributes of the nation. Let us consider the modes of articulation between these principles in historical context.

Islam as nationalism

Nationalist sentiments often originated in the confrontation with the European powers from the nineteenth century onwards. These confrontations were conceived by many in the Ottoman, Persian and Indian worlds as being between religious communities: Islam versus Christendom. The problematic of decline, weakness and backwardness in relation to Europe generated discourses of remedies and responses. The conservatives asserted that it was the departure of Muslims from strict observance of their religion and the application of their law that detracted from their solidarity and resolve, not to mention God's blessing, which led to their weakness vis-à-vis the infidels. The enemies of Islam were seen as holding on to their religious solidarity: witness the support of the European powers for the local Christian communities, contributing to their security and prosperity; witness, too, the support of Europeans for the independence movements and secessions from the Ottoman state of the Christian nations of the Balkans. Politics was thus reduced to religious communitarianism.

> Whenever Egyptians see European statesmen acting in concert against Egyptian interests or sentiments and agreeing on measures which postpone the day of their independence, they tend to contrast their fortune with that of the Balkan domains of the Ottoman Empire. They conclude that these dependencies won their independence through European intervention, because their inhabitants are Christians. The impression is thereby gained that there is a certain kind of unity among the Christians in Europe, and consequently they wish for unity among the Muslims capable of protecting their interests. As Christian unity saved the Balkan countries from the yoke of Muslim Ottomans, Muslim unity would save Egyptians from European hegemony. This, we believe, is a naïve idea engendered by a faulty understanding of European politics in the East.[2]

Religious communalism, for long the basis of local solidarities and conflicts, comes to be generalized as a model of international relations, and of the politics of confrontation between a Christian Europe and the Muslim domains.

Reformists, on the other hand, sought to strengthen the lands of Islam against European ascendancy by adopting European models of social, political and military organization. The Muslim reformers among them, such as Afghani (1838–97) and Abduh (1849–1905), whom we encountered in Chapter 4, argued that such reforms were not incompatible with Islam, but indeed original to it. The original Islamic community of the Prophet and his companions embodied all the virtues of the European models of constitutionalism, democracy, rationality, love of science and knowledge, social justice and so on. So progress and authenticity could be united. It was the intervening centuries of tyranny and corruption (often blamed by Arabs on Turks, by Persians on Arabs and by Turks on both) that led to the decline and backwardness of Muslims and the distortion of religion. This distortion was identified with the common beliefs and practices of popular Islam, as well as the ignorance and obscurantism of the traditional ulama. The reform of al-Azhar (the foremost university of Sunni Islam, in Cairo) was one of the main projects of Abduh's life, and one in which he largely failed. Reform was aimed at the perceived corruption and superstition of popular Sufism, the worship of saints and visitations to tombs, and magical cults. The reformed religion would be rational, based on scriptures and a modern inter-pretation and formulation of the sources and the law.[3] In this stance the religious reformers coincided on the one side with the secular nationalists, including Ataturk, and on the other with the radical fundamentalists and Salafists. They all shared an antagonism to the common people and their religion in the name of progress, religious or national purity/authenticity and righteousness. 'The people' are the raison d'être of nationalism, for they are the nation and the bearers of its cultural essence. Yet they are recalcitrant, refusing to exhibit this essence as defined by the ideologies of nationalism. They have to be awakened (Gellner's 'Sleeping Beauty'). The metaphor of awakening is common to nationalists and religious ideologues from Ataturk to Khomeini.

Islam as nationalism, then, does not pertain to territory or state, but is often raised in the context of particular countries and their politics. Its logic is pan-Islamic, but its reality is often particular. The early pan-Islamists, notably Afghani, had their primary focus on resisting the colonial powers, especially Britain. Afghani was a cosmopolitan activist who stirred ideas and movements in India, Afghanistan, Iran, Egypt and Turkey, and, as such, was a rare phenomenon in the history of Islamic reform. As against the European powers, he postulated indeterminate entities, such as 'the East' (anticipating the much later Third Worldist entity of 'the South'). The qualities of Islam and the East then pertained to all the countries in question, each waging its own struggles. Afghani's ideal was for a unification of effort between the admittedly distinct countries; but a political unity of all Muslims in one state was not on the agenda.[4]

Islam and Arabism

The ideology and political movements of pan-Arabism developed in the process and aftermath of Ottoman collapse. They developed alongside notions of pan-Islamism and a renewed caliphate – preferably an Arab caliphate – as well as regional nationalisms. Many Arab nationalists, and many Arab Islamists, have argued that there is no contradiction between Arabism and Islam, but have variously constructed the interrelations between the two. Secular Arab nationalists, notably Ba'th ideologues, have lauded Islam as the peculiar genius of the Arab nation and the crowning glory of its history. This was the creed of Michel Aflaq (1910–89), one of the founders of the Ba'th Party and a Syrian Christian. For him, Islam was the national culture of the Arabs. It was 'a veritable image and a perfect and eternal symbol of the nature of the Arab self'; Muhammad was 'all the Arabs'.[5] This construction, however, does not find favour with Islamists, especially when it comes from Christian theoreticians. For Arab Islamists, religion is not merely a historical heritage of the Arabs, but a living system of politics and law to be applied in contemporary societies. They also point out that Arab prominence in history was only accomplished through Islam and its conquests. Additionally, Islam assigned a place of honour to the Arabic language as the medium of holy scriptures and Prophetic tradition. Language played a central role for both Arabists and Islamists. Both strenuously resisted ideas of language reform, modernization and the incorporation of regional colloquial dialects into the written language, as bordering on blasphemy – against religion and the unity of the nation.[6]

As a rule, Muslim reformists – and even militants – in the early decades of the twentieth century did not see a contradiction between Arab nationalism and an Islamic programme. Perhaps the most important figure in this respect was Rashid Rida. A Syrian who lived and worked in Egypt, Rida was not only a disciple of Muhammad Abduh, as discussed in Chapter 3, but also his biographer. Abduh was the main figure of the reforms, but one who veered more in 'fundamentalist' directions. Rida wrote at a time when there was much resentment in many Arab quarters against Ottomans and Turks, occasioned by the increasingly nationalist directions taken by the Young Turks and the persecution of Arabist elements, especially in Syria in the years leading up to and during World War I. In Egypt the Turkish ruling and military elite was much resented, which was one of the causes of the Urabi revolt in 1882 that culminated in the British occupation of the country.[7] Rida declared that as a Muslim, he was a brother to all Muslims, and as an Arab, a brother to all Arabs, and that he saw no contradiction between the two. Nevertheless, like his mentor Abduh and many others, he blamed the Turks for the decline and weakness of Islam, and thought of the Arabs as its champions and defenders. Comparing the conquests of the Turks to those of the Arabs, Rida argued that the Arab conquests established Islam in the world, while those of the Turks (in Europe and elsewhere) brought a burden on Islam:

> [T]he greatest glory in the Muslim conquests goes to the Arabs, and that religion grew and became great through them; their foundation is the strongest, their light the brightest, and they are indeed the best *umma* brought forth to the world [a Quranic reference] ... a little knowledge of past and present history shows that most of the countries where Islam was established were conquered by the Arabs ...[8]

Rida was also sympathetic to the restoration of the Arab caliphate, as opposed to Ottoman claims.

What, then, of the unity of the Muslim Umma? While keen on uniting the will and solidarity of Muslims, and on Islam as the basis for social and political organization, Rida was realistic about the chances of political union. His advocacy of a revived caliphate to unite Muslims did not conceive a unitary state for all Muslims, but of a caliph who would assume the functions of a supreme *mujtahid* who would hold authority over spiritual matters for Muslims living under various political authorities and national arrangements. The caliph was conceived as a pope-like figure, presiding over diverse nation-states. Islamic unity would not supersede national identity.[9]

Subsequent Islamic ideologues in the first half of the twentieth century would not have disagreed. Abduh and Rida were the giants of reform, but remained theoreticians and publicists. The following generation – that of the previously discussed Muslim Brotherhood, founded in Egypt in 1928 – were activists and organizers of mass mobilization. They were competing in the political arena with varieties of nationalism: with liberals as well as fascists. They also faced struggles with the left. What all these groups had in common was an anti-colonialist stance calling for an end to British occupation and control, later extending to anti-Zionism and support for the Palestinians. The Muslim Brotherhood conceived all these issues in Islamic terms, and saw no contradiction between Arabism and Islam. Tariq al-Bishry, in *Bayna al-Islam wal-uruba* (Between Islam and Arabism) written during the course of the 1980s, quotes Hassan al-Banna, founder of the Muslim Brotherhood, who reiterated sentiments similar to Rida's: 'The Arabs are the mainstay of Islam and its guardians ... and it is a duty of every Muslim to work for the revival and support for Arab unity'.[10]

A distinguished historian and lawyer, al-Bishry, like many Egyptian intellectuals, started his political career as a Marxist, then veered towards pan-Arab nationalism of the left (fitted together with Nasirism), and ultimately, after the Iranian revolution, to Islamism. He thus speaks with good perspective – and hindsight – on Egyptian and Arab political life and culture in his book.[11] Al-Bishry quotes with approval the twentieth-century Islamists on the consistency between nationalism and Islam. He adds that the antagonism between the two is only generated as a result of the secularist bent of so many nationalists. Islamists, he argues, objected to the subordination of Islam to Arabism in the ideologies of Ba'thists and Nasirists, who glorified Islam only as the heritage of the Arab people, then abandoned it as a social and political system and as the source of all legislation.

Al-Bishry also offered insights into why Sayyid Qutb and the radicals who followed him rejected nationalism in favour of Islam. While the Islamists of the earlier decades of the twentieth century shared with the nationalists the objective of ending colonial domination, the Islamists under Nasir were firmly repressed and persecuted by a nationalist regime after the British had been ejected. Qutb conceived of the Nasirist regime as a *jahiliya* – an age of barbarism and ignorance – to be confronted by true Muslims fortified by faith, and following in the footsteps of the first Islamic vanguard of Muhammad and his followers. Faith, in this scenario, replaces nation as the basis of solidarity and struggle, establishing the sovereignty of God as against that of the nationalist tyrant. Al-Bishry traced this rejection of the nation primarily to Indian Islamic thought – notably, that of Abu al-A'la Mawdudi. Indian Muslims, argued al-Bishry wanted to create a Muslim community, as distinct from the Indian nation, and thus rejected nationalism (and also, he could have added, a nationalism based on Muslim identity but not on the Islamic Shari'a, *à la* Jinnah, founder of Pakistan). Mawdudi had considerable influence over the more militant Islamists of the Arab world, including Qutb.[12]

The Qutbic strand of Islamic anti-nationalism persists, however, and is widespread among radical Muslims. Contrary to al-Bishry's pronouncements, they insist on the firm link of nationalism to secularism, and of both to an intrinsic hostility to Muslim unity and faith. Emmanuel Sivan studied the pronouncements on Arabism in the taped sermons of a variety of radical Islamic preachers at the height of the Islamic resurgence in the 1970s and 1980s. A Palestinian–Jordanian preacher, Abdallah Azzam, proclaimed that 'Arab nationalism was conceived in sin and born in corruption and dissolution'.[13] A common theme is that Arab nationalism is a Western import, encouraged by Orientalists and colonialists to divide and weaken the Islamic Umma, to separate Arab from Turk, and to demolish the caliphate. And it is asked, who were its Arab agents and ideologues? Answer: Christians, in league with their Western co-religionists – people like Jirji Zaydan and George Antonius, to be followed in subsequent generations by Michel Aflaq, the primary progenitor of Ba'th ideology, then George Habbash of the Popular Front for the Liberation of Palestine. This tendency to denounce Arab Christians as agents and conspirators feeds into the question of the equality of all faiths in common citizenship, so central to nationalist aspirations. Much as the reformists, such as al-Bishry, cling to this principle and dress it in Islamic garb, the radicals delight in denouncing such equality. Islam tolerates infidel *dhimmis* ('people of the Book'), they argue, providing they pay the poll tax and keep to their

place as protected and subordinate communities. Radical preachers, like the Egyptian Shaykh Kishk, in the 1970s denounced Copts
for departing from this role and assuming positions and stances of
prominence and equality. A particular bête noire of the Islamists was
Boutros Boutros-Ghali, the Egyptian former secretary general of the
UN, whose international prominence was attributed to his being a
Christian, and 'one of them'. Preachers also denounced Arab hypoc-
risy – specifically, the claims to unity and solidarity belied by the
selfish conduct of so many Arabs, especially the rich of Saudi Arabia
and the Gulf, spending lavishly on forbidden pleasures while the
majority of their fellow Arabs and Muslims lived in poverty. Kishk
told stories of the drinking, gambling and whoring of these Arabs in
Cairo's Pyramid Street.[14]

The idea of nationalism and the nation-state as forms of idolatry,
worshipping a reified nation as a substitute for God, is a common
theme not only among radical Islamist constructions, but also in some
sophisticated intellectual ones – notably among the Turkish theorists
of the Umma, such as Ali Bulaç, who attributes many of the ills of
the modern world to nationalism and blames Hegel for deifying
the nation and its state. Nationalism, he argues, is the path to ethnic
cleansing and genocide – demonstrated by the largely peaceful coexistence between religions and ethnicities under the Ottomans, followed
by the massacres and atrocities of the twentieth century, all in the
name of nationalism. His solution is a kind of liberal communalism – a
multiplicity of 'law communities' coexisting under a minimal state.[15]

The territorial nation

Pan-Arabism and pan-Islamism have been dreams and aspirations,
while the territorial nation-state is the only concrete political reality – as nation and as state. But there are many forms of articulation
between these territorial nationalisms and Islam. An important element in many nation-states of the region has been the existence of
non-Muslim groups, primarily Christians, as citizens. Where this
is the case – as in Egypt, Syria, Lebanon, Palestine and Iraq – it has
become an issue of contention between nationalism and Islam, as

we have seen. But there are countries in which Islam has coincided with citizenship to a large extent: this is the case in the Maghreb countries and in Turkey.

Country nationalism: Turkey

Turkey is perhaps the most interesting country in this respect. The Turkish Republic was proclaimed 'secular' in its foundational period. Kemalism proclaimed the European identity of Turkey and celebrated the ancient history of the pre-Islamic Turks. Even before Kemalism, Zia Gokalp argued that the Turkish people had a distinctive culture, the product of their long history from before Islam, their language, territory and stock (in line with the German theories of the nation so popular with Arab nationalists).[16] This culture was historically linked to Muslim civilization, which was now, by the early twentieth century, in a state of decline and decadence. At that historical juncture, Turkish culture was to be reoriented towards European civilization. Islam, then, remained as one element in the Turkish cultural heritage – a kind of cement of social solidarity (à la Émile Durkheim). Kemalist secularism, in line with these ideas, firmly subordinated religion to Turkish nationalism. Yet the Turkish Republic emerged with a primarily Muslim population. National identity was withheld from non-Muslim inhabitants of Turkey, in contrast with Christian and Jewish Arabs. They were Armenians and Greeks for the most part, largely ethnically cleansed in the massacres and exchange of populations of the early decades of the twentieth century. These episodes of conflict and violence reinforced the identification of Turkish identity with Islam. Though there remain non-Muslim citizens of the Republic, it is difficult to classify them as 'Turks'; Sunni Islam (of the Hanafi school) is implicitly a criterion of true Turkish citizenship.[17] Kurds are Sunnis, but of the Shafi'i school; and Alevis – mostly in peasant communities in Eastern Anatolia, some Kurds and some Turks – constitute a sect considered heretical by orthodox Muslims. This fact has facilitated the coexistence of Turkish nationalism and Islamist ideology in much of the Turkish Islamic revival, as well as in ultra-right activism.

The thrust of Gokalp's theories and of Kemalism, however, was to separate Turkish Islam from that of its neighbours, and from the historical association with them: it was precisely the Arab and Persian heritages that were seen as a burden of backwardness and corruption within the pure Turkish heritage. Turkish Islamism, though opposed to this secular nationalism and often declaring the unity of Islam, nevertheless took specifically Turkish forms. Much of Turkish Islamism depended organizationally and ideologically on the revivals of and continuities with older Sufi orders – mainly branches of the Nakshbandi. There were thus few organizational links with the Arab world, and certainly not with Shi'i Iran. In effect, Turkish Islamism is national, and often nationalist.[18]

The question of EU membership is relevant here. In the 1990s the Islamic Party – including its leaders at the time of writing, Tayip Erdogan and Abdullah Gul – opposed Europe as a Christian club, and proposed instead closer links with the Muslim world. This all changed in recent years, with the party becoming one of the foremost advocates of EU membership. But it may be argued that they have an ulterior motive: EU membership will weaken the military grip on Turkish government and society and usher in greater democracy, from which the Islamists will benefit. Yet the shift shows a pragmatic orientation towards national politics, to the extent of orienting policy towards the supposedly Christian Europe, and against (unrealistic) Islamic links. After 2005, the increasingly emphatic rejection of Turkish membership by several major EU countries has led to subtle changes of orientation. While keeping European membership on the agenda, the Justice and Development Party government has inclined towards closer relations with Turkey's Arab and Iranian neighbours, and fostered a cooling of relations with Israel – policies that have enhanced its popularity with the Turkish public.

In the Maghreb countries, Islam largely coincided with Arab and national identity, as well as providing a basis for national unity between Arab and Berber. There were no native Christians, and the thriving Jewish communities of old identified firmly with the French colonial presence, and were thus counted out of the national sphere. Ben Badis (d. 1940), a prominent reformist, like other Algerian ulama in the first half of the twentieth century, resisted the colonial thrust to make Algeria French with the slogan, 'Islam is my religion, Arabic my language, Algeria my fatherland'. Islam was an important component of the independence movements, unencumbered by the Mashriqi (eastern Arab world) problem of multiple communities of faith. Islam played different roles in the distinctive polities and histories of the three countries of the Maghreb, which are too complex to outline here.

Country nationalism: Egypt

Egypt is the country in the region with the most firmly established territorial and historical identity, buttressed by a long history of centralized and effective government. It is also the Arab country with the longest history of modernity and direct European dominance, starting with the Napoleonic invasion at the end of the eighteenth century, through the modernizing dynasty of Muhammad Ali, to European domination and British occupation in 1882. All the political trends of the region surfaced in Egypt: Ottomanism, constitutionalism, different brands of nationalism and Islamism, and then the leftist trends. The sense of Egypt as politically Arab – and as leader of the Arab world – was late to surface (after the Nasirist revolution of the mid-1950s), and was thrust upon bewildered Egyptians, who happily acquiesced in the lionization of Nasir and his leadership of the Arab and Third Worlds. For much of its modern history, however, Egyptian nationalism has been – and continues to be – in the ascendancy.[19]

A modernist, liberal Egyptian nationalism was proclaimed by many intellectuals in the earlier decades of the twentieth century, the most prominent being Taha Hussein, who we briefly met in Chapter 4 – writer, academic and educationalist, and at one point minister of education. His book, *The Future of Culture in Egypt*, published in 1937, raised a storm of controversy and was attacked by traditionalists and Islamists.[20] In it, Hussein attaches Egypt and its history to the Mediterranean and Hellenic world. Egypt's Islam, he argued, was no hindrance to this identification. Many centuries ago, Europe married Hellenism to Christianity, thus making Christianity rational and forward looking. Muslims, too, looked to the Greeks for logic and order, and led the medieval world in discovering and translating Aristotle. The march towards rationality and progress in Islam, however, was halted by the Turkish invasions and Ottoman rule. Egypt shared a common culture with Europe until the fifteenth century, when the Europeans started on the path of modernity, while Egyptians were prevented from sharing in this progress by the burden of Ottoman rule – only to resume the march in the nineteenth century. Nothing should now stop Egyptians from pursuing this path of modernity and progress. It is not clear from Hussein's discourse whether this prognosis applies to all Arabs and Muslims, or specifically to Egypt; the emphasis on the Mediterranean and the Hellenic worlds suggests the latter.

Few Egyptians today would subscribe to this vision, in a country swept by a wave of narrow religious moralism and chauvinistic paranoia. Yet one suspects that underlying all that is still a bedrock of Egyptian nationalism. Various strands of anti-imperialism, as well as the preoccupation with the problems between Palestine and Israel, dispose most political pronouncements to be solidaristic with Arabs and Muslims; yet the focus of all political manoeuvring is the nation and its state.

The Islamic Republic and Iranian nationalism

Iranian nationalism in the modern period separated Iranian history from that of the Arabs. It celebrated the pre-Islamic past and insisted on the continuity of Iranian culture, despite Islam and the Arab conquest. Indeed, it celebrated the penetration of that culture into Islamic civilization, and its role in shaping it with its themes and motifs. Iranian Islam, too, was seen as distinct, and its Shi'ism as a continuity with pre-Islamic spiritual themes. The Pahlavi regime played on these themes and celebrated the antiquity of Iranian or Arian monarchy. These themes were overtly secular, and accompanied by disparagement of the clerical establishment in its backwardness and reaction – while that establishment reciprocated with equal hostility and accusations of alien affiliation to the West, with its decadence and hostility to Islam and Muslims. Khomeini was particularly virulent in his condemnation of secularism and the Pahlavi pretensions. Despite the distinctness of Shi'i Islam and the historical antipathy towards its Sunni counterpart, Khomeini and his supporters emphasized the unity of the Muslim world and its common mission.[21]

The ideology of the Islamic Republic, then, was overtly internationalist. It proclaimed the project of liberation and solidarity for the whole Islamic world, and it openly attempted to export the Revolution. It was thus seen as subversive by the Arab regimes, and much celebrated by Islamists everywhere as a demonstration of Islam's revolutionary powers and appeal to the masses, as against the 'imported' secular ideologies. Here was a popular revolution, not an Arab-style military coup: the masses were mobilized in the name of Islam, their authentic creed. It swayed not only Islamists but many nationalists and leftists in the Arab world.

Yet the politics of the Islamic Republic operated in many registers, some with a distinctly nationalist flavour. While at one level it proclaimed Islamic universalism, there was never any doubt about the Shi'i identity of Iran. The Constitution of the Islamic Republic specified that Iranian nationality be a condition for citizenship of the Republic. Article 15 specified that the president must be Iranian by both origin and citizenship, and have a 'convinced belief in the ... official school of thought in the country' – that is to say, he must be Shi'i. Jaloddin Farsi, a long-time disciple of Khomeini, was prevented from standing in the presidential election of 1980 because his mother was Afghan. At the same time, Iranian Christians, Jews and Zoroastrians are accorded citizenship rights, short of assuming positions of political leadership.[22] The war with Iraq sharpened the sense of national identity of the Revolution as Iranian and Shi'i, against a hostile Arab, predominantly Sunni, world. Khomeini and the other leaders spoke frequently of the Muslim nation of Iran. The Iranian nation, in their discourse, was the vanguard of the Islamic revolution in the world. The direction of revolutionary propaganda and subversion to other parts of the region – notably Syria and Lebanon – followed the logic of Iranian national interest. The analogy drawn by many observers is with Russia and communism: internationalist rhetoric and nationalist foreign policy, the logic of 'socialism in one country'. In Iran, too, the failure of the rest of the Muslim world to follow in the path of revolution (on Iranian terms) and the hostilities of enemies led to a retrenchment of the Islamic Republic as a national project, which fits in with the older forms of Iranian nationalism. Predictably, with the waning of the initial revolutionary flush and rhetoric, the Islamic Republic has become routinized into a national state like the others, with a distinct Iranian identity in terms of religion, culture and politics.

The left, Third Worldism and Islamic authenticity

The 1950s and 1960s saw the success of liberation struggles against colonial powers and the rise of independent states in Africa and Asia that were strident in their politics of liberation. This was in the context of the Cold War, in which these countries emerged as 'non-aligned'. This non-alignment was ideologically directed against the Western former colonists (while still often dependent on them) and much cultivated by the Soviet camp, which traded with these countries and supplied them with arms. Such was the case in Nasir's Egypt, then in Ba'thist Syria, Iraq under Qasim and then the Ba'th, and many other Arab countries. These arms were ranged against the old Arab monarchies, the shah's Iran and NATO Turkey – all counted in the Western camp, or the ironically labelled 'Free World'. It was in this context that the revisionist Soviets under Khrushchev, having ditched Stalinist orthodoxies, advanced the doctrine of the 'non-capitalist path to socialism', especially to accommodate its new allies in the Third World – notably Nasir, and then the Ba'th. Under this rubric the Arab communist parties, including the powerful Iraqi Communist Party, were pressured to align themselves with these nationalist 'socialists', even when these regimes were persecuting them, as under Nasir, the 'Arif regime in 1960s Iraq and then the Ba'th. The Syrian Communist Party became a subordinate partner of Asad's Ba'th, complicit in its repression, as did the Iraqi Communist Party in a common front with Saddam in the mid-1970s, until he turned on them in a massacre.

Communism, then, became integrated into the Third Worldist nationalist regimes friendly to the Soviets, and their rhetoric in the Arab world concurred with that of the nationalists, especially on anti-West and anti-Israel issues. At the same time, 'socialism' was sported as a joint label for nationalist parties, such as Nasir's Arab Socialist Union and the Ba'th Arab Socialist Party. In terms of policy and politics, 'socialism' meant statism and state ascendancy in economy and society – a feature of the consolidated totalitarianism of these regimes. On the positive side, however, this articulation gave nationalism a universalist scope, insofar as it was not confined to a particular nation but presented itself as part of a universal liberation struggle of oppressed people against colonialism and imperialism, tied to the idea of socialist reform. This was particularly significant in relation to the Palestinian liberation movement, which found a niche within this complex and became a cause not only for liberationists from the Arab world, but also for supporters and volunteers from Iran, Turkey and even South America; Palestinian Liberation Organisation factions, some Marxist, were located first in Jordan, then (after a massacre in 1971) in Lebanon. It was this universalist articulation that faded in later times into religio-ethnic identification.[23]

Secular nationalists, such as Nasir and the Ba'th, assumed government powers in the 1950s and 1960s. The initial success of Nasir in the 1956 Suez episode, and the subsequent failed invasion by Britain, France and Israel, gave his leadership and regime great prestige and enthusiastic support throughout the region. Land reforms and nationalization gave it populist credentials. Equally, the spectacular defeat in the Six Day War with Israel in 1967 led to great popular disillusionment, accompanied by the realization that these now totalitarian regimes had failed on the military and economic fronts, and the realization of their apparent corruption. Two overlapping themes entered the ideologies of opposition and protest: leftist insurrectionism (Mao Zedong and Che Guevara) and nativist authenticity. Both were forms of anti-imperialism, and the figure who combined them was Frantz Fanon, with his Algerian connections.[24] Iran saw ideas and movements that combined an anti-Western search for authenticity with liberationist nationalism, best exemplified in the ideologies of Al-e Ahmed and Ali Shari'ati. Maoist and Guevarist insurrectionism, and the glorification of peasants and subalterns, appeared in various factions among Iraqi communists and in the Palestinian liberation movement. This insurrectionist leftism proved to be a passing trend, while the nativist return to authenticity persisted and deepened.

The Iranian ideological field in the 1970s saw the most coherent forms of this combination of leftist liberationism with Islamic orientations: Marx and Fanon combined with romanticized constructions of Hussein and the martyrs as revolutionary symbols. 'Red Shi'ism', for Shari'ati, was an exemplification of this revolutionary liberation, against the 'Black Shi'ism' of the clerics, of law and ritual. Marx and Fanon were hidden behind Hussein and Fatima (daughter of the Prophet), and Marx was explicitly rejected.[25] This combination of leftist ideologies with Islamic themes found its most sophisticated forms in Iran, but it also surfaced in the Arab world, mostly in Egypt. After the success and the euphoria of the 1979 Iranian Revolution, Iran's successful defiance of the USA and the extended humiliation of American diplomats in the following year, many Arab nationalists turned to Islamism. In Egypt, prominent Marxist intellectuals such as Adel Hussein and Tariq al-Bishry turned to Islam as a source of inspiration and mobilization of the masses. 'The people' were the carriers of revolution and liberation for both socialists and nationalists, and the Iranian Revolution was read as indicating that Islam was the genuine, authentic idiom of the people. Adel Hussein, an economist and journalist, and the editor of the populist *Al-Sha'b* – the newspaper of the Labour Party – shifted his nationalist and anti-imperialist themes to align with Islam, supporting the Muslim Brotherhood and their offshoots (although the Muslim Brotherhood never really trusted those intellectuals). Hussein's economic and political thought – dependency theory in economics and anti-imperialism in politics – remained constant through its successive articulations in reference to Marxism, then Nasirism and ultimately Islam.[26]

Behind this gravitation of nationalists and leftists to 'nativist' themes, including religion, was a cultural disillusionment with aspects of modernity, and a search for native authenticity against

Western capitalism. These trends were most explicit in Iran. In the early stages of modernization under Reza Shah (r. 1925–41), many intellectuals supported the process in spite of Reza's dictatorial repression. State centralization; secularization against the power of the clergy, the tribes and the backward bazaaris; the liberation of women; the establishment of modern education, health, uniform law and administration – all these were highly desirable to the modern intellectuals and in accord with nationalist aspirations. In many respects, Reza modelled himself on Ataturk, much to the consternation of the clerics and the conservatives. Reza was toppled in 1941 by a joint force of the British and the Soviets anxious to prevent the shah's plan for a neutral Iran favourable to the Axis powers. The period that followed, under occupation and thereafter until 1953, was the most vital and open in Iranian politics and, although turbulent, the nearest to pluralism and democracy. The communist Tudeh Party and its trade union affiliates were a largely open and popular political force, growing ever more powerful with the support of intellectuals, students and many popular elements. The clerics re-emerged as a political force after being suppressed and contained by Reza and were now free to advocate reactionary gender laws and the re-veiling of women. The nationalist coalition formed by Mohammad Mossadeq as the National Front was elected to power in free parliamentary elections, and Mossadeq served as prime minister from 1951 to 1953 – that is, during the turbulent years of the nationalization of Iranian oil, to the chagrin of Western oil companies and their governments, as well as of the young Mohammad Reza Shah, who succeeded his father. The National Front was supported by the Tudeh Party and by sectors of the clergy on a nationalist platform. However, the coalition was split by many lines of fissure, prominently on religious–secular issues, and especially on questions of gender and the political enfranchisement of women. Ultimately, the religious elements turned against Mossadeq and the seemingly secular thrust of his supporters; they sided with the powers activated by the American and British governments in the 1953 coup against Mossadeq, leading to the restoration of dictatorial rule by the young shah and his ever more powerful security service and repressive apparatus.[27] The clerics were at first happy with the new regime and the apparent defeat of the secularizing liberals and leftists, but would later suffer from the renewed zeal for secular modernization of the second Pahlavi shah. And it was partly this episode and its pro-Western, repressive aftermath that led some of the leftist intellectuals into cultural nostalgia and a religious orientation.

Over the decades that followed, the repressive Iranian regime was identified with the USA and the West. At the same time, rapid modernization from above and the processes of economic modernity were causing major dislocation and alienation in Iranian society. The shah, the court and the Westernized elite were ever more ostentatious in their displays of wealth and glamour. Western models of lifestyle, dress, media and consumption were more ubiquitous, alongside repression and poverty. Land reforms in the early 1960s (with disputed benefits to the peasantry) caused a great exodus to the cities, resulting in further dislocation and the break-up of traditional family and community bonds. Religious associations formed in the cities, some with connections to dissident clerics like Khomeini, who had been exiled to Turkey and then Iraq in 1964, but who maintained clandestine networks of supporters active in Iran. Most interesting, however, were the changing ideological orientations among intellectuals. The movements of the earlier twentieth century saw the West as a model of political order, education, science and rationality. Religion and its authority were obstacles, even in the view of the religious reformers who were seeking accommodation with a desirable type of modernity. The left – in the form of the Tudeh Party, as well as social-democratic orientations in some sections of the National Front – generated the dominant discourses and motifs of intellectual and secular politics, and even recruited several religious thinkers. The transformations of post-1953 Iran saw subtle shifts in leftist thought, with the entry of religious and traditional elements. The West in these terms was no longer the model of political order and rationality, but the source of cultural imperialism and consumerist capitalism, seen as the basis for the corruption of Iranian culture and society. It was associated with the tyranny and repression of the shah's regime, and the dislocation and corruption in society and culture.

The one constantly potent issue in the contests and debates was that surrounding women, sexuality and gender.[28] Even for modernists favouring the liberation and unveiling of women, sexuality remained a question surrounded by great hesitation and ambivalence. And this was one of the central issues to emerge in the ideological developments of the 1960s and 1970s – only this time in the context of anti-capitalism and national authenticity. The exploitative consumption culture of capitalism was most prominently embodied in the fashions, make-up and lifestyle of Westernized elite women – and, increasingly, in the new middle classes. Frivolity, erotic representations in films, magazines, advertising and pop culture – all these were seen as the most offensive manifestations of the Western capitalist invasion of Iran. Remedies were sought in the return to a traditional ideal and cultural authenticity. These were the dynamics that brought about a kind of convergence between the left and the religious thinkers, not only in politics, but also in culture and lifestyle. The women of the leftist (Maoist) militant Fedayeen-e Khalq, while not veiled, were uniformly clad in shapeless Mao shirts and rigorously rejected make-up, and even sex, as bourgeois corruption.[29] Ali Shari'ati held up Fatima, the daughter of the Prophet and wife of Ali, as a model for womanhood – steadfast in her religion and struggle for justice, standing alongside her martyred husband and sons – as a great contrast to the frivolous, empty-headed modern woman, exploited and manipulated, financially and sexually, by Western capitalism and its corrupting culture.[30] Note that many of these ideas and thinkers drew on Western critiques of modernity and capitalism from Friedrich Nietzsche, Marx, Fanon and Jean-Paul Sartre. Although seeking cultural authenticity with Shi'i Islam at its root, this trend continued to have universalist aspirations to liberate the 'wretched of the earth' (later, *al-mustaz'efin*), reading this universalism into the path of the imams and martyrs.

The 1979 Revolution saw the acquiescence of leftist forces in the leadership of Khomeini and his clerical establishment. Indeed, in the first year of the Revolution and the Islamic Republic, the communists and the Maoist Fedayeen supported Khomeini against the more liberal elements and the women's movement, who were alarmed by the growing signs of theocratic despotism. In their logic, 'liberals' were bourgeois counter-revolutionaries playing into the hands of the imperialists. Not long after, the clerics turned against their erstwhile leftist supporters in the campaigns of repression that started in 1980. This was reinforced by the war with Iraq, whose end in 1988 saw an intensification of the repression and a veritable massacre of opposition forces in Iranian prisons. After the death of Khomeini in 1989, there was a cautious and pragmatic liberalization under Hashimi Rafsanjani. Thereafter, liberal and leftist opposition to the clerics was only openly expressed in Islamic terms – urging the separation of religion and government, citing Islamic sources and precedents – as in the work of intellectuals such as Abdel-Karim Soroush and Akbar Ganji. There is no mistaking the secular thrust of these advocacies.

Islam in Iranian nationalism, then, took different forms. Shari'ati, Al-e Ahmed and their followers pursued a cultural nationalism, seeking historical authenticity against capitalism and imperialism and their colonization of mind and culture. In that respect, they retained a universalist orientation to human liberation, in which they saw the 'authentic' Islam of the imams and the martyrs as a precedent. Shari'ati explicitly denounced the Black Shi'ism of the clerics, of ritual and law, in favour of the Red Shi'ism of the martyrs, the true liberationist example. But it was Black Shi'ism that was to triumph in the Islamic Republic. This, in turn, was also to express Iranian nationalism and appeal to the imams and martyrs – especially during and after the war with Iraq (1980–88). Iranian identity merged with Shi'ism against the Sunni Arab world, which sided with Saddam Hussein. But this nationalism was far from the intellectual universalism of the earlier intellectuals. As we have seen, the apparent universalism of pan-Islamism was a disguise for Iranian power and influence, much as Soviet internationalism was an instrument of Russian nationalism. The resentment towards clerical power and Islamic imposition led to an intellectual and cultural movement for secular reform (although often expressed in religious language) – and a generation of cynical and frustrated youth.

Iran is a unique case, but with illuminating contrasts to other countries in the region. The assumption of power by a clerical establishment that appropriated religious nationalism has led to a revisionist, if not outwardly secular, opposition. The clerical government, while repressive, had not succeeded in establishing a unitary or dynastic centre of power in the manner of its Arab neighbours (though the Ahmadinejad regime is attempting to do just that); political and cultural ferment continues and is expressed in a degree of political pluralism, at the time of writing under threat from renewed repression. Intellectual and cultural innovations, religious and secular, flourish despite repression, and their content often transcends the narrow confines that seem to characterize the more stereotypical offerings of Iran's Arab neighbours.

The Arab world is diverse, but religion seems to be hegemonic in the culture and politics of most countries. Ruling cliques, mostly dynastic, try to monopolize religion as a prop to their increasingly repressive and stagnant regimes. Saddam Hussein in Iraq, starting with a militantly secular Ba'th, moved full circle to religious advocacy in the 1990s, as a means of social control under adverse circumstances. Opposition and discontent were equally expressed in Islamic idioms. Secular nationalism and socialism had become discredited clichés as the ideologies of bankrupt regimes. Over and above the discontent of poverty and repression, the primary form of political expression is the denunciation of the USA, the West and, above all, Israel, which is seen as the source of all evil and of conspiracies against Arabs and Muslims. Virulent anti-Semitism is a central ingredient in this religio-ethnic nationalism. This has become the main form of nationalism – a superimposition of the Umma over the Arab nation, in the face of the hostility of Christians and Jews. A religious, communalist model of international relations has been rejuvenated. A few intellectual, universalist voices have been raised against this xenophobia, but have been largely drowned by the acquiescence, if not support, of mainstream journalists, writers and academics. *The Protocols of the Elders of Zion* is widely read and cited as a work of historical record.[31] Secularism has become a dirty word. In Egypt, Islamic discourse is so dominant that even the old leftist party dare not deny the Shari'a, instead advocating a liberal version of it. Liberals, such as they are, take refuge in Islamic reformism – more timid than its nineteenth-century predecessor – without intellectually advancing on it. The main innovation in Arab Islamic thought came from Sayyid Qutb and his militant radicalism in the 1950s, which still animates jihadist trends. Otherwise, the Salafist shaykhs and their supporters are the most vociferous, often tacitly endorsed by the regime and its media as a means of social control, with feeble opposition from those who try to present a more liberal version of Islam.

The contest over national and cultural identity in Turkey has always featured contests and debates about the place of Islam. Conservative and patriarchal currents have always simmered below the modernizing surface, and continue as an undercurrent in Turkish politics. What is interesting for the present discussion, however, is the place assigned to religious heritage in modern and reformist thought. Even the most modernist and positivist thought before Ataturk – such as that of Gokalp – endeavoured, as we saw above, to find a place for religion. More committed religious thought, such as that of Said Nursi, continued to play a part in the cultural and political ferment, first clandestinely and then openly.[32] To what extent were these features of 'nationalism'? The polarization of religious advocacy against the militantly secular thrust of the dominant nationalist ideology may have blunted overtly nationalist elements. However, as many writers have noted, Sunni Islam has remained a potent component of Turkish nationalism and national identity, and emerged as such more explicitly from the 1970s onwards. While a kind of 'Umma nationalism' animates these sentiments, especially in contrast to the Christian West, it did not usually include common identification with Arabs or Kurds, let alone Shi'ite *'ajam* (Persians). Islam also entered into intellectual currents in original ways. The Turkish–Islamic Synthesis was one such movement with mild nationalist overtones. The other was based on the already mentioned community-centred ideas of Bulaç and his group, who were explicitly anti-nationalist. Its critique of modernity, drawing on Western currents such as critical theory, included a denunciation of the nation-state as tyranny and idolatry, in favour of a plurality of voluntarily chosen religious communities: a kind of utopian anarchism. But, those currents aside, one gets the impression that Turkish nationalism in the current situation is not so different from that of its neighbours, containing a powerful dose of anti-American and anti-Jewish sentiment, enriched by conspiracy theories, and with various degrees of affinity with or rejection of religion not making much of a difference. All of this is masked by the apparent pragmatism and moderation of a governing party with Islamic roots.

In a world of spectacular and protracted American military adventurism, potent nationalist reactions are not surprising. The presentation of these conflicts as an attack on the Islamic Umma appears to be convincing to many, and even effective in drawing an American reaction – as in President Obama's address to the 'Islamic world' soon after his inauguration, in effect conceding its unity. Of course, the conflicts in Afghanistan, Iraq and Palestine are not about Islam or religion, but are concerned with issues of geopolitics, strategy and domination. Yet, under the present circumstances, the religious presentation seems to echo popular sentiment in many quarters. It is predominantly in Iran that strong currents of popular sentiment and intellectual orientation apparently resist this religio-political identification, perhaps for obvious reasons.

* * *

The religious current in politics and culture does not go unchallenged: it is the subject of open or covert contention in many countries. Turkey is one extreme, where secularism is a founding principle of the state – and one that is upheld by powerful constituencies, confronting the religious orientations of the current government and its supporters. In many respects, however, there is some convergence within Turkish nationalism between the religious and the secular. Egypt is at the other end of the spectrum, where religious discourse and sentiment are so hegemonic that secularists – who include many important figures – are pushed into defensive stances, and often present themselves as advocates of a reformist or liberal Islam. Iran is also most interesting in this respect, in that the theocratic repression and moralistic impositions have spawned widespread disillusion and cynicism, and a desire among many – especially the young – to separate religion from government and culture. Iraq has been largely secular for much of the twentieth century, in the orientations of successive regimes and in its cultural manifestations. The religious current is intertwined with sectarian conflicts aggravated by the closing years of the Ba'th regime and the subsequent invasion. There are now many signs of secularist revival. 'Umma nationalism', however, seems to be ever more dispersed among ideologies, sentiments and movements all over the world, fuelled by American military adventurism and the 'war on terror'.

Notes

Introduction

1 See Zubaida (2003b): 182–219.
2 The most prominent advocates of these themes of multiple or alternative modernities have been writers associated with S. N. Eisenstadt; see Schasemaier et al. (2002), S. N. Eisenstadt (1987) and Salvatore (1997).
3 Eisenstadt (2002): 144.
4 Salvatore (2007): 10.
5 Geertz (1971).
6 Mitchell (2002): 80–122.
7 On these themes, see the subtle analyses in Afary (2009), esp. 111–233.
8 On Abdul-Hamid II's policies and ideology, see Deringil (1998).
9 On the paradoxes of piety, desire and modernity in Iran and Egypt, see Bayat (2007), esp. 136–86. On the cultures of consumption in Egypt, see Abaza (2006), esp. 165–228.
10 The clerics and the moralists are especially incensed about the popularity of St Valentine's Day rituals of cards, flowers and courtship among the young, and keep threatening participants with hellfire, as well as urging authorities to curb the practice.
11 Taylor et al. (1994): 64.
12 'Salafi' designates those who adhere to the principles and examples of *al-salf al-salih*, 'the righteous ancestors'. In the initial age of reform in the nineteenth and earlier twentieth centuries, this term applied to reformers who, ostensibly, revived the principles of the early and original Islam.

More recently, it has come to designate conservative fundamentalists such as the Saudi ulama and jihadist activists.

13 On those themes in relation to France, see the research-based International Crisis Group report (2006).

14 Ramadan (2004). For an incisive discussion of issues of Islam in the West, see Roy (2004): 201–31.

15 See Zubaida (2003b), esp. 182–219.

16 These views were expressed in a widely disseminated and discussed *New York Times* article, 'Why Shariah?' (16 March 2008), and then a book, Feldman (2008). Among the many critical responses to the article, see esp. Said Amir Arjomand's (2008) blog, 'Why Sharia?', *The Immanent Frame*, at <http://blogs.ssrc.org/tif/2008/28/why-sharia/> (30 July 2010).

17 Hoexter et al. (2002).

18 Ibid.: 15.

19 Zubaida (2003b): 109–13. For a biography of Abussu'ud, see Imber (1997).

20 Horii (2002).

21 Marcus (1989): 182–88. The picture of the credit transactions and interest payments that emerges here for Aleppo was not exceptional for Ottoman cities: interest rates of 10 to 12 per cent were reckoned reasonable and enforceable in court; only excessive rates were disapproved of.

22 Sayid Tantawi, former Shaykh al-Azhar, famously allowed the legitimacy of normal interest in a 1989 fatwa. He reviewed the controversies on the subject and the opinions of the reformers in Tantawi (2001).

23 Zubaida (1990): 152–61.

24 Mir-Hosseini (2000) details those debates from a viewpoint championing 'Islamic feminism'. For a more critical approach, see Afary (2009): 292–322.

25 Zubaida (2003b): 147–53, 165–73.

26 Afary (2009): 263–91.

27 El-Rouayheb (2005). See also Afary (2009): 79–108; Najmabadi (2005).

28 Afary (2009): 79–108.

29 Hanioglu (2008): 105.

30 Saliba (1994). See also note 31.

31 Gutas (2002). Note the author's deliberate usage of the term 'Arabic', and not 'Islamic'.

32 Huff (1993). George Saliba's review and the subsequent debate are available at <http://baheyeldin.com/history/toby-huff-1.html>, <http://baheyeldin.com/history/george-saliba-1.html> and <http://baheyeldin.com/history/goerge-saliba-2.html> (2 August 2010). These were in the *Jordanian Review of Inter-Faith Studies*, 2002.

Chapter 1

1 Crone has written extensively on early Islam. See in particular Crone and Cook (1977) and Crone (1980). Hall (1985) offers yet another statement of the 'uniqueness of the West' thesis, with a chapter on Islam (84–110). Mann (1986) advances a conceptual framework for analysis and classification of forms of power in state and society that highlights the success of the West in achieving integration and a balance between the two. Crone has also written a general book (1989) that treads similar ground. Gellner made his own contribution to these themes in the philosophy of history (1988).

2 Sadowski (1993): 17–20.

3 For an earlier critique of Gellner's contrast between Islam and Christianity in terms of their respective involvement in the mechanisms of power, see Asad (1986), which anticipates many of the themes pursued here.

4 Gellner (1983).

5 Gellner (1992). Gellner (1983) is a collection of his essays on the subject. The discussion in this paper concentrates for the most part on the first chapter, 'Flux and Reflux in the Faith of Men' (1–85), which states the general model of Muslim society.

6 al-Azmeh (1982): vii.

7 Ibid.: 1–9. Al-Azmeh's two books on Ibn Khaldun (1981, 1982) are particularly enlightening in this respect. In the former (199–222), al-Azmeh argues that Maghrebi historiography of that period shared in the mythology of the age, which tended to represent events in terms of genealogies and stereotypes of traditional tribal alliances and antagonisms. In fact, tribal designations often had vague or multiple referents. French historians of the Maghreb mostly adopted Ibn Khaldun's chronicles, which fitted in well with their own trans-historical anthropology of 'nomads' and their 'natural' propensities. Gellner carries on in that tradition.

8 Gellner (1983): 40–41.

9 Ibid.: 41–45.

10 Ibid.: 55.

11 Ibid.: 73.

12 Ibid.: 77.

13 Ibid.

14 Ibid.: 55–56.

15 Hall (1985): 89.

16 Gellner (1983): 79.

17 Hall (1985): 107–8.

18 Gibb and Bowen (1957): 122–6.

19 Repp (1977): 277.

20 Heyd (1961); Levy (1971); Chambers (1978).

21 Shaw (1976): 273–77.

22 Ibid.: 170–1.

23 For accounts and discussions of the reforms and the struggles surrounding them, see Heyd (1961), further developed in the volume dedicated to Heyd, Baer, ed. (1971), 'Introduction by the Editor' (1–12) and Levy (1971). For an account of nineteenth-century legal reforms in the Ottoman Empire, see Zubaida (2003b): 121–57.

24 Levy (1971): 15.

25 Ibid.: 19.

26 Ibid.; Heyd (1961).

27 Chambers (1978).

28 Hourani (1968).

29 Ibid.: 48.

30 Ibid.: 50.

31 Ibid.

32 Hanbali is one of the four orthodox Sunni schools of law, alongside Hanafi, Shafi'i and Maliki. It is the most strict literalist school. Ash'ari is the dominant Sunni school of theology.

33 Gellner (1983): 42.

34 Ibid.: 48–51.

35 Ibid.: 115.

36 Ibid.: 50.

37 Birge (1994 [1937]): 13–14.

38 Gellner (1983): 77–81.

39 Ibid.: 78.

40 This fear of the Devil and his traps is shared with Protestantism. Protestant participation in the witch-hunts of seventeenth-century Europe, and later in New England, casts doubt on the Weberian characterization of Protestantism as 'rational' and anti-magic: to persecute witches you must believe in magic!

41 Arberry (1964): CXIII, 668.

42 Mauss (1972).

43 Arberry (1964): LXXII, 611.

44 Gellner (1983): 80.

45 Zubaida (2009): 99–120.

46 Bouhdiba (1982) elaborates on positive attitudes to sexuality. Sabbah (1984) considers the matter from a critical feminist viewpoint, arguing

that the Islamic tradition fetishizes sexuality, denuding it of erotic, affective and intellectual dimensions. Women in this perspective become objects of possession like other riches bestowed by God on favoured male believers. This sexual order is confirmed by the model of Paradise (Sabbah [1984]: 91–97), which, although admitting both men and women, seems to cater only for the sexual pleasure of men, in the form of eternally virgin *houris*. For the purpose of the present discussion, both books confirm the preoccupation with sexuality in the Muslim tradition, the permissive allowances it makes for men's sexuality within generous legal limits, and the continuation of this indulgence into the sacred afterlife.

47 Quran, II, 223, Arberry (1964): 31.

48 Sabbah (1984): 110–17.

49 Ibid.: 93–97

50 Arberry (1964): LVI, 12–22, 560.

51 On the prevalence of homoerotic relations, mostly between men and boys, in Iran, and of male concubinage, see Afary (2009): 79–108; see also the Introduction to this volume.

52 Sabbah (1984): 10–12.

53 See Houtsma et al. (1987 [1913–36]), 'al-Suyuti' entry.

54 Ibid.

55 Waines (1994) tells us that in the tenth century intoxicating beverages were widely prepared and consumed, and their merits for health and gastronomy discussed. Medical treatises, such as those of al-Razi and al-Balkhi, included chapters on wine and its benefits. Al-Razi's book has been printed in successive modern editions, starting in 1888 in Cairo. It was only in the 1985 Beirut edition that the editor penned an introduction denouncing the chapter on wine: 'the offending chapter was excised from the edition, only the chapter title remaining in its allotted place on an otherwise empty page' (Waines 1994: 113). This episode is significant for our later argument that censorious puritanism is a product of recent ideological developments, rather than a feature of historical Islam.

56 For a brief and clear exposition of legal positions and arguments on wine and intoxicants in Muslim jurisprudence, see Hattox (1985): 46–57.

57 Lane (1895): 153.

58 Ibid.

59 Heine (1982); Waines (1994). For more accounts on drinking cultures in more recent contexts, see Chapters 4 and 5.

60 Marcus (1989).

61 Hattox (1985).

62 Rida (1970): fatwa no. 196: 512.

63 Gellner (1983): 80.

64 For debates on early Ottoman history, see Kafadar (1995).

65 Philby (1968).

66 Habib (1978).

67 Holt (1968).

68 Gellner (1992): 5–22.

69 Ibid.: 19.

70 Ibid.: 20.

71 Ibid.: 17.

72 Ibid.: 18.

73 A *mujtahid* is a cleric of sufficiently high rank to deliver independent judgement on matters of dogma and law. *Ijtihad*, the activity of so doing, is a feature of Iranian Shi'ism. Traditional Sunni ulama, though they do similar things, cannot call it ijtihad for doctrinal reasons that need not concern us here. Modernist Sunnis have, for the most part, restored *ijtihad*, but without the institutional setting of the Iranian practice.

74 Khomeini (n.d.).

75 Ibid.: 70–74.

76 Mottahedeh (1985): ch. 5, esp. 182–85.

77 See Haeri (1989) for an excellent exposition on the law and practice of this form of marriage, and its place in the politics and social life of the Islamic Republic. See also Afary (2009): 50–78.

78 Ramazani (1993); Afary (2009): 292–322.

79 See Mallat (1993); Schirazi (1997); Zubaida (2003b): 182–219.

80 Kepel (1985): 172–90.

81 In an interview with *Civil Society*, a human rights newsletter issued in Cairo, Hussein Ahamad Amin, an eminent diplomat and scholar, and a liberal Muslim, had this to say:

> Al-Azhar is traditionally used as a tool by ruling regimes to legitimize their policies. Contemporary history shows Al-Azhar supporting Egyptian President Gamal Abd El-Nasser in his decision to fight Israel, while later on supporting Sadat's peace treaty with that same country.
> (*Civil Society* III(33) September 1994: 27)

He then goes on to say that, after the Iranian Revolution and the subsequent ascendancy of militant Islam, Al-Azhar had to assume greater autonomy from the regime or lose credibility. This was facilitated by an increasingly cautious regime, anxious to prove its Islamic credentials against its radical opponents, and therefore more tolerant of an autonomous Azhar.

82 Zubaida (2009): xiv–xiii, xxv–xxxi.

83 Roussillon (1988); Zubaida (1990).
84 Bilici (1993).

Chapter 2

1 Gibb and Bowen (1950; 1957).
2 Ibid.: II: 70.
3 For an account of this hierarchy, see Gibb and Bowen (1957): 122–26, and Inalcik et al. (1994): 556–61. An illustration of positions, careers and 'nepotism' is afforded by a biography of Ebussu'ud, the Shaykhulislam of Suleyman (Imber [1997]).
4 For an example of *awqaf* in an Ottoman city and its politics, see van Leeuwen (1999); for accounts of *awqaf* in more recent times, see Bilici, ed. (1994).
5 Gibb and Bowen (1957): 171–78.
6 van Leeuwen (1999).
7 On judicial institutions, see Zubaida (2003b): 60–6, Gibb and Bowen (1950/57): 123–37 and Inalcik et al. (1994): 556–61.
8 See the studies in Barnes, ed. (1992); Zubaida (2003b): 104–7; Quataert (2000): 161–3; Birge (1937): 13–14.
9 Naguib Mahfouz's novel *Malhamat al-Harafish* (Epic of the Rabble) (Cairo: Maktabat Misr, 1977) (English translation by Catherine Cobham, *The Harafish* [New York: Doubleday, 1994]) presents a vivid picture of life and politics in the old urban quarters, illustrating the role of local Sufi orders and their shaykhs in local politics.
10 Batatu (1978): 207–23.
11 Burke (1989): 47–48.
12 Ibid.: 48.
13 al-Jabarti (n.d.), 1: 621–2.
14 See the history of the Mahdiyya by Holt (1970).
15 See Makdisi (2000) for an analysis of these events in Lebanon, and Fawaz (1994) on Lebanon and Damascus.
16 On the politics of Aleppo in the eighteenth century, see Marcus (1989) and Thieck (1985).
17 McGowan in Inalcik et al. (1994): xx–xx.
18 Baer (1977).
19 Ibid.: 228–42.
20 Raymond (1973): 432–33.
21 Walzer (1966): 1.
22 Ibid.: 16.
23 On the economic, legal and administrative transformations in Ottoman

lands, see Quataert (1994; 2000), Deringil (1998), Mardin (1962), Berkes (1998 [1964]) and Zubaida (2003b: 121-57). On Iran, see Algar (1969), Abrahamian (1982) and Keddie (1981).

24 Berkes (1998 [1964]): 94-99; Zubaida (2003b): 125-40.

25 Deringil (1998).

26 Quataert (2000): 110-39.

27 Berkes (1998 [1964]): 277-78; Mardin (1989): 136-38.

28 Hourani (1983): 161-92, 271-73; Berkes (1998 [1964]): 169-72.

29 Note that the Young Ottomans are distinct from the later Young Turks. The first were a group of modern intellectuals and reformers that started in the 1860s; the second were the Committee of Union and Progress, authors of the constitutional revolution of 1908.

30 The classic work on the Young Ottomans and their milieu is Mardin (1962).

31 On Abdul-Hamid's reign, see Deringil (1998).

32 Baer (1968): 142-47.

33 This is part of the continuing vitality of the bazaars in Iranian cities to the present. See Mottahedeh (1985): 345-56; Abrahamian (1982): 432-33.

34 Quataert (1994): 765.

35 On the Young Turks, or Committee for Union and Progress, see Ahmad (1969).

36 Quataert (1994): 769.

37 Berkes (1998 [1964]): 278.

38 Ibid.: 277.

39 Cole (1993): 115-26.

40 Baer (1968).

41 For accounts of Iranian politics, society and religion from the later nineteenth century, see Algar (1969), Keddie (1966; 1972) and Martin (1989b).

42 Martin (1989a): 165-200; Enayat (1982): 164-69.

43 Martin (1989a).

44 Abrahamian (1982): 50-101.

45 Abrahamian (1968): 201-7.

46 Katouzian (1999).

47 Abrahamian (1968): 202.

48 Ibid.: 203 and Abrahamian (1982): 281-325.

49 On the politics of the Mossadegh era, see Katouzian (1999) and Abrahamian (1982): 261-80.

50 Abrahamian (1982): 270-72.

51 For accounts of this episode, see Moin (1999), and Algar (1969).

52 Abrahamian (1982): 496-524; Zubaida (2009): 64-82.

53 See Chapter 6 for an expansion on this theme.

54 There is a vast amount of literature on the Iranian Revolution and the Islamic Republic. See particularly Abrahamian (1993), Arjomand (1988), Keddie (1981) and Zubaida (2009): 1–63.

55 For an analysis of the situation in Iran at the time of writing, see Ali Ansari (2010), 'The Revolution will be Mercantilized', *National Interest Online*, 11 February, at <www.nationalinterest.org/Article.aspx?id=22602> (5 August 2010).

56 See Batatu (1978): 709–925, and Farouk-Sluglett and Sluglett (1990). See also Zubaida (1991).

57 Baram (1997): 110–26.

58 Owen (2004): 132–33 .

59 Keinle (2001): 51–67.

60 Owen (2004): 134–36.

61 Singerman (1995).

62 See also Ismail (2006) for a study of popular and informal politics in modern Cairo.

63 Qutb (1990); Moussalli (1992).

64 For an expansion of this typology of Islamism, see Zubaida (2000).

65 Kepel (2002): 276–98.

66 The main account of the formation and development of the Muslim Brotherhood is Mitchell (1969). For subsequent developments see Kepel (2002): 43–80, 276–98.

67 Roy (1994) is further developed in Roy (2004).

68 There is a voluminous amount of literature on jihadism and the 'war on terror'. Roy (2004: 290–325) is one of the most cogent and informative. See also Burke (2003).

69 For France, see International Crisis Group (2006): 5, which suggests that a secular outlook is still dominant among Muslims in France.

70 Roy (2004): 100–200.

Chapter 3

1 For a discussion of those strands in social theory, see Anderson (1979): 462–550.

2 On Moroccan cities, see Naciri (1986): 249–70.

3 Kafadar (1995): 1–2.

4 Sherrard (1973): 182–99.

5 On Pontic Greeks, see Ascherson (1996): 176–96.

6 Personal communication.

7 On population movements in the nineteenth century, see Quataert (1994): 777–97.

8 On the Young Ottomans, see Mardin (1962). On Afghani and Abduh, see Hourani (1983).

9 Zubaida (2003b): 121–57.

10 Hussein (1937).

11 Parla (1985).

12 Stoke (1992).

13 Zubaida (2004): 407–20.

14 Terzibasoglu (2001).

15 Cagaptay (2006), 61–82.

16 van Bruinessen (1996): 7–10.

17 On the history and politics of the shrine cities, see Cole (2002).

18 See Deringil (1990).

19 For a history of Iraqi Shi'a and their differences from their Iranian co-religionists, see Nakash (1994).

20 Sha'ban (2002).

21 Zubaida (2005).

22 See Zubaida (2006).

23 al-Jawahiri (1988).

Chapter 4

1 Two collections of essays on cosmopolitanism are Meijer, ed. (1999), and Vertovec and Cohen, eds (2002). Each include an essay by the present author.

2 al-Jabarti (n.d.), vol. 1: 633–34.

3 See Hourani (1983): 245–59.

4 Quataert (2000): 110–39.

5 See Mardin (1962).

6 For an exposition of Namik Kemal's ideological formulations, see Berkes (1998 [1964]): 208–22.

7 The most comprehensive source on freemasonry is Zarcone (1993), esp. 177–300. An unusually objective, though not always accurate, modern Arabic account is al-Wardi (1992): 329–83 (see also 266–328).

8 Zarcone (1993): 98–99.

9 Ibid.: 208–10.

10 Ibid.: 209.

11 Ibid.: 99.

12 Ibid.: 149–54.

13 The Donmeh are Jews who converted to Islam in the seventeenth century, after the failure and conversion of Sabbatai Sevi, the so-called False Messiah. Though formally Sunni Muslim, they divided into distinct sects and communities, and were prominently present in Ottoman Salonica. Many of their intelligentsia became enthusiastic supporters of liberal constitutionalism and then of the Kemalist Republic.

14 See Mazower (2004): 252–57.

15 Ibid.: 272–85; Zarcone (1993): 241–70.

16 Zarcone (1993): 241.

17 Privileges and immunities granted to nationals of favoured countries.

18 Zarcone (1993): 243; Mazower (2004): 272–73.

19 Mazower (2004): 282–85.

20 Hanioglu (2008): 150–202.

21 Zarcone (1993): 250–54.

22 Hanioglu (2008): 167–77.

23 Zarcone (1993): 288–90; al-Wardi (1992): 276–80.

24 Which was among al-Afghani's papers that were apparently kept in the archives of the Iranian parliament, and published in a book in 1963, cited by al-Wardi (1992): 276, fn. 22.

25 Zarcone (1993): 289.

26 Ibid.: 288; al-Wardi (1992): 278.

27 al-Wardi (1992): 322–33.

28 Ibid.: 283–6; 313–18.

29 In particular, Kedourie (1997 [1966]).

30 Zarcone (1993): 301–26.

31 al-Wardi (1992): 334.

32 Ibid.: 379–83.

33 Ibid.: 377–78.

34 Goodwin (2006 [1994]): 87–89.

35 Kafadar (1995): 150.

36 Georgeon (2002): 7–30.

37 Ibid.: 17.

38 Ibid.: 19–23.

39 Related in Navaro-Yashin (2002): 19.

40 See Fahmy (2004a, 2004b), and Mabro (2004).

41 Hussein (1937).

42 A brief account appears in a booklet accompanying the recording *Congres du Caire 1932*, Muhammad al Qubbanji, Dawud Hosni, Muhammad Ghanim et al. (1988), 2 vols, compact disc, France: Édition Bibliothèque Nationale, APN 88–9, 10: 33–37. See also Racy (2003).

43 Evans-Pritchard delivered these lectures at the Faculty of Arts at the Egyptian (later Cairo) University after his appointment there in 1932. A later version was published as Evans-Pritchard (1965).

44 See Zürcher (1993): 231–322.

45 These themes in German Romantic nationalism and its emphasis on language are recounted in Kedourie (1993 [1960]), esp. 44–86.

46 There is extensive literature on the Muslim Brotherhood. See the now classic Mitchell (1969) and Kepel (1985).

47 See Chapter 6.

48 See Human Rights Watch (2004).

49 For interesting insights in some of these areas, see Sennett (2002): 42–47.

Chapter 5

1 Habermas (1989); a collection of critiques and debates followed in Calhoun, ed. (1992).

2 Hoexter et al. (2002).

3 Ibid.

4 Mahfouz (1994, 1999).

5 For a description of an *imaret* in Konya, see Faroqhi (1984).

6 Hattox (1985).

7 The Arabic word for coffee, *qahwa*, previously referred to wine.

8 Marcus (1989): 229–37.

9 Pamuk (2002).

10 Marcus (1989): 231.

11 See Goodwin (2006): 87–89.

12 On the debauchery of judges and dignitaries, see Tyan (1960): 293–332.

13 The first modern printing of this book was in Bulaq 1888, Beirut edition in 1985.

14 See Waines (1994): 111–26.

15 Cook (2003).

16 Ibid.: 57.

17 Cook (2003): 58.

18 Nafisi (2003).

19 Anderson (1983).

20 Mannheim (1960 [1936]).

21 See Berkes (1998 [1964]): 270–78.

22 Cole (1993): 115–26.

23 For a discussion on Rida, see Dallal (2000) and Zubaida (forthcoming).

24 See Armbrust (1996) and Armbrust, ed. (2000).

25 See Bayat (2007): 136–86.
26 Schirazi (1997).
27 Ibid.: 171–72.
28 Abaza (2006).

Chapter 6

1 Quoted in Mortimer (1982): 271.
2 Lutfi al-Sayid, quoted in Ahmad (1960): 61.
3 On Abduh and the reform movement, see Hourani (1983): 130–60.
4 On Afghani, see Hourani (1983): 103–29 and Keddie (1983); see also Chapter 5.
5 Quotes from Hourani (1983): 357.
6 On the debates on language, nation and religion, see Suleiman (2003).
7 Rogan (2009): 123–32.
8 Haim (1962): 22–23.
9 Hourani (1983), 239–44.
10 al-Bishry (1998): 52.
11 al-Bishry (1998).
12 Qutb's ideas on these issues are expressed in Qutb (1990). See also Kepel (1985), Moussalli (1992) and Zubaida (2009): 51–55.
13 Sivan (1997): 211.
14 Ibid.: 226–28.
15 On Ali Bulac, see Meeker (1991) and Zubaida (1996).
16 On Gokalp, see Davison (1995).
17 Hanafi and Shafi'i are two of the four Orthodox Sunni schools of law, mutually accepting each other as different but equally valid.
18 Zubaida (1996); Cagaptay (2006).
19 For a general history of modern Egypt, see Marsot (1984) and Rogan (2009): 61–84, 175–210, 277–318.
20 Hussein (1937); Hourani (1983): 324–40.
21 On some of these themes in the history of modern Iran, see Abrahamian (1982), Keddie (1981) and Mottahedeh (1985).
22 Zubaida (1997).
23 For a general survey and analysis of the political history of the Middle East at these junctures, see Owen (2004).
24 Fanon (1925–61) became a cult figure in the 1960s and 1970s. His celebrated book *The Wretched of the Earth*, published in 1961, was highly influential.
25 Rahnama (1998); Zubaida (2009): 20–34.

26 Zubaida (1988): 1–32.

27 Katouzian (1999).

28 Afary (2009): 263–322 contains subtle accounts and analyses of these movements from the left to Islamic authenticity, especially with regard to women and sexuality.

29 Afary (2009): 274–77.

30 Zubaida (2009): 20–26.

31 *The Protocols* purports to be a record of the conspiratorial deliberations of Jewish elders, including the Rothschilds, on plans to dominate the world by instigating wars and revolutions. It was shown to be a forgery published by the Tsarist secret police in Russia at the turn of the twentieth century. It has since been widely revived as a prop to anti-Jewish sentiments, notably in the Middle East in recent times.

32 Mardin (1989).

Bibliography

Abaza, Mona (2006), *Changing Consumer Cultures in Modern Egypt: Cairo's Urban Reshaping*, Leiden: Brill.

Abrahamian, Ervand (1968), 'The Crowd in Iranian Politics 1905-1953', *Past and Present* 41: 184-210.

—— (1982), *Iran Between Two Revolutions*, Princeton, NJ: Princeton University Press.

—— (1993), *Khomeinism: Essays on the Islamic Republic*, London: I.B.Tauris.

Afary, Janet (2009), *Sexual Politics in Modern Iran*, Cambridge: Cambridge University Press.

Ahmad, Feroz (1969), *The Young Turks: The Committee for Union and Progress in Turkish Politics, 1908-1914*, Oxford: Clarendon Press.

Ahmad, Jamal Mohammed (1960), *The Intellectual Origins of Egyptian Nationalism*, Oxford: Oxford University Press.

Al Qubbanji, Muhammad, Hosni, Dawud and Ghanim, Muhammad et al. (1988), *Congres du Caire 1932*, 2 vols, compact disc, France: Édition Bibliothèque Nationale, APN 88-9, 10: 33-37.

Algar, Hamid (1969), *Religion and the State in Iran, 1785-1906: The Role of the Ulama in the Qajar Period*, Berkeley: University of California Press.

Amin, Hussain Ahmad (1994), 'Interview', *Civil Society* 3 (33): 27.

Anderson, Benedict (1983), *Imagined Communities: Reflections on the Origins and Spread of Nationalism*, London: Verso.

Anderson, Perry (1979) *Lineages of the Absolutist State*, London: Verso.

Ansari, Ali (2010), 'The Revolution will be Mercantilized', *National Interest Online*, 11 February, available at <www.nationalinterest.org/Article.aspx?id=22602> (5 August 2010).

Arberry, J. A. (1964), *The Koran Interpreted*, Oxford: Oxford University Press.

Arjomand, Said Amir (1981), 'The Ulama's Traditionalist Opposition to Parliamentarism', *Middle Eastern Studies* 17 (2): 174-89.

—— (1984), *The Shadow of God and the Hidden Imam: Religion, Political Order and*

Societal Change in Shi'ite Iran from the Beginning to 1890, Chicago: University of Chicago Press.

—— (1988), *The Turban for the Crown: The Islamic Revolution in Iran*, Oxford: Oxford University Press.

Armbrust, Walter (1996), *Mass Culture and Modernism in Egypt*, Cambridge: Cambridge University Press.

—— ed. (2000), *Mass Mediations: New Approaches to Popular Culture in the Middle East and Beyond*, Berkeley: University of California Press.

Asad, Talal (1986), *The Idea of an Anthropology of Islam*, Washington, DC: Center for Contemporary Arab Studies, Georgetown University.

Ascherson, Neal (1996), *Black Sea: The Birthplace of Civilisation and Barbarism*, London: Vintage.

al-Azmeh, Aziz (1981), *Ibn Khaldun in Modern Scholarship: A Study in Orientalism*, London: Third World Centre for Research and Publishing.

—— (1982), *Ibn Khaldun*, London: Routledge.

Baer, Gabriel (1968), 'Social Change in Egypt: 1821-1962', in P. M. Holt, ed., *Political and Social Change in Modern Egypt*, London: Oxford University Press: 135-61.

—— ed. (1971), *The Ulama in Modern History: Studies in Memory of Professor Uriel Heyd*, Jerusalem: Israel Oriental Society.

—— (1977), 'Popular Revolt in Ottoman Cairo', *Der Islam* 54 (2): 213-42.

Baram, Amatzia (1997), 'Neo-Tribalism in Iraq: Saddam Hussein's Tribal Policies 1991-96', *International Journal of Middle East Studies* 29: 1-31.

Barnes, John Robert, ed. (1992), *Introduction to Religious Foundations in the Ottoman Empire*, Berkeley: University of California Press.

Batatu, Hanna (1978), *The Old Social Classes and the Revolutionary Movements of Iraq: A Study of Iraq's Old Landed and Commercial Classes, and of its Communists, Ba'thists and Free Officers*, Princeton, NJ: Princeton University Press.

Bayat, Asef (2007), *Making Islam Democratic: Social Movements and the Post-Islamist Turn*, Berkeley: University of California Press.

Berkes, Niyazi (1998 [1964]), *The Development of Secularism in Turkey*, London: Hurst.

Bilici, Faruk (1993), 'Sociabilité et expression politique islamistes: les nouveaux waqfs en Turquie', *Revue Francaise de Science Politique* 43 (3): 412-34.

—— ed. (1994), *Le waqf dans le monde musulman contemporain (XIXe–XXe siecles): fonctions sociales, économiques et politiques*, Istanbul: Institut Français d'Études Anatoliennes/Edition Isis.

Birge, John Kingsley (1994 [1937]), *The Bektashi Order of Dervishes*, London: Luzac.

al-Bishry, Tariq (1998), *Bayna al-islam wa-al-'uruba: fi al-mas'alah al-islamiyah al-mu'asirah*, [Between Islam and Arabism: on the current Islamic question], Cairo: Dar al-Shuruq.

Bouhdiba, Abdelwahab (1982), *Sexuality in Islam*, London: Routledge.

Burke, Edmund (1989), 'Towards a History of Urban Collective Action in the Middle East: Continuities and Change, 1750-1980', in Kenneth Brown, Bernard Hourcade, Michele Jole, Claude Liauzu, Peter Sluglett and Sami Zubaida, eds, *État, ville et mouvements sociaux au Maghreb et au Moyen-Orient* (Urban Crises and Social Movements in the Middle East), Paris: L'Harmattan: 47-48.

Burke, Jason (2003), *Al-Qaeda: Casting a Shadow of Terror*, London: I.B.Tauris.

Cagaptay, Soner (2006), 'Passage to Turkishness: Immigration and Religion in Modern Turkey', in Haldun Gulalp, ed., *Citizenship and Ethnic Conflict: Challenging the Nation-State*, London: Routledge: 61-82.

Calhoun, Craig, ed. (1992), *Habermas and the Public Sphere*, Cambridge, MA: MIT Press.

Chambers, Richard L. (1978), 'The Ottoman Ulama and the Tanzimat', in Nikki R. Keddie, ed., *Scholars, Saints and Sufis*, Berkeley: University of California Press: 33-46.

Chehabi, H. E. (1991), 'Religion and Politics in Iran: How Theocratic is the Islamic Republic?', *Daedalus* 120 (3): 69-91.

Cole, Juan (1993), *Colonialism and Revolution in the Middle East: Social and Cultural Origins of Egypt's Urabi Movement*, Princeton, NJ: Princeton University Press.

—— (2002), *Sacred Space and Holy War: The Politics, Culture and History of Shi'ite Islam*, London: I.B.Tauris.

Cook, Michael (2003), *Forbidding Wrong in Islam*, Cambridge: Cambridge University Press.

Crone, Patricia. (1980), *Slaves on Horses: The Evolution of the Islamic Polity*, Cambridge: Cambridge University Press.

—— (1989), *Preindustrial Societies*, Oxford: Blackwell.

Crone, Patricia and Michael Cook (1977), *Hagarism: The Making of the Islamic World*, Cambridge: Cambridge University Press.

Dallal, Ahmad (2000), 'Appropriating the Past: Twentieth-Century Reconstruction of Pre-Modern Islamic Thought', *Islamic Law and Society* 7 (3): 325-58.

Davison, Andrew (1995), 'Secularization and Modernization in Turkey: The Ideas of Ziya Gokalp', *Economy and Society* 24 (2): 189-224.

Deringil, Selim (1990), 'The Struggle Against Shiism in Hamidian Iraq', *Die Welt des Islam* XXX: 45-62.

—— (1998), *The Well-Protected Domains: Ideology and the Legitimation of Power in the Ottoman Empire, 1876-1909*, London: I.B.Tauris.

Eisenstadt, Shmuel N. (1987), *Patterns of Modernity*, London: Pinter.

—— (2002) 'Concluding Remarks', in Miriam Hoexter, Shmuel N. Eisenstadt and Nehemia Leftzion, eds, *The Public Sphere in Muslim Societies*, Albany: SUNY Press: 139-62.

El-Rouayheb, Khaled (2005), *Before Homosexuality in the Arab-Islamic World*, Chicago: Chicago University Press.

Enayat, Hamid (1982), *Modern Islamic Political Thought: The Response of Shi'i and Sunni Muslims to the Twentieth Century*, London: Macmillan.

Evans-Pritchard, Edward E. (1965), *Theories of Primitive Religion*, Oxford: Oxford University Press.

Fahmy, K. (2004a), 'Towards a History of Alexandria', in Anthony Hirst and Michael Silk, eds, *Alexandria, Real and Imagined*, Aldershot: Ashgate: 281-306.

—— (2004b) 'For Cavafy with Love and Squalor: Some Critical Notes on the History and Historiography of Modern Alexandria', in Anthony Hirst and Michael Silk, eds, *Alexandria, Real and Imagined*, Aldershot: Ashgate: 263-80.

'Egyptian Literary Images of Alexandria', in Anthony Hirst and Michael Silk, eds, *Alexandria, Real and Imagined*, Aldershot: Ashgate: 307–22.

Fanon, Frantz (2006 [1961]), *The Wretched of the Earth*, London: Pluto Press.

Faroqhi, Suraiya (1984), *Towns and Townsmen in Ottoman Anatolia: Trades, Crafts and Food Production in an Urban Setting, 1520–1650*, Cambridge: Cambridge University Press.

Farouk-Sluglett, Marion and Peter Sluglett (1990), *Iraq since 1958: From Revolution to Dictatorship*, London and New York: I.B.Tauris.

Fawaz, Leila (1994), *An Occasion for War: Civil Conflict in Lebanon and Damascus in 1860*, London: I.B.Tauris.

Feldman, Noah (2008), *The Fall and Rise of the Islamic State*, Princeton, NJ: Princeton University Press.

Geertz, Clifford (1971), *Islam Observed: Religious Development in Morocco and Indonesia*, Chicago: Chicago University Press.

Gellner, Ernest (1983), *Muslim Society*, Cambridge: Cambridge University Press.

—— (1988), *Plough, Sword and Book: The Structure of Human History*, London: Collins.

—— (1992), *Postmodernism, Reason and Religion*, London: Routledge.

Georgeon, François (2002), 'Ottomans and Drinkers: The Consumption of Alcohol in Istanbul in the Nineteenth Century', in Eugene Rogan, ed., *Outside In: On the Margins of the Modern Middle East*, London: I.B.Tauris: 7–30.

Gibb, H. A. R. and Harold Bowen (1950), *Islamic Society and the West*, vol. I, part 1, Oxford: Oxford University Press.

—— (1957), *Islamic Society and the West*, vol. II, part 2, Oxford: Oxford University Press.

Goodwin, Godfrey (2006), *The Janissaries*, London: Saqi.

Gutas, Dimitri (2002), 'The Study of Arabic Philosophy in the Twentieth Century: An Essay on the Historiography of Arabic Philosophy', *British Journal of Middle Eastern Studies* 29 (1): 5–26.

Habermas, Jürgen (1989), *The Structural Transformation of the Public Sphere*, Oxford: Polity.

Habib, John S. (1978), *Ibn Sa'ud's Warriors Of Islam: The Ikhwan of Najd and Their Role in the Creation of the Sa'udi Kingdom, 1910–1930*, Leiden: Brill.

Haeri, Shahla (1989), *Law of Desire: Temporary Marriage in Shi'i Iran*, London: I.B.Tauris.

Haim, Sylvia, ed. (1962), *Arab Nationalism: An Anthology*, Berkeley: University of California Press.

Hall, John A. (1985), *Powers and Liberties: The Causes and Consequences of the Rise of the West*, Harmondsworth: Penguin.

Hanioglu, Sukru (2008), *A Brief History of the Late Ottoman Empire*, Princeton, NJ: Princeton University Press.

Hattox, Ralph S. (1985), *Coffee and Coffeehouses: The Origins of a Social Beverage in the Medieval Near East*, Seattle: University of Washington Press.

Heine, Peter (1982), *Weinstudien: Untechungen zu Anbau, Produktion und Konsum des Weins im arabisch-islamischen Mittelalter*, Wiesbaden: Harrassowitz.

Heyd, Uriel (1961), 'The Ottoman Ulama and Westernization in the time of Selim III and Mahmud II', in Uriel Heyd, ed., *Studies in Islamic History*, Jerusalem: Magnus Press: 63–96.

Hoexter, Miriam, Shmuel N. Eisenstadt and Nehemia Leftzion, eds (2002), *The Public Sphere in Muslim Societies*, Albany: SUNY Press.

Holt, P. M., ed. (1968), *Political and Social Change in Modern Egypt*, London: Oxford University Press.

—— (1970), *The Mahdist State in the Sudan, 1881–1898: A Study of its Origins, Development and Overthrow*, Oxford: Oxford University Press.

Horii, Satoe (2002), 'Reconsideration of Legal Devices (*Hiyal*) in Islamic Jurisprudence: The Hanafis and the "Exits" (*Makharij*)', *Islamic Law and Society* 9 (3): 312–57.

Hourani, Albert (1968), 'Ottoman Reforms and the Politics of Notables', in William Roe Polk and Richard L. Chambers, eds, *Beginnings of Modernization in the Middle East: The Nineteenth Century*, Chicago: Chicago University Press: 41–68.

—— (1983), *Arabic Thought in the Liberal Age, 1798–1939*, Cambridge: Cambridge University Press.

Houtsma, Martijn Theodoor et al., eds. (1987 [1913–38]) *The Encyclopædia of Islam: A Dictionary of the Geography, Ethnography and Biography of the Muhammadan Peoples*, 4 vols. and Suppl., vol. VII, entry on 'Al-Suyuti', Leiden: Brill: 273–75.

Huff, Toby (1993), *The Rise of Early Modern Science: Islam, China and the West*, Cambridge: Cambridge University Press.

Human Rights Watch (2004), *In A Time of Torture: The Assault on Justice In Egypt's Crackdown on Homosexual Conduct*, 29 February, New York and London: Human Rights Watch. Available at <http://www.hrw.org/en/reports/2004/02/29/time-torture> (8 August 2010).

Hussein, Taha (1937), *Mustaqbal al-Thaqafa fi Misr*, Cairo: Matba'at al-Ma'arif.

Imber, Colin (1997), *Ebu's-Su'ud: The Islamic Legal Tradition*, Edinburgh: Edinburgh University Press.

Inalcik, Halil, Suraiya Faroqhi, Bruce McGowan, Donald Quataert and Sevket Pamuk (1994), *An Economic and Social History of the Ottoman Empire, vol. 2: 1600–1914*, Cambridge: Cambridge University Press.

International Crisis Group (2006), *France and Its Muslims: Riots, Jihadism and Depoliticisation*, Brussels: IRG.

Ismail, Salwa (2006), *Political Life in Cairo's New Quarters*, Minneapolis: University of Minnesota Press.

Jabar, Falah (2003), 'Sheikhs and Ideologues: Deconstruction and Reconstruction of Tribes under Patrimonial Totalitarianism in Iraq', in Falah Jabar and Hosham Dawod, *Tribes and Power: Nationalism and Ethnicity in the Middle East*, London: Saqi: 69–109.

Jabar, Falah and Hosham Dawod (2003), *Tribes and Power: Nationalism and Ethnicity in the Middle East*, London: Saqi.

al-Jabarti, Abdul-Rahman (n.d.), *Tarikh 'Aja'ib al-Athar fi'l-Tarajim w'al-Akhbar*, 3 vols, Beirut: Dar al-Jil.

al-Jawahiri, Muhammad Mahdi (1988), *Dhikrayati* ('My Memoirs'), vol. 1, Damascus: Dar al-Rafidain.

Kafadar, Cemal. (1995), *Between Two Worlds: The Construction of the Ottoman State*, Berkeley: University of California Press.

Katouzian, Homa (1999), *Musaddiq and the Struggle for Power in Iran*, London: I.B.Tauris.

Keddie, Nikki R. (1966), *Religion and Rebellion in Iran: The Iranian Tobacco Protest of 1891–1892*, London: Cass.

—— (1972), 'The Roots of the Ulama's Power in Modern Iran', in Nikki R. Keddie, ed., *Scholars, Saints and Sufis: Muslim Religious Institutions since 1500*, Berkeley: University of California Press: 211–230.

—— (1981), *Roots of Revolution: An Interpretive History of Modern Iran*, New Haven: Yale University Press.

—— (1983), *An Islamic Response to Imperialism: Politics and Religion in the Writings of Sayyid Jamal Al-Din 'Al-Afghani'*, Berkeley: University of California Press.

Kedourie, Elie (1993 [1960]), *Nationalism*, Oxford: Blackwell.

—— (1997 [1966]), *Afghani and Abduh: An Essay on Religious Unbelief and Political Activism in Modern Islam*, London: Cass.

Keinle, Eberhard (2001), *A Grand Delusion: Democracy and Economic Reform in Egypt*, London: I.B.Tauris.

Kepel, Gilles (1985), *The Prophet and Pharaoh: Muslim Extremism in Egypt*, London: Saqi.

—— (2002), *Jihad: The Trail of Political Islam*, transl. A. Roberts, London: I.B.Tauris.

Khomeini, Ayatullah R. (n.d.), *Al-Hukuma Al-Islamiyya: Wilayat al-Faqih*, Beirut: Dar-ul-Tali'ah.

Lane, Edward W. (1895), *An Account of the Manners and Customs of the Modern Egyptians Written in Egypt During the Years 1833–1835*, London and the Hague: East–West Publications.

Laoust, Henri. (1971), 'Ibn Taymiyya', in *Encyclopedia of Islam*, vol. III, Leiden: Brill: 951–55.

Levy, Avigdor (1971), 'The Ottoman Ulama and Military Reforms of Sultan Mahmud II', in Gabriel Baer, ed., *The Ulama in Modern History: Studies in Memory of Professor Uriel Heyd*, Jerusalem: Israel Oriental Society: 179–85.

Mabro, Robert (2004), 'Egyptian Literary Images of Alexandria', in Anthony Hirst and Michael Silk, eds, *Alexandria, Real and Imagined*, Aldershot: Ashgate: 307–22.

Mahfouz, Naguib (1977), *Malhamat al-Harafish* (Epic of the Rabble), Cairo: Maktabat Misr; English transl. C. Cobham (1994), *The Harafish*, New York: Doubleday.

—— (1999) *Awlad Haretna*, Cairo: Dar Misr [1959]; English transl. P. Stewart, *Children of Gebelawi*, New York: Doubleday.

Makdisi, Ussama (2000), *The Culture of Sectarianism: Community, History and Violence in Nineteenth-Century Ottoman Lebanon*, Berkeley: University of California Press.

Mallat, Chibli (1993), *The Renewal of Islamic Law*, Cambridge: Cambridge University Press.

Mann, Michael (1986), *The Sources of Social Power*, vol. I, Cambridge: Cambridge University Press.

Mannheim, Karl (1960 [1936]), *Ideology and Utopia*, London: Routledge.

Marcus, Abraham (1989), *The Middle East on the Eve of Modernity: Aleppo in the Eighteenth Century*, New York: Columbia University Press.

Mardin, Şerif. (1962), *The Genesis of Young Ottoman Thought: A Study in the Modernization of Turkish Political Ideas*, Princeton, NJ: Princeton University Press.
—— (1989), *Religion and Social Change in Modern Turkey: The Case of Bediuzzaman Said Nursi*, Albany: SUNY Press.
Marsot, Afaf Lutfi al-Sayyid (1984), *Egypt in the Reign of Muhammad Ali*, Cambridge: Cambridge University Press.
Martin, V. A. (1989a), 'Shaikh Fazlallah Nuri and the Iranian Revolution', *Middle Eastern Studies* 23 (1): 40–41.
—— (1989b), *Islam and Modernism: The Iranian Revolution of 1906*, London: I.B.Tauris.
Mauss, Marcel (1972), *A General Theory of Magic*, London: Routledge.
Mazower, Mark (2004), *Salonica: City of Ghosts: Christians, Muslims and Jews 1430–1950*, London: HarperCollins.
Meeker, Michael E. (1991), 'The New Muslim Intellectuals in the Republic of Turkey', in Richard Tapper, ed., *Islam in Modern Turkey: Religion, Politics and Literature in a Secular State*, London: I.B.Tauris: 130–46.
Meijer, Roel, ed. (1999), *Cosmopolitanism, Identity and Authenticity in the Middle East*, London: Curzon Press.
Mir-Hosseini, Ziba (2000), *Islam and Gender: The Religious Debate in Contemporary Iran*, London: I.B.Tauris.
Mitchell, Richard P. (1969), *The Society of Muslim Brothers*, Oxford: Oxford University Press.
Mitchell, Timothy (2002), *Rule of Experts: Egypt, Techno-Politics, Modernity*, Berkeley: University of California Press.
Moin, Baqer (1999), *Khomeini: Life of the Ayatollah*, London: I.B.Tauris.
Mortimer, Edward (1982), *Faith and Power: The Politics of Islam*, London: Faber.
Mottahedeh, Roy (1985), *The Mantle of the Prophet: Religion and Politics in Iran*, Harmondsworth: Penguin.
Moussalli, Ahmad S. (1992), *Radical Islamic Fundamentalism: The Ideological and Political Discourse of Sayyid Qutb*, Beirut: American University of Beirut Press.
Naciri, M. (1986), 'Regard sur l'évolution de la citadinité au Maroc', in Kenneth Brown et al., eds, *Middle Eastern Cities in Comparative Perspective*, London: Ithaca: 249–70.
Naff, Thomas and Roger Owen, eds (1977), *Studies in Eighteenth-Century Islamic History*, Carbondale and Edwardsville: Southern Illinois University Press.
Nafisi, Azar (2003), *Reading Lolita in Tehran: A Story of Love, Books and Revolution*, London: I.B.Tauris.
Najmabadi, Afsaneh (2005), *Women with Moustaches and Men without Beards: Gender and Sexual Anxieties of Iranian Modernity*, Berkeley: University of California Press.
Nakash, Yitzhak (1994) *The Shi'is of Iraq*, Princeton, NJ: Princeton University Press.
Navaro-Yashin, Yael (2002), *Faces of the State: Secularism and Public Life in Turkey*, Princeton, NJ: Princeton University Press.
Owen, Roger, (2004) *State, Power and Politics in the Making of the Modern Middle East*, London: Routledge.
Pamuk, Orhan (2002), *My Name is Red*, transl. Erdag Gokner, London: Faber.

Parla, Taha (1985), *The Social and Political Theories of Ziya Gokalp 1876-1924*, Leiden: Brill.

Philby, H. St John (1968), *Sa'udi Arabia*, Beirut: Librarie de Liban.

Quataert, Donald (1994), 'The Age of Reforms, 1812-1914', in Inalcik, Halil, Suraiya Faroqhi, Bruce McGowan, Donald Quataert and Sevket Pamuk (1994), *An Economic and Social History of the Ottoman Empire, vol. 2: 1600-1914*, Cambridge: Cambridge University Press: 759-933.

—— (2000), *The Ottoman Empire, 1700-1992*, Cambridge: Cambridge University Press.

Qutb, Sayyid (1990), *Milestones*, Indianapolis: American Trust Publications.

Racy, A. J. (2003), *Making Music in the Arab World: The Culture and Artistry of Tarab*, Cambridge: Cambridge University Press.

Rahnama, Ali (1998), *An Islamic Utopian: A Political Biography of Ali Shari'ati*, London: I.B.Tauris.

Ramadan, Tariq (2004), *Western Muslims and the Future of Islam*, Oxford: Oxford University Press.

Ramazani, Nesta (1993), 'Women in Iran: The Revolutionary Ebb and Flow', *Middle East Journal* 47 (3): 407-28.

Raymond, André (1968), 'Quartiers et mouvements populaires au Caire au XVIIIème siècle', in P. M. Holt, ed., *Political and Social Change in Modern Egypt*, London: Oxford University Press: 104-16.

—— (1999), *Artisans et commerçants au Caire au XVIIIe siècle*, 2 vols, Damascus: Institut Français d'Études Arabes de Damas [1973], reprinted Cairo: Institut Français d'Archéologie Orientale.

Repp, R. C. (1977), 'The Altered Nature of the Role of the Ulama', in Thomas Naff and Roger Owen, eds, *Studies in Eighteenth-Century Islamic History*, Carbondale and Edwardsville: Southern Illinois University Press: 277-87.

Rida, Rashid (1970), *Fatawa al-Imam Muhammad Rashid Rida*, Beirut: Dar Al-Kitab al-Jadid.

Rogan, Eugene (2009), *The Arabs: A History*, London: Allen Lane.

Roussillon, Alain (1988), *Sociétés islamiques de placement des fonds et 'ouverture économique'*, Cairo: Dossiers de CEDEJ.

Roy, Olivier (1994), *The Failure of Political Islam*, transl. Carol Volk, Cambridge, MA: Harvard University Press.

—— (2004), *Globalised Islam: The Search for a New Ummah*, London: Hurst.

Sabbah, Fatnah A. (1984), *Woman in the Muslim Unconscious*, New York: Pergamon.

Sadowski, Yahya (1993), 'The New Orientalism and the Democracy Debate', *Middle East Report* 183: 14-21.

Saliba, George (1994), *A History of Arabic Astronomy: Planetary Theories During the Golden Age of Islam*, New York: New York University Press.

Salvatore, Armando (1997), *Islam and the Political Discourse of Modernity*, Reading: Ithaca.

—— (2007), *The Public Sphere*, New York and Basingstoke: Palgrave.

Schasemaier, Dominic, Jens Reidel and Shmuel N. Eisenstadt, eds (2002), *Reflections on Multiple Modernities: European, Chinese and Other Interpretations*, Leiden: Brill.

Schirazi, Asghar (1997), *The Constitution of Iran: Politics and the State in the Islamic Republic*, transl. John O'Kane, London: I.B.Tauris.

Sennett, Richard (2002), 'Cosmopolitanism and the Social Experience of Cities', in Steven Vertovec and Robin Cohen, eds (2002), *Conceiving Cosmopolitanism: Theory, Context, and Practice*, Oxford: Oxford University Press: 42–47.

Sha'ban, Abdul-Hussein (2002), *Man huwa al-Iraqi? Ishkaliyat al-jinsiya wal-la-jinsiya fi al-qanunayn al-Iraqi wal-duwali*, Beirut: Markaz al-Dirasat al-Sharqiya.

Shaw, Stanford (1976), *History of the Ottoman Empire and Modern Turkey*, vol. I, Cambridge: Cambridge University Press.

Sherrard, Philip (1973), 'Church, State and the Greek War of Independence', in Richard Clogg, ed., *The Struggle for Greek Independence*, London: Macmillan: 182–99.

Singerman, Diane (1995), *Avenue of Participation: Family, Politics and Networks in Urban Quarters of Cairo*, Princeton, NJ: Princeton University Press.

Sivan, Emmanuel (1997), 'Arab Nationalism in the Age of Islamic Resurgence', in James Jankowski and Israel Gershoni, eds, *Rethinking Nationalism in the Arab Middle East*, New York: Columbia University Press: 207–28.

Stoke, Martin (1992), *The Arabesk Debate: Music and Musicians in Modern Turkey*, Oxford: Clarendon.

Suleiman, Yasir (2003), *The Arabic Language and National Identity: A Study in Ideology*, Edinburgh: Edinburgh University Press.

Tantawi, Sayid (2001), *Mu'amalat al-Bunuk wa Ahkamuha al-Shar'iyya* (Bank Dealings and their Islamic Legal Status), Cairo: Nahdat Misr.

Taylor, Charles, K. Anthony Appiah, Jürgen Habermas, Steven C. Rockefeller, Michael Walzer, Susan Wolf and Amy Gutmann (1994), *Multiculturalism: Examining the Politics of Recognition*, Princeton, NJ: Princeton University Press.

Terzibasoglu, Yucel (2001), 'Landlords, Refugees and Nomads: Struggles for Land around Late Nineteenth-Century Ayvaluk', *New Perspectives on Turkey* 24 (Spring 2001): 51–82.

Thieck, Jean-Paul (1985), 'Décentralisation ottomane et affirmation urbain à Alep à la fin du XVIIIème siècle,' in Mona Zakaria et al., eds, *Mouvements communautaires et espaces urbains au Machreq*, Beirut: Centre d'études et de recherches sur le Moyen-Orient contemporain: 117–68.

Tyan, Émile (1960), *Histoire de l'organisation judiciaire en pays de l'Islam*, Leiden: Brill.

van Bruinessen, Martin (1996), 'Kurds, Turks and the Alevi Revival in Turkey', *Middle East Reports* 200 (Summer 1996): 7–10.

van Leeuwen, Richard (1999), *Waqfs and Urban Structures: The Case of Ottoman Damascus*, Leiden: Brill.

Vertovec, Steven and Robin Cohen, eds (2002), *Concerning Cosmopolitanism: Theory, Context and Practice*, Oxford: Oxford University Press.

Vertovec, Steven and Ceri Peach, eds (1997), *Islam in Europe: The Politics of Religion and Community*, London: Macmillan.

Waines, David (1994), 'Abu Zayd al-Balkhi on the Nature of Forbidden Drink: A Medieval Islamic Controversy', in Manuela Marín and David Waines, eds, *La Alimentación en las Culturas Islámicas*, Madrid: Agencia Española de Cooperación Internacional: 111–26.

Walzer, Michael (1966), *The Revolution of the Saints: A Study in the Origins of Radical Politics*, London: Weidenfeld & Nicholson.

al-Wardi, Ali (1992), *Lamahat ijtima'iya min tarikh al-Iraq al-hadith* ('Social aspects of Iraqi Modern History'), vol. III, London: Kufan Publishing.

Zarcone, Thierry (1993), *Mystiques, philosophes, et francs-maçon en Islam: Riza Tevfik, penseur ottoman 1868-1949*, Paris: Maisonneuve.

Zubaida, Sami (1988), 'Cultural Nationalism and the Left', *Review of Middle East Studies* 4: 1-32.

—— (1990), 'The Politics of the Islamic Investment Companies in Egypt', *Bulletin of the British Society for Middle East Studies* 17 (2): 152-61.

—— (1991), 'Community, Class and Minorities in Iraqi Politics', in Robert Fernea and William R. Louis, eds, *The Iraqi Revolution of 1958: The Old Social Classes Revisited*, London: I.B.Tauris: 197-210.

—— (1996), 'Turkish Islam and National Identity', *Middle East Report* 26 (2): 10-15.

—— (1997), 'Is Iran an Islamic State?', in Joel Beinin and Joe Stork, eds, *Political Islam: Essays from Middle East Report*, London: I.B.Tauris: 103-19.

—— (2000), 'Trajectories of Political Islam: Egypt, Iran and Turkey', in David Marquand and Ronald Nettler, eds, *Religion and Democracy (Political Quarterly Special Issues)*, Oxford: Blackwell: 60-78.

—— (2003a), 'Islam in Europe', *Critical Quarterly* 45 (1/2): 88-98.

—— (2003b), *Law and Power in the Islamic World*, London: I.B.Tauris.

—— (2004), 'Islam and Nationalism: Continuities and Contradictions', *Nations and Nationalism* 10 (4): 407-20.

—— (2005), 'Communalism and Thwarted Aspirations to Iraqi Citizenship', *Middle East Report* 35 (4): 8-11.

—— (2006), 'Al-Jawahiri: Between Patronage and Revolution', *Revue des mondes musulmans et de la Mediterranee (L'Irak en perspective)*, 117-18: 81-97.

—— (2009), *Islam, the People and the State: Political Ideas and Movements in the Middle East*, 3rd edn, London: I.B.Tauris.

—— (forthcoming) 'Contemporary Trends in Muslim Legal Thought and Ideology', in *New Cambridge History of Islam*, vol. 6.

Zürcher, E. J. (1993), *Turkey: A Modern History*, London: I.B.Tauris.

Index